Th
Ge
The ...European Union, ranging from
gen ...assessments of key institutions and actors, issues, policies
and policy processes, ...the role of member states.

Books in the series are written by leading scholars in their fields and reflect the most up-to-date research and debate. Particular attention is paid to accessibility and clear presentation for a wide audience of students, practitioners and interested general readers.

The series editors are **Nell Nugent**, Professor of Politics and jean Monnet Professor of European Integration, Manchester Metropolitan University, and **William E. Paterson**, Founding Director of the Institute of German Studies, University of Birmingham and Chairman of the German British Forum. Their co-editor until his death in July 1999, **Vincent Wright**, was a Fellow of Nuffield College, Oxford University.

Feedback on the series and book proposals are always welcome and should be sent to Steven Kennedy, Palgrave Macmillan. Houndmills, Basingstoke, Hampshire RG21 6XS, UK, or by e-mail to s.kennedy@palgraye.corn

General textbooks

Published

Desmond Dinan **Encyclopedia of the European Union**
[Rights: Europe only]
Desmond Dinan **Europe Recast: A History of European Union**
[Rights: Europe only]
Desmond Dinan **Ever Closer Union: An Introduction to European Integration (3rd edn)**
[Rights: Europe only]
Mette Eilstrup Sangiovanni (ed.) **Debates on European Integration: A Reader**
Simon Mix **The Political System of the European Union (2nd edn)**
Paul Magnetic **What is the European Union? Nature and Prospects**
John McCormick **Understanding the European Union: A Concise Introduction (4th edn)**
Brent F. Nelsen and Alexander Stubb **The European Union: Readings on the Theory and Practice of European Integration (3rd edn)**
[Rights: Europe only]
Neill Nugent (ed.) **European Union Enlargement**
Neill Nugent **The Government and Politics of the European Union (6th edn)**
[Rights: World excluding USA and dependencies and Canada]

John Peterson and Elizabeth Bomberg **Decision-Making in the European Union**
Ben Rosamond **Theories of European Integration**

Forthcoming

Laurie Buonanno and Neill Nugent **Policies and Policy Processes of the European Union**
David Howarth **The Political Economy of European Integration**

Also planned

Theories of European Union Governance

Series Standing Order (outside North America only)
ISBN 0-333-71695-7 hardback
ISBN 0-333-6935Z-3 paperback
Full details from www.palgrave.com

Monetary Integration in the European Union

Michele Chang

First published 2009 by
PALGRAVE MACMILLAN

Palgrave Macmillan in the UK is an imprint of Macmillan Publishers Limited,
registered in England, company number 785998, of Houndmills, Basingstoke,
Hampshire RG21 6XS.

Palgrave Macmillan in the US is a division of St Martin's Press LLC,
175 Fifth Avenue, New York, NY 10010.

Palgrave Macmillan is the global academic imprint of the above companies
and has companies and representatives throughout the world.

Palgrave® and Macmillan® are registered trademarks in the United States,
the United Kingdom, Europe and other countries

ISBN-13: 978–0–230–54284–6   hardback
ISBN-10: 0–230–54284–0   hardback
ISBN-13: 978–0–230–54285–3   paperback
ISBN-10: 0–230–54285–9   paperback

This book is printed on paper suitable for recycling and made from fully
managed and sustained forest sources. Logging, pulping and manufacturing
processes are expected to conform to the environmental regulations of the
country of origin.

A catalogue record for this book is available from the British Library.

A catalog record for this book is available from the Library of Congress.

10 9 8 7 6 5 4 3 2 1
18 17 16 15 14 13 12 11 10 09

Printed and bound in China

Contents

Figures, tables and boxes

Boxes

Abbreviations

BEPG	broad economic policy guidelines
BIS	Bank for International Settlements
CAP	common agricultural policy
CEEC	Central and Eastern European country
EBRD	European Bank for Reconstruction and Development
EC	European Community
ECB	European Central Bank
ECJ	European Court of Justice
Ecofin	Economic and Financial Affairs Council
ECU	European Currency Unit
EDP	excessive deficit procedure
EEC	European Economic Community
EES	European employment strategy
EFC	Economic and Financial Committee
EMF	European Monetary Fund
EMI	European Monetary Institute
EMS	European Monetary System
EMU	Economic and Monetary Union
EP	European Parliament
EPC	Economic Policy Committee
ERM	exchange rate mechanism
ESCB	European system of central banks
EURIMF	European coordination body on International Monetary Fund
HICP	harmonized index of consumer prices
IGC	intergovernmental conference
IMF	International Monetary Fund
JAP	joint assessment paper
MPC	Monetary Policy Committee
MTO	medium-term objective
NAP	National Action Plan

NCB	national central bank
OLAF	European Anti-Fraud Office
OMC	open method of coordination
RTGS	real time gross settlement
SCIMF	EU sub-committee on IMF matters
SGP	Stability and Growth Pact
TABS-MFIs	total aggregate balance sheet – monetary financial institutions
TARGET	Trans-European automated real-time gross settlement express transfer system
TEU	Treaty on European Union (Maastricht Treaty)

Preface

The idea for this book came shortly after I joined the Department of European Political and Administrative Studies at the College of Europe, where I teach a course on the European Union's economic and monetary policy. Given that my primary research interest is in monetary integration, I am frequently assumed to be an economist. While much of the literature on monetary integration has long been found in the field of economics, over the last few decades political scientists/political economists have been increasingly active in this field. This book is an attempt to recognize the contributions from both fields while placing them in historical context.

I would like to thank everyone who helped me in this project. Neill Nugent has been an invaluable colleague/collaborator/mentor for me. His assistance made this book possible, and I owe him a deep debt of gratitude both intellectually and personally. Other members of the Palgrave team that I would like to thank are Steven Kennedy and Stephen Wenham. Neill Nugent, Iaian Begg, Patrick Crowley, William Paterson and Benjamin Cohen have kindly read drafts of sections and made comments, though all errors remain my own.

I would also like to thank the Centre for European Policy Studies, in particular its director, Daniel Gros, for allowing me to participate in its activities as a Fulbright Scholar. I would like to thank the Fulbright Commission, especially Margaret Nicholson, for financing a year of research in Brussels. I would also like to thank my home institution, the College of Europe, and its staff, in particular Rector Paul Demaret, Dieter Mahncke, Sieglinde Gstöhl, Katrin Gunst, Dominik Hanf, Renée Maeyaert, Marc Mermuys, Angela O'Neill, Jacques Pelkmans, Eric De Souza and Mirko Widenhorn. The Politics Department also boasts a dedicated team that I would also like to thank: Joerg Monar, Rina Balbaert, Mauro Gagliardi, Thomas Kostera, Ugo Lopez, Andrea Maier, Daniele Marchesi, Elisa Molino, Skander Nasra, Jérémie Pélerin, Ariadna Ripoll-Servent and Mathieu Rousselin. I also thank Ramesh de Silva for the idea of organizing the theoretical portion around ideas, interests and institutions.

This book draws upon previous work that I have done on the topic, so I would like to thank the institutions and the individuals that allowed me to pursue this research. Prior to coming to Europe I worked at Colgate University. Its financial support, in particular the Picker Grant, allowed me to conduct some of the research that appears in this book. I would like to thank some of my students, in particular Vaughn Crowe, Venelin Saltirov, Jarrod Singer and Parker Laite for inspiring me to do better work. I would also like to thank Stephan Haggard, my advisor and mentor since my days as a graduate student.

I would like to thank several institutions and individuals for allowing me to use their work. I thank the Directorate General for Economic and Financial Affairs, European Commission for the permission to use Table 4.1, 'A schematic representation of the EU governance regimes', Figure 6.1, 'Flow chart of the streamlined policy coordination cycle', and Table 6.4, 'The old and new SGP: two readings', from documents previously published.

Table 4.3, 'Standard procedures for decision making on economic policy coordination' is from U. Puetter, 'Providing venues for contestation: the role of expert committees and informal dialogue among ministers in European economic policy coordination', *Comparative European Politics* 5(1): 18–35 (2007), and is reprinted with the permission of Palgrave Macmillan.

Table 5.4, 'Possible distribution of countries into ECB voting groups', was originally published as a briefing paper for the European Parliament. I thank Daniel Gros for his permission to reproduce it here.

Table 8.2, 'Banknotes in circulation', was published in W. Becker, 'Euro riding high as an international reserve currency', EU Monitor 46 (2007). I thank the *EU Monitor* for allowing its reprint.

Table 8.6, 'Selected international fora and member countries', was originally published in A. Ahearne and B. Eichengreen, 'External monetary and financial policy: a review and a proposal', in A. Sapir (ed.), *Fragmented Power: Europe and the Global Economy* (Brussels: Bruegel, 2007), and I would like to thank the Bruegel Institute for allowing me to reprint it. Its publications are available at www.bruegel.org.

I would like to thank my personal support network for letting me bounce off various ideas, allowing me to draw on their expertise in their respective fields, and helping me to think about European integration in different ways: Carolyn Hsu, Erika Eriksson, Nicole Germay, Massimiliano Giannandrea, Karen Leahy, Michelle Mueller, Frédéric Muhl, Francisco Rodriguez Jiménez and Mauricio Ruiz.

Finally I would also like to thank my family: Wayne, Adoracion, Robert, William and Michelle.

Michele Chang

Chapter 1

Introduction

On 1 January 1999 the European Union ushered in a new era with the successful transition from national currencies to the euro. Today the euro is one of the world's major currencies, and only the US dollar surpasses it in terms of its usage and global influence. It is currently used by 320 million people in 16 countries, and with the exceptions of Britain and Denmark (which received derogations from Economic and Monetary Union (EMU) participation), all EU Member States are eventually obliged to adopt it as their currency, thus ensuring the growth and continuation of its influence.

The single currency represents the culmination of decades of efforts to unite Europe for economic and political reasons, and is the most visible symbol of European integration today. Although the final stage of monetary union began over a decade ago, the story is far from over: the eastward expansion of the Eurozone, the rapid rise of the euro to the position of the world's number two reserve currency, and the continuing negotiations between governments and institutions in the maintenance of monetary union do not grab headlines like the signing of the Maastricht Treaty in 1992, but they are vital components of European integration as well as international monetary relations.

The purpose of this book is to provide a theoretically informed account of EMU, drawing on both economic and political research. While on the surface monetary integration has been a technical exercise dominated by central bankers, it is an intensely political process that has had a major impact on European integration and national politics. The reverse is also true, as domestic politics and European developments have reverberated to affect the monetary integration process. In particular the following questions will be addressed.

1

FIGURE 1.1   2008 Eurozone Member States

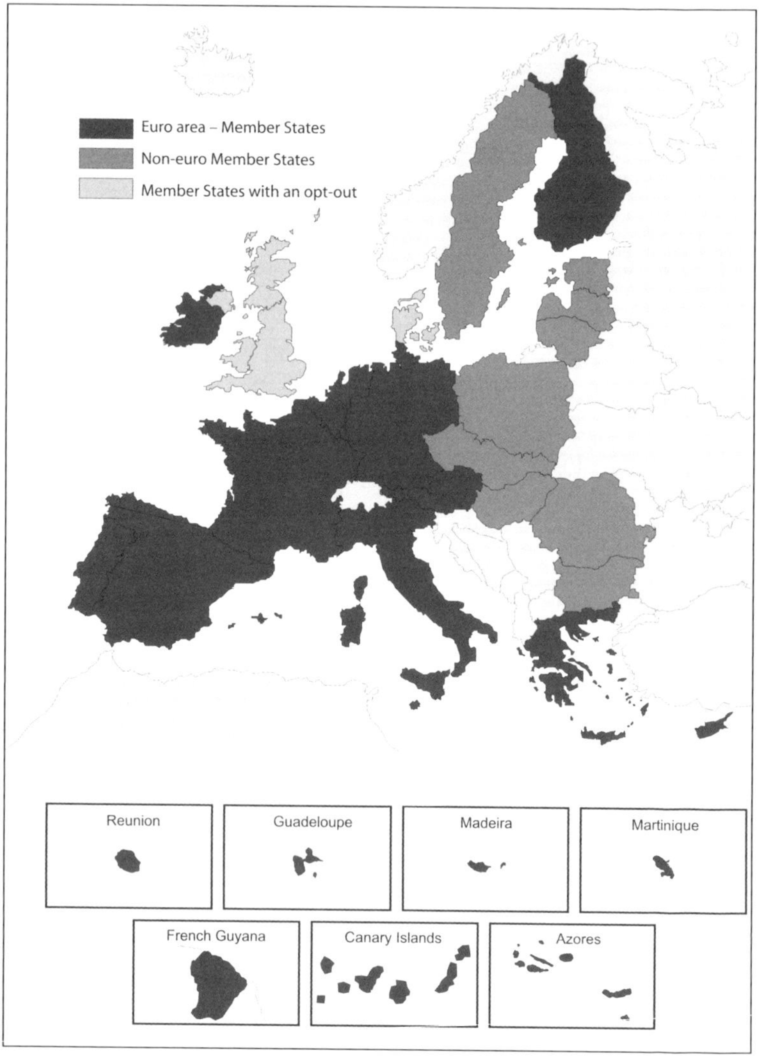

Euro area – Member States
Non-euro Member States
Member States with an opt-out

Reunion

Guadeloupe

Madeira

Martinique

French Guyana

Canary Islands

Azores

Source: based on Directorate General for Economic and Financial Affairs, European Commission.

1. Why did monetary union take on its particular form?

This question needs to be approached from a number of perspectives. First of all, does economic theory indicate that monetary union is either desirable or feasible? Of course, the answer is not so straightforward when (as in the case of EMU) political imperatives outstripped the pace of economic research. The economic benefits of EMU were (and still are) hotly contested, indicating the need to examine how political incentives converged with certain economic ideas to make EMU attractive to a critical mass of Member States.

Second, why did monetary union take place when it did? This is important because it points to the political incentives that were driving integration, at times allowing for a permissive consensus and other times obliging governments to take a more critical/sceptical approach, depending on the timing and how monetary cooperation interacted with other international, European and domestic political events. The idea for monetary union in Europe dates back several decades, and the fact that EMU succeeded in becoming a reality at the end of the twentieth century is related to numerous political developments. Moreover, the subsequent policies that were undertaken to support monetary union also were negotiated within a specific economic and political context which limited the options of negotiators and made certain outcomes more likely than others.

Third, to what extent were the preferences at the time institutionalized? Students of politics are well aware of the stickiness of institutions, and EMU is no different. The ability of actors to lock in preferences through institutions will determine to a large extent the room for manoeuvre that their successors enjoy, for good or ill. The institutions supporting EMU could have been constructed along a variety of different models. Why an independent European Central Bank (ECB)? Why is there no political counterweight? Why are fiscal and economic policies coordinated rather than delegated to an EU-level authority the way that monetary policy was? The institutions reflect power struggles between major actors, and such struggles may continue long after the initial agreements are signed. The 2008 French presidency of the European Union, for example, raised the issue of the ECB's accountability, stopping short of once again calling for a political counterweight to the institution but nonetheless encouraging political leaders to engage in more debate with the ECB. Despite the legal issue of the ECB's independence having been settled long ago, as a political issue it continues to attract attention.

2. Does monetary union work the way that it was supposed to?

Even though preferences may be institutionalized, this does not guarantee the successful implementation of policy. In particular when dealing with actors like sovereign nation states, the incentives for respecting international obligations may be weaker than the rewards for breaking them. In addition, the functioning of monetary union deals with not only the implementation of rules but unforeseen consequences. Despite the best efforts of academics to predict the effects of monetary integration on things like trade flows or further political integration, reality does not always correspond to theory. This book will contrast the economic and political expectations of the actors at the time with the results of the first decade of monetary union, analysing the reactions of politicians and political economists. The success of monetary union is not restricted to fulfilling original expectations, but it is important to understand why expectations were not met, both in determining which actors may be to blame (should the ECB run a looser monetary policy, for example? Or do the Member States need to implement more reforms?) and in considering the lessons that may be drawn for non-EMU states (including those who may join the Eurozone in the future as well as non-European states interested in monetary cooperation). This book therefore evaluates the success of monetary union along a number of criteria, including but not limited to the stated objectives of the founders of EMU as well as its perceived success among the citizenry of current and future Eurozone states.

3. Is monetary union harmed by not including all of the EU Member States?

Prior to the Maastricht Treaty, integration happened at the same time for all members of the European Community. Along with the creation of the European Union, the Maastricht Treaty also introduced a multi-speed Europe (or Europe à la carte, variable geometry: choose your term). Originally this only pertained to a few Member States, all of them wealthy countries from the EU-15. The EU enlargements in 2004 and 2007 complicated the situation and raised the stakes by making the creation of a wealthy core and lower income periphery within the European Union a stronger possibility. Given that EMU membership is not automatic but a country must qualify for it, the

Eurozone threatened to embody this core–periphery within the European Union, with the Eurozone countries on the inside and the newer Member States on the outside.

In addition to the central and eastern countries (CEECs), other EU countries (Britain, Denmark and Sweden) have also remained outside of the Eurozone but do not appear to have suffered either economically or politically. This presents a challenge to the economic and political rationale for monetary integration. It is significant not only for monetary cooperation but for European integration more generally, as the actual costs and benefits of membership can be examined given the alternative models provided by the European Union – without EMU membership.

4. How does monetary union contribute to the international prestige of the European Union?

In other words, did the introduction of the euro sound the death knell for the dollar? As the world's international reserve currency since the end of the Second World War, the dollar and the US government have enjoyed extraordinary (or, in the words of former French President Charles de Gaulle, exorbitant) privileges. Some analysts have gone so far as to argue that the benefits of a single currency extend beyond economics and the realm of 'soft power', and view a currency as an instrument of hard power. The stakes are quite high, and the weakness of the dollar vis-à-vis the euro in recent years, coupled with the corresponding weakness of the US economy in the wake of rising energy prices, make the dethroning of the dollar a stronger possibility than ever before. What exactly are the benefits associated with issuing the international reserve currency, and what are the costs? The latter are considered less frequently than the former, but are particularly important for the Eurozone given that it is not a nation state like the United States and therefore may not be able to distribute any negative effects across the constituent states. Understanding the Eurozone's and ECB's policies regarding the internationalization of the euro requires a more nuanced understanding than directly comparing the European Union with the United States.

5. What is the impact of monetary integration on European integration?

The *raison d'être* of European integration continues to occupy the thoughts of policymakers, academics and citizens. Given the ambiguous economic benefits of monetary integration, the real justification for monetary union lies in the political realm. Indeed, the spillover effects of policies have been studied since the beginning of integration, and monetary integration can be viewed as both a consequence of spillover (stemming from the internal market project) and the source of spillover (prompting cooperation in employment policy and the subsequent Lisbon Agenda, for example). The issue of spillover in the European Union is complicated by the lack of agreement on the future of the European Union. The crisis surrounding the European Union after the failed constitutional referenda in 2005 led to a period of reflection that resulted in the little-changed Lisbon Treaty, which was then rejected in the Irish referendum in 2008. The future of the European Union and the role that monetary union can and should play in further integration remain uncertain, given the current climate at both the elite and grassroots levels. The financial crisis that spread to Europe in late 2008 demonstrated that better coordination mechanisms (possibly necessitating more institutions or delegation to existing institutions) are needed to deal with a rapidly transforming international economic environment.

Understanding monetary integration – ideas, interests and institutions

This study of European monetary integration thus goes beyond either an historical retelling of the events of the late 1980s and early 1990s or an analysis of its institutions. It takes a holistic approach to understanding EMU, looking at history, theories, policies, institutions and external euro area relations. Each chapter will conclude with a section dedicated to academic research done by economists and political scientists, divided according to the sub-headings of ideas, interests and institutions.

The role of ideas: the political economy of monetary integration

The role of politics in forming economic and monetary policies is an uneasy one. Most of the earlier work done on monetary integration was done by economists, and during the last few decades, monetary policymaking has deliberately been promoted as a policy space best left to technocratic central bankers who can better manage the economy with long-term interests in mind, rather than the next electoral cycle. The ECB is one of the most independent central banks in the world and has zealously guarded this independence from political pressure. However, the importance of political factors is evident throughout every step of monetary integration. The initiation of monetary integration in the late 1980s and early 1990s was at the behest of not central bankers, but rather political actors. Indeed, political concerns played a more important role than adherence to specific economic ideas, a point repeated by academic economists and central bankers alike.

Ideas-based theories include both economic as well as political ideas. The economic ideas most relevant to EMU are those concerning the advantages of a fixed exchange rate system, optimum currency area theory, the benefits of central bank independence and the need for fiscal and economic policy coordination. A survey of the economics literature on these topics highlights both accepted conventional wisdom as well as some of the disagreements that may exist within the economics profession. Economic logic or necessity is often used to justify policies, but when the economics are indeterminate, the political influences and manipulation of ideas become more apparent.

This is not to say that the use of economic ideas is purely instrumental, as genuine beliefs may have formed and policy learning may have taken place. Indeed some of the policymaking procedures (in particular the open method of coordination) were specifically designed to promote such learning. Therefore the ideas-based theories coming from the political science literature will largely be drawn from those using constructivist theories which argue that policy preferences are not exogenously determined by material interests, but that such interests are formed endogenously.

A related strand of theorizing, referring to the legitimacy of monetary integration and European integration more generally, is also incorporated in this section, as the legitimacy of European monetary integration is closely tied to conceptions of the *raison d'être* of European integration more generally. For those that imagine the European Union as a regulatory state that should minimally infringe on the policies of the Member States, the loose coordination of economic and fiscal policy may be preferable. On the other hand, for those that view monetary integration as a stepping-stone towards greater political integration, such governance structures could be frustrating. Such different conceptions of monetary integration could be tied to larger issues of legitimacy, or they could be linked to interest-based explanations.

Competing interests in monetary cooperation: conflict and compromise

Interest-based theories argue that actors pursue power and material interests. This can refer to the interests of governments (at different levels) as well as the interests of other actors (like financial interests). For example, intergovernmental theories argue that the larger Member States tend to be more influential in decision making than smaller countries; therefore EU policies tend to reflect their preferences. The interests of the Member States are derived from domestic commercial and financial interests as well as domestic actors and institutions. Thus the interests at stake are not only those of the EU Member State governments (and EU institutions) but also domestic actors and institutions.

Explaining the motivation of government policies and whose interests are served is important in understanding monetary cooperation, especially when the economic benefits are either indeterminate or accrue primarily to a select group. Governments face policy choices, and which policy is chosen may not make sense from a purely economic perspective. The economic interests of a country may be ambiguous, and even when the social welfare may improve as a result of following a certain policy, in the short to medium term, there are winners and losers involved. In the most pernicious case, a policy might be detrimental to the economy as a whole but will be adopted anyway due to the inordinate influence of specific actors, such as those with an interest in international trade and finance. The Eurozone, its institutions and policies reflect the interests of the aforementioned actors and their strategic interactions with one another. Moreover because these interests are not static, neither are the policies (and even institutions) of EMU: they constantly evolve as these different interests vie to promote their objectives.

Economic governance and the institutionalization of monetary union

Such diverging policy preferences necessitated the rather complicated governance structure of monetary union. Political scientists have long recognized that 'institutions matter' in structuring preferences as well as determining outcomes. At the European level, institutions like the ECB and the Commission have a set of preferences that influence the type of policies that they pursue, which are distinct from and at times at odds with those of the Member States. The official procedures for policymaking become important, as more ambiguous structures leave room for conflict and necessitate a negotiated solution that is politically acceptable. Similarly institutions within Member States (like national central banks, finance ministries and electoral cycles) influence the preferences of Member States and make some political outcomes more likely than others.

EMU divides power primarily between Community institutions and Member States, most importantly the ECB and the Economic and Financial Affairs (Ecofin) Council. While monetary policy is handled by the ECB, fiscal and economic policy coordination is done through the Ecofin Council and allows Member States to decide on the specific policies they will follow to achieve agreed-upon objectives. Thus EMU governance has strong centralizing tendencies as well as decentralizing ones. Although the ECB and national governments play the most important roles, other institutions such as the Commission and the European Parliament also are involved in the governance of the Eurozone. In addition, the Eurogroup (the subset of Ecofin comprised of Eurozone members) lacked formal status until the Lisbon Treaty but nevertheless became an important forum for the sharing of ideas and building of consensus.

This division of labour is one born of both political compromises as well as path dependence. Indeed, political rather than economic logic dictated the delegation of some policies and the retention by the Member States of other policies. The result is that both the economic outcomes and the political rationalizations have been sub-optimal, as economic and political rationales do not always predict the same policy. For example, according to some economists the delegation of monetary policy to a Eurozone-level body should have been accompanied by the delegation of fiscal policy. However, Member States were loath to give up their right to tax and spend. The compromise was the Stability and Growth Pact (SGP), in which deficit targets were set at the EU level but it was up to the Member States to decide on the specific policy mix that would achieve these targets.

This seemed like a reasonable compromise. Nevertheless it proved difficult for governments to restrain spending during economically difficult times, and respecting European rules like the SGP did not provide a strong enough reason to prevent numerous countries from breaking the SGP deficit limits. Thus the SGP is an example of political compromise that led to frustrating economic and political outcomes. The Eurozone is distinctive in that its governance structure has multiple sources of authority, making policy disagreements and the pursuit of incompatible objectives more likely.

With the introduction of the euro, new actors like the ECB and the Eurogroup became important stakeholders in the governance of monetary union, alongside the Commission and Member States. These institutions are struggling to build their own constituency and to define their role in the governance process while existing institutions try to maintain or expand their respective influence. At times this brings institutions and governments into conflict with one another. Furthermore the relatively wide array of relevant actors makes it difficult for the Eurozone to speak with a single voice and thus have as much influence in international financial circles as its economic strength would suggest.

Conflicting ideas, different preferences, contradictory incentives and a complex governance structure make political analysis essential to understanding the formation and operation of EMU. Monetary union has achieved much in the first decade, surprising critics but perhaps disappointing its more ardent supporters. How the Eurozone fares in the coming decade in promoting economic objectives (price stability, employment, growth), political objectives (greater political integration, extension of EU competences into issue areas like employment and social policy), and external objectives (challenging the dollar as the international reserve currency, reducing the vulnerability of the euro and European financial markets to market speculation) will depend on a myriad of factors, making monetary integration one of the most interesting and important EU policies for those interested in political economy and financial issues.

Plan of the book

Of course these three analytic constructs of ideas, interests and institutions are not completely distinct from one another, and overlap exists. Nevertheless such categories provide a useful starting point of analysis and make it possible to provide some structure to the growing literature on economic and monetary policy. This book will provide an empirical and theoretical account of economic and monetary integration. Each chapter begins with a description of the major historical events and a description of the institutional configuration, when appropriate, followed by a summary of the theoretical analyses. The theoretical section is generally divided into theories based on ideas, interests and institutions, with some deviations from this structure depending on the specific chapter. Of course this book cannot give an exhaustive account of all of the theories used, but a broad overview is given of economic and political theories of monetary and economic cooperation.

Chapter 2 provides a history of monetary integration from the Bretton Woods system up until the hard phase of the European Monetary System (EMS). The history of monetary cooperation continues in Chapter 3, which covers the Maastricht Treaty negotiations up until the present day. International influences are considered in addition to those found at the European and domestic levels, given the importance of the US dollar in the international monetary system. Taking a long-term view of economic and monetary cooperation in Europe allows one to see the changing ideas and subsequent institutionalization of such ideas in policies like exchange rate cooperation and central bank independence. The inordinate influence of France and Germany in shaping monetary integration is also readily apparent, as cooperation in this area serves important economic and political interests in these countries. These interests and ideas led to the current governance structure that continues to impact monetary and economic policymaking in the European Union.

Chapters 4 and 5 introduce the decision-making structure of EMU, and cover the functions of the major institutions of EMU as well as their relationship with one another. The institutions included in this study are the ECB, the Eurogroup, the Ecofin Council, the Economic and Financial Committee (EFC, formerly the Monetary Committee), the Commission and the European Parliament. The reasons for the rather complicated division of labour, the functions each institution serves, and how well the governance system has worked thus far are considered. Chapter 5 provides a more in-depth analysis of the history, structure and policies of the ECB. This chapter explains the primary duties of the ECB as an institution and how well it has fared in achieving the objectives set by the European Union. However, before it even came into operation the ECB was criticized for being too independent, lacking adequate mechanisms of accountability with other institutions that could provide legitimacy. Theories on central bank independence are therefore discussed, considering both its merits and its limitations.

Chapter 6 looks at fiscal and economic policy coordination in EMU. It first considers the political impetus behind the creation of the SGP and the economic rationalizations that were later used to justify it. Indeed, the utility of the SGP in both its original and current form was hotly debated among economists, and ultimately its course followed a political logic, as large Member States like France and Germany ignored the policy prescriptions associated with the pact until the Ecofin Council altered the pact to suit the policy imperatives of Member States in March 2005. The story of the reform of the SGP incorporates elements of intergovernmentalism (large states not being punished for transgressions), domestic politics (in particular the French government's willingness to violate the pact in the interest of pursuing further growth), institutionalism (the difficulties of the relationship between the ECB and the Eurogroup given their at times unclear mandates) and the dissemination of ideas (regarding the relationship between technocratic and political bodies and economic ideas on the efficacy of fiscal policy coordination).

In addition to the coordination of fiscal policy under the SGP, the economic arm of the EMU relies on the coordination of economic policy, largely using the open method of coordination. Monetary policy cannot be effective in isolation from other economic policies, as actions in one area can run counter to other economic policies. The Broad Economic Policy Guidelines (BEPG), European Employment Strategy (EES) and the Lisbon Agenda have all employed the open method of coordination (OMC), which has alternately been described as a first step towards further integration and as a new method that essentially amounts to a talk shop with little chance of influencing actual policy. The open method operates as a system of benchmarking whereby Member States learn from one another's best practices through a system of peer review, and a section is devoted to both the praise and criticism that the open method has elicited.

Chapter 7 considers the countries outside of the Eurozone. The three EU15 countries of the United Kingdom, Denmark and Sweden are considered as well as the countries that acceded to the EU in 2004 and 2007. The economic and political rationale for each EU15 country's decision to remain outside of EMU are analysed, as well as how this decision has affected these countries economically and politically in terms of their relationship with EU insiders. In the case of the 2004 and 2007 accession countries, each one's prospects for future membership is considered, along with how their inclusion could affect the functioning of the Eurozone. The chapter concludes with a reflection on the impact a multi-speed EMU has had on European integration more generally. Theories explaining these developments, including those based on power politics (in particular a country's ability to remain influential while outside the Eurozone), institutions (the stickiness of the Maastricht Treaty despite the arguably inappropriate application of its convergence criteria to the new Member States), and constructivism (the prevalence of more neoliberal ideas in the new Member States and how that affects their relationship with current Eurozone members) are also covered.

Chapter 8 focuses on the international role of the euro, how a single currency has affected the European Union as an economic entity, and the impact that it has made internationally. In particular, the ability of the euro to challenge the dollar's hegemony has been the topic of much discussion. What it takes to be a key currency, why the dollar has been able to hold the top position for decades despite the macroeconomic challenges it has faced (such as its twin deficits) and the impact the Eurozone could have on international financial management, comprise much of this chapter. In addition, although the Eurozone as an international financial actor is still a work-in-progress, the internal difficulties it faces in speaking with a single voice pose a substantial obstacle to its ability to fulfil its potential in this regard, and the reasons behind this are taken into account. Some recent public disagreements between various actors in the Eurozone (such as the ECB and Ecofin members) are recounted in order to illustrate the continued weakness of the Eurozone in acting as a coherent political body.

Chapter 9 gives an initial balance sheet of EMU after its first few years of operation. Its economic and political triumphs and difficulties are considered. The extent to which it has functioned as originally planned, how it has conformed to or defied predictions, and its ability to produce economic and political benefits for the European Union as an organization and its respective member states are considered. After a decade since its launch, an appraisal of how the Eurozone is functioning thus far is in order, along with a consideration of how problems are being handled by the European Union.

Chapter 10 revisits the themes presented in Chapter 1. The backdrop to monetary integration has always been political calculations, which include the contribution it makes to European integration and the extent to which it empowers the European Union and its Member States. The politicization of monetary integration is emphasized, pointing out instances in which institutional solutions were derived as the result of political (as opposed to economic) imperatives, and how theories from political science and international political economy have increased our understanding of European integration and monetary integration as a case study of this. The tension between international, European and domestic imperatives is reconsidered, and so are the future prospects of the euro in terms of promoting (or perhaps hindering) further integration and its impact on the international system.

Chapter 2

The origins of economic and monetary union

Monetary cooperation in postwar Europe did not begin with a drive towards monetary union and a single currency. These ideas gained support in later decades, but in the 1950s the importance of monetary cooperation was widely recognized as a global issue rather than a strictly European one. Indeed, for much of the postwar period concerns over European exchange rates took a back seat to international regimes dedicated to exchange rate cooperation. After the collapse of the Bretton Woods system in the early 1970s, however, European exchange rate cooperation took on newfound significance as a mechanism to protect European trading interests and later as a means to further develop European integration more generally. This chapter outlines these events and how the EU states progressed from an international exchange rate regime under Bretton Woods to a weakly enforced European regime (the Snake) to a more credible regime (the European Monetary System (EMS)) before graduating to a single currency in 1999. Economic theories explaining the rationale behind EU policy decisions are highlighted (and explained in further depth in later chapters), and the political rationale behind their eventual adoption is also considered.

Bretton Woods and the return to fixed exchange rates

Europe's interest in fixed exchange rates began with the Gold Standard during the nineteenth century. This era saw an unprecedented amount of international economic transactions between nation states, and the exchange rate system based on gold contributed to the stability of the international economy. The First World War disrupted the Gold Standard, but after the war's conclusion states were eager to revert to this system that had served them well during the previous era. However, the political and economic environment during the interwar period had changed substantially from previous decades, and the level of commitment to the fixed exchange rate system was much weaker (Eichengreen 1992a; Simmons 1994). Indeed, as economic conditions deteriorated during the 1920s and 1930s governments became prone to devaluing their currencies in order to gain a temporary price advantage over their trading partners (beggar-thy-neighbour devaluations). This type of behaviour was symptomatic of the general deterioration of international economic cooperation, which also manifested itself in rising trade protection. The result was heightened tension between countries, contributing to poor political relations as well as worsening economic conditions and the Great Depression. It was in this historical context that the leaders met in 1944 in Bretton Woods (New Hampshire) to discuss the post-war international economic system.

Creating the new international monetary system

Constructed largely by the leading international economic powers of the United States and (to a lesser extent) Great Britain, the Bretton Woods system was based on the idea that international economic transactions should be promoted via free trade and fixed exchange rates. The International Trade Organization (which would later become the much less institutionalized series of trade rounds, the General Agreement on Tariffs and Trade, before being resurrected as the World Trade Organization in 1995) was to govern international trade. The International Monetary Fund (IMF) would manage the international monetary system, in particular by providing assistance to governments suffering from balance of payments problems that would jeopardize the fixed exchange rate regime. The decision to revert to a fixed exchange rate system was based on the assumption that it promoted international economic exchange and stability, an assumption that was backed up by memories of the Gold Standard of the nineteenth century and the more recent experience with exchange rate instability during the interwar period. However, instead of a gold exchange standard the countries committed to a dollar-exchange standard: the dollar was fixed to gold at the price of $35/ounce and the other currencies were fixed to the dollar. The central exchange rate around which the currencies pivot was adjustable, and there was additional flexibility built in with the adjustment bands of plus or minus 1 per cent. Exchange rate changes were expected to take place in case of a 'fundamental disequilibrium' (a concept which remained undefined), thus allowing the exchange rate to reflect changing economic conditions. However, frequent exchange rate realignments were not expected, as this would have undermined the goal of promoting exchange rate stability. Therefore governments needed to prevent their exchange rates from varying too widely.

Although the Bretton Woods agreement was signed in 1944, it could not immediately go into operation because of the lack of convertibility of many currencies, including European currencies. The European economies were hit by a depression after the Second World War and had only a small amount of gold reserves with which to conduct international economic transactions. Instead, the European countries conducted trade via bilateral agreements where an agreed-upon line of credit was used between country pairs but was not transferable to trade with third countries. In order to resolve the convertibility problem, in 1948 the Organization for European Economic Cooperation (OEEC) stepped up to the task as part of its effort to distribute and put to use the aid given by the United States as part of the Marshall Plan. Thus in 1950 the European Payments Union (EPU) went into operation, composed of the 18 participants of the OEEC (Gros and Thygesen 1998: 4–7). The EPU was essentially created as a clearinghouse for trade between members. Indeed, exports rose 1.7 times from 1948–55, with trade between participating EPU members increasing 2.3 times (Gillingham 2003: 39). Had convertibility been restored immediately, the European currencies would have been devalued, which would have had a negative effect on income and likely destroyed the postwar social pact (Eichengreen 1995).

By 1958 convertibility was restored and the European Monetary Agreement was established. This set the fixed but adjustable exchange rate system between European economies as part of the Bretton Woods agreement. The six members of the newly formed European Economic Community (EEC) (Belgium, France, Germany, Italy, Luxembourg and the Netherlands) along with the United Kingdom, Ireland and Sweden, narrowed their fluctuation bands relative to the US dollar from plus or minus 1 per cent to plus or minus 0.75 per cent in order to avoid the de facto fluctuation band of 4 per cent between non-US dollar currencies (Apel 1998: 24–5).

The 1950s and 1960s saw rapid economic growth in Europe and the United States. International trade grew under the General Agreement on Tariffs and Trade, which was able to accommodate the creation of the EEC's regional trade preferences. The issue of monetary cooperation in the nascent EEC was a moot point given the undisputed leadership role of the United States in international monetary affairs (Tsoukalis 1977: 52). Indeed, when Italy faced a balance of payments crisis in 1963–64, its central bank turned to the United States and IMF for a loan, not other EEC countries (Tsoukalis 1977: 58). The Europeans took a back seat to the United States in the functioning of the international monetary system, with the IMF regarded largely as an outpost of US power and interests rather than a truly international institution (Oatley and Yackee 2004). Figures 2.1, 2.2 and 2.3 demonstrate how the European economies bounced back from the devastating war to create growth and stability.

Rising instability and the Triffin dilemma

Despite the relative stability of the first decade of the Bretton Woods system and its success in re-establishing international monetary cooperation, the sustainability of the system in the long term was put into question early on. Economist Robert Triffin (1960) described what would later be called the 'Triffin dilemma' in which the fixed exchange rate system of Bretton Woods was based on confidence in the US dollar and a US economy that would

FIGURE 2.1   Annual GDP growth, 1961–73

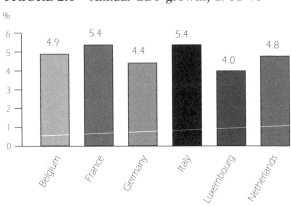

Source: data from Eurostat.

FIGURE 2.2   Unemployment rate, 1961–73

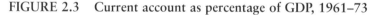

Source: data from Eurostat.

FIGURE 2.3   Current account as percentage of GDP, 1961–73

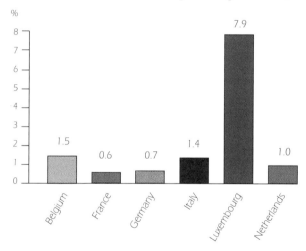

Source: data from European Commission.

serve as the engine for international economic growth. The international economy had become dependent on the United States running a balance of payments deficit, a situation that continued after the end of the dollar glut in 1958 and the start of the period of dollar overhang (Cohen 2002). Continued US deficits meant the Bretton Woods system would ultimately suffer from a liquidity problem: the continuation of US monetary policy in the 1960s would lead to rising inflation worldwide (as currencies were tied to the dollar), provoking an exchange rate crisis. However, reining in US inflation would have the effect of reining in international economic growth as well, hence the dilemma.

By the 1960s, however, a number of forces conspired to overturn the system, and by the early part of the next decade it was officially dead. First was the rising mobility of international capital. Along with the increased power of multinational corporations, the very success of international economic openness had made it easier for financial market actors to evade capital restrictions, thus making them less effective. Governments were now unable to offset destabilizing exchange rate fluctuations without resorting to politically and economically costly intervention in the markets (normally through interest rate increases, foreign exchange intervention, or some combination of the two). Indeed, despite the 1961 revaluation of the German mark and the Dutch guilder, speculation against these currencies continued. A coordinated European response, however, was not forthcoming, leading to 'the first serious exchange crisis in the post-war international monetary system [that] had immediate repercussions within the Community' (Tsoukalis 1977: 54). Various actors within the EEC made proposals in the wake of the crisis: the European Parliament (EP) called for greater coordination of national monetary policies, the Monetary Committee advocated establishing a system to provide assistance to countries experiencing balance of payments difficulties, and the Commission proposed greater economic and monetary consultation via the creation of a Committee of Governors of Central Banks, a Budgetary Policy Committee and a Medium-Term Policy Committee (Tsoukalis 1977: 56)

Second, maintaining the system required adjustments by governments which they were no longer willing to make. By 1969 France and Germany had been forced to engage in exchange rate realignments. Although the economics and effects of exchange rate adjustments are generally not well understood by the general public, the devaluation of a currency nonetheless conjures up images of economic mismanagement and policy failure (Chang 2004). Weaker currencies like the French franc suffered from lost credibility, and stronger currencies like the German mark were forced to revalue upwards, making their exports less competitive. The fixed exchange rate system had become more constraining and costly for its participants.

Moreover, the situation of the dollar became ever more precarious during this period as the US government simultaneously engaged in expansionary foreign and domestic policies. In order to finance the Vietnam War and Johnson's Great Society program, the United States printed more dollars. Thus the United States effectively exported inflation to the other countries, which were expected to continue to accept US dollars at the price of $35/ounce, despite the fact that more dollars were now in circulation. The French government under Charles de Gaulle criticized this policy and the United States' misuse of its 'exorbitant privilege' as holder of the world's key currency. The French government went so far as to demand that some of its dollar reserves be paid back in gold, thus demonstrating publicly French scepticism regarding the system as well as having the effect of further destabilizing the dollar. Financial markets also questioned the ability of the United States to continue such a policy, and the dollar's exchange rate became volatile.

Despite the ultimate demise of the system, several features were established early on that would remain hallmarks of the international monetary system. First, the success of international monetary cooperation rested with the willingness to accept the interference of partner countries in domestic political matters, as seen in the success of the EPU (Gros and Thygesen 1998: 7). This readiness to accept infringements on sovereignty would be a key determinant of the waxing and waning of European monetary cooperation throughout the postwar era. Second, in 1951 Germany was running a surplus, a condition that would also become a staple of the international monetary system. Third, the burden of adjustment fell disproportionately on the country running a deficit. As we shall see, even when a system is specifically designed to engender symmetry as the EMS was (see below), the onus of adjustment still shifted to the deficit country (Gros and Thygesen 1998: 7). Finally, the dominance of France and Germany in monetary affairs also was established early on (Tsoukalis 1977: 80).

The end of Bretton Woods and the beginning of European monetary cooperation

Planning for monetary union in Europe: the Werner Plan

The European economies took a proactive stance to the rising instability in the international monetary system. European economies are more open than that of the United States, thus they suffer more from exchange rate fluctuations as it disrupts international trade, which forms a larger part of their economy. In addition, the proper functioning of the common agricultural policy (CAP) also required exchange rate stability (Giavazzi and Giovannini 1989). As early as 1965 the idea of monetary union was being floated by the Commission, alternately (tacitly) supported by and rebuffed by French policymakers and widely acknowledged by states like Germany and the Netherlands as a likely consequence of European integration (Tsoukalis 1977: 60–1). The May 1968 crisis in France provoked exchange rate speculation on the franc–mark rate, and in August 1969 the French government devalued its currency. This was followed by the German government's revaluation of its mark in October, prompting EEC countries to construct a European facility to assist in balance of payments adjustments. The pound's devaluation in November 1967 had already hardened views that a regional solution was needed (Tsoukalis 1977: 36).

The Barre Plan of February 1969 recommended the coordination of economic policies in addition to the creation of a system of monetary support for EC countries. Thus on 17 July 1969, the Council passed a resolution that created a system of short-term monetary support, which went into effect in February 1970. Each Member State's central bank would furnish funds not in excess of a specified ceiling (the equivalent of its debtor quota) to other Member States' central banks that were undergoing problems with their balance of payments (Apel 1998: 31).

At the Hague Summit in December 1969, German Chancellor Brandt endorsed European monetary integration (a departure from Germany's previous preference for IMF-based solutions), an objective shared by French President Pompidou (Tsoukalis 1977: 84–5). With political support at the highest levels in place, in 1970 the Werner Plan articulated the goal of European monetary union by 1980. This would insulate the European economies from the movements of the dollar, which had become increasingly unstable. Monetary union would be achieved in three stages. The first stage involved reducing currency fluctuation margins in Europe, the setting of broad Community-level economic policy guidelines, fiscal policy coordination and changes to the Treaties of Rome in anticipation of EMU progression. The second step referred to financial market integration, removing capital restrictions, eliminating exchange rate fluctuations, and short-term economic and fiscal policy coordination. The final step included the irrevocable setting of exchange rates, economic policy convergence, and a Community-level system of central banks (Werner Plan 1970).

Creating this plan exposed divergences within Europe on the best way to proceed with monetary union, as it advocated harmonizing economic policies prior to monetary union (Tsoukalis 1977: 98). Many of these debates would haunt monetary cooperation in later decades. On the one hand, the monetarists (not to be confused with monetarists in economics, who believe in controlling the money supply in order to keep inflation in check) advocated that convergence between the economies would naturally result from monetary integration, thus there was no pressing need to coordinate and harmonize economic and monetary policies in advance of monetary union. France was at the vanguard of this group along with Belgium and Luxembourg. On the other hand, the economists, led by Germany and including the Netherlands and to a lesser extent Italy, argued that economic convergence in advance of integration was vital to the credibility and sustainability of cooperation (Tsoukalis 1977: 90–3). This debate would be an enduring one between the two groups and would be resurrected during the debates surrounding monetary integration in the late 1980s and early 1990s.

Another important element of the Werner Plan was the expectation that it would lead to political union (Werner Plan 1970: 12). This indicates how monetary union can contribute to European integration more generally, and disagreement over this point would continue into the 1990s. Finally, unlike the Maastricht Treaty which would ultimately bring about monetary union two decades later, the Werner Plan incorporated fiscal union as part of monetary union: 'the margins within which the main budget aggregates must be held both for the annual budget and the multi-year projections will be decided at the Community level'. Both academics and politicians would hotly debate the necessity of fiscal coordination in the 1990s.

The rise and fall of the Snake

The 1970s turned out to be an inauspicious time for international monetary cooperation. By the second half of 1970 the US balance of payments deficit had reached new highs as a result of its deteriorating trade deficit and capital flight, which had the effect of causing inflationary pressure and the need to raise domestic interest rates. The French and German governments disagreed on how to handle the crisis when the EEC finance ministers met in an emergency meeting in May 1971. While the French government advocated the use of capital controls, the German government insisted on continuing its policy of capital mobility, resulting in the 'agreement to disagree: the German and Dutch allowed their currencies to float and the other European currencies imposed capital controls' (Tsoukalis 1977: 112–13).

On 15 August 1971 the US government 'closed the gold window' (Gowa 1983) as it refused to convert dollars into gold, signalling the end of Bretton Woods. The Smithsonian Agreement of December 1971 established new central rates for the currencies and expanded the fluctuation margins to 2.25 per cent. By extension, the reciprocal rates between any two EEC currencies became 4.5 per cent, an unacceptably large level given the level of stability required by the CAP. The EEC therefore reduced intra-EEC bands to 2.25 per cent in February 1972. Moreover, exchange market interventions would cease to be done in dollars, only EEC currencies would be used (Tsoukalis 1977: 121). European monetary integration was picking up momentum.

On 24 April 1972 the Snake came into existence, with Belgium, France, Germany, Italy, Luxembourg and the Netherlands as the original participants; the United Kingdom, Denmark and Norway joined the following month. But continued speculation in currency markets prompted the withdrawal of the United Kingdom in June, followed by Denmark (the latter rejoining in October). Despite the devaluation of the dollar, continued speculation against European currencies led to new capital restrictions to control the inflows (Tsoukalis 1977: 122). The decision to float the dollar in March 1973 intensified tensions in the Snake, forcing considerable amounts of intervention by the Bundesbank as the Snake splintered off into a group of strong currencies (German mark, Dutch guilder and Norwegian krone) and weak currencies (French franc, Belgian-Luxembourg franc, Danish krone and Swedish krona) (Gros and Thygesen 1998: 16). France had a particularly rocky history, withdrawing in 1974, returning in 1975 and withdrawing again in 1976 (see Table 2.1). The Snake featured regular exchange rate realignments as well, as the German mark, Dutch guilder, Norwegian krone, Belgian franc, Danish krone and Swedish krona all made exchange rate adjustments. The Snake would continue to eke out an existence over the next few years, but given its unstable membership as numerous realignments occurred and participants

TABLE 2.1 *Chronology of the Snake membership*

Date	Country	Action
1972		
24 April	Belgium, France, Germany, Italy, Luxembourg, the Netherlands	Form the Snake
1 May	United Kingdom, Denmark	Join
23 May	Norway	Joins
23 June	United Kingdom	Withdraws
27 June	Denmark	Withdraws
10 October	Denmark	Returns
1973		
13 February	Italy	Withdraws
19 March	Sweden	Joins
1974		
19 January	France	Withdraws
1975		
10 July	France	Returns
1976		
15 March	France	Withdraws
1978		
12 December	Norway	Withdraws

Source: Gros and Thygesen (1998: 17).

dropped out and back into the system over the years, it no longer served as a credible foundation for monetary integration. By the latter half of the decade, the Snake essentially operated as a mark zone, with Belgium, Denmark and the Netherlands tightly shadowing the movements of the German mark.

The problem with the Snake rests in the aforementioned loss of monetary sovereignty, also referred to as the 'n – 1 problem', in that a fixed exchange rate system required an anchor currency and participants had to follow the movements of that anchor or their currency would suffer from market speculation. Thus all the participants (save for Germany) sacrificed monetary sovereignty in adhering to a fixed exchange rate. Given the disparity between economic policies followed by the European countries at the time, this involved a greater amount of adjustment than most European governments were willing to bear.

The European Monetary System and the road towards EMU

The 1970s was a volatile decade for the international economy. The US government's policy of benign neglect towards the dollar led to a substantial amount of exchange rate fluctuation for the European currencies. This damaged the trade relations of these relatively open economies. The green rates of the Common Agricultural Policy also came under threat. Exchange rate instability threatened European business and agricultural interests to the extent that exchange rate cooperation was once again relaunched in 1978. French President Valéry Giscard d'Estaing and German Chancellor Helmut Schmidt took the initiative in resuming exchange rate cooperation in Europe so as to create a 'zone of monetary stability' in an uncertain international environment (Ludlow 1982). Although it dealt with the technocratic world of exchange rates, negotiations were handled at the highest levels, with heads of government meeting in order to construct what would become the EMS.

The European Monetary System

The EMS was launched in March 1979 with eight Member States: Belgium, Denmark, France, Germany, Ireland, Italy, Luxembourg and the Netherlands. It was unclear at the start whether Ireland and Italy would become full participants, and a combination of side

TABLE 2.2   *Chronology of monetary integration 1979–92*

1979	EMS launched.
1986	Single European Act signed.
1987	Basel-Nyborg agreement.
1988	Hanover European Council, objective of EMU confirmed, Delors Committee appointed.
1989	Delors Report submitted; Fall of the Berlin Wall; Strasbourg European Council: agreement to convene the IGC on EMU before the end of 1990; Guigou Report submitted.
1990	Dublin European Council: IGC and a parallel conference on political union would be ready to be ratified before the end of 1992; Phase 1 of EMU begins: capital controls lifted.
1992	Maastricht Treaty signed.

payments (for both) and a wider fluctuation band (for Italy) permitted their involvement. The EMS had much in common with its predecessor, the Snake. They were both fixed but flexible exchange rate systems in which participating currencies could fluctuate within a certain band from the central rates. For most of the currencies this was 2.25 per cent, although Italy negotiated a 6 per cent margin. This exchange rate commitment was the heart of the EMS and was formally known as the Exchange Rate Mechanism (ERM).

The EMS boasted two institutional innovations, a new nominal anchor and the divergence indicator. These were designed to make the EMS more symmetrical than the Snake, and required both the strong currency country and the weak currency country to adjust to exchange rate pressure. The European Currency Unit (ECU) was composed of the currencies of European Community countries, and it served as the official anchor. However, although the ECU had been intended to help make the EMS a more symmetric system than the Snake, in practice financial markets also took into account the bilateral exchange rates between the currencies (in particular a currency's rate of exchange with the German mark), undermining the symmetrical effect that had been intended. Similarly, the divergence indicator failed to induce greater symmetry. The idea behind it was to compel the governments of both the strong and the weak currencies to intervene when the exchange rate had crossed 75 per cent of the band, thus preventing the currency band from being breached. Once the system went into operation, however, the governments of the weak currency countries would intervene to boost their currency before the divergence indicator was crossed. The feeling was that markets would interpret allowing the currency to reach the threshold as a sign of weakness, and that it then would be too late to save it from a realignment.

Britain had opted out of participating in further initiatives involving closer European cooperation. The Labour government was expecting a tough election, and European integration was highly divisive within Britain in general and unpopular with trade unions, the Labour Party's core constituency. When the Thatcher government came to power later that year, the pound was officially brought into the EMS, though the government refused to fix the pound within the ERM. Fixing the pound to the other European currencies would have brought the government no political benefits from the still-sceptical British public, and the economic case also provoked controversy given the dissimilar economic cycle that

Britain found itself in, as well as the effects of the discovery of oil in the North Sea.

The early years of the EMS saw modest results. Admittedly it was an inauspicious time for exchange rate cooperation. The European economies had emerged from the stagflation of the 1970s in poor economic shape, and the second oil shock did little to help matters (see Figures 2.4 to 2.7). In addition, European integration in general had suffered, with 'Eurosclerosis' settling in and no initiatives prompting and propelling further cooperation. The EMS was realigned seven times during its first four years.

The French U-turn and rise of the hard EMS

The turning point came in 1983 with the French U-turn. Socialist president François Mitterrand had been elected in 1981, and this combined with the inclusion of the Communist Party in his first government provoked massive capital flight. In addition, the pursuit of numerous public works projects and the nationalization of key industries contributed to high inflation, which led to the weakening of the French franc against the German mark and prompted several devaluations. After the 1983 municipal elections, the liberal wing of the Socialist party seized command, and the French government followed a *franc fort* policy in which monetary policy closely followed that of the German government's as economic policy and became increasingly market oriented (Bauchard 1986; Hall 1985, 1986; Ross 1996).

FIGURE 2.4   Average annual GDP growth rates, 1974–85

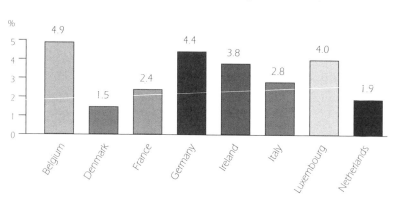

Source: data from Eurostat.

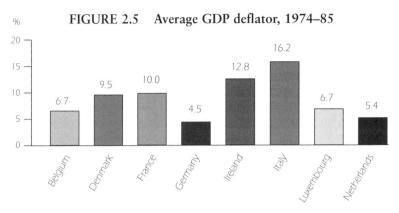

FIGURE 2.5   Average GDP deflator, 1974–85

Source: data from Eurostat.

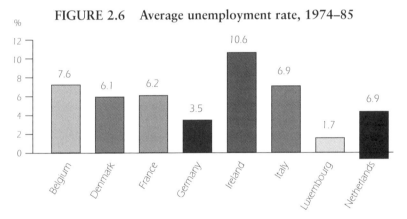

FIGURE 2.6   Average unemployment rate, 1974–85

Source: data from Eurostat.

The subsequent period of 1983–86 saw an EMS that served as a stronger constraint than it had during its initial years of operation. Inflation levels began to decline and interest rates also converged to a lower level. Economists explained this as 'the advantage of tying one's hands' (Giavazzi and Pagano 1988). Domestic monetary policymakers often lacked credibility when setting policy because market actors knew that they had strong incentives to run cyclical monetary policy for their own political

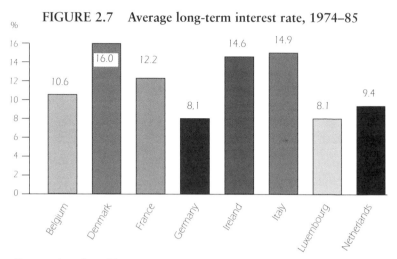

FIGURE 2.7   Average long-term interest rate, 1974–85

Source: data from Eurostat.

advantage. For example, a government might announce that it would follow a tight economic and monetary policy in order to combat inflation. However, prior to an election a government might be interested in pursuing the contradictory policy of increasing public spending so as to give the impression of an economic boom and win additional votes (Hibbs 1977; Nordhaus 1975). Knowing such incentives exist, markets distrust the policy promises of governments and act as if they expect a government to engage in inflationary policies (whether or not such policies are put into place). This harms the economy's overall performance, and it is also difficult for a government to establish market credibility (Kydland and Prescott 1977; Barro and Gordon 1983). The solution is to delegate monetary policy to a body that has different incentives than that of politicians: that is, one that values price stability (see Chapter 5 on the ECB for more details). In the German case, this came in the form of delegating monetary policy to an independent central bank, the Bundesbank. The EMS countries, however, essentially delegated monetary policymaking to the Bundesbank via their participation in the ERM.

In 1986 the Single European Act was signed, giving new life to European integration and generating spillover effects in the call for further monetary integration in order to reap its expected benefits. It would create 'an area without internal frontiers in which the free movement of goods, persons, services and capital is ensured in accordance with the provisions of this Treaty' (SEA). Another impetus for further monetary integration was contained in its provision for the free movement of capital. While some states like Germany and the United Kingdom had lifted capital restrictions a long time before, many Member States still resorted to their use in order to manage currency speculation. However, they were becoming less useful in stemming capital outflows and were out of line with the more market-oriented economic policy that had begun to take over the advanced industrial democracies.

The Basel–Nyborg agreement of 1987 institutionalized the existing norm of defending exchange rate parities while implementing changes to try to cope with rising capital mobility. Central bankers were to utilize the intramarginal intervention bands instead of buying up the currency of the weaker country. In addition, in the event of exchange rate pressure national governments were now expected to implement changes at the level of domestic policies in order to rectify the imbalance (Mayes and Viren 2001). The EMS was thus more flexible and therefore better able to soothe market expectations. But for the French government, and finance minister Edouard Balladur in particular, the agreement still did not address adequately the asymmetric nature of the EMS, nor did it outline a strategy towards the dollar, both issues that would continue to be priorities for the French government (Dyson and Featherstone 1999: 163).

The period from 1987–92 saw the EMS bands 'harden' (see Table 2.3) in that markets (and governments) essentially treated the exchange rates as if they were fixed. Save for the devaluation of Italy in 1990 in conjunction with its move from the wider fluctuation bands to the narrow ones used by other ERM members, there were no realignments during this period after the January 1987 revaluation of the mark. The success of the EMS in stabilizing exchange rates had resulted in lower inflation rates and interest rate convergence. Although other OECD currencies saw similar economic developments (see Figure 2.8), many attributed it to the success of the EMS, the primary strategy of which was the delegation of monetary policy to the Bundesbank.

Single market spillover and plans for monetary union

The end of the 1980s also corresponded to the end of Eurosclerosis in Europe and the rise of Europhoria in the wake of the

TABLE 2.3   *EMS realignments against central rates, 1979–93*

Date	Belgian franc	Danish krone	French franc	German mark	Dutch guilder	Irish punt	Italian lira	Portuguese escudo	Spanish peseta
24 September 1979		-2.9		+2.0			-6.0		
31 November 1979		-4.8					-3.0		
2 March 1981	-4.8								
5 October 1981			-3.0	+5.5	+5.5				
22 February 1982	-8.5	-3.0							
14 June 1982			-5.75	+4.25	+4.25		-2.75		
21 March 1983	+1.5	+2.5	-2.5	+5.5	+3.5	-3.5	-2.5		
21 July 1985	+2.0	+2.0	+2.0	+2.0	+2.0	+2.0	-6.0		
7 April 1986	+1.0	+1.0	-3.0	+3.0	+3.0				
4 August 1986						-8.0			
12 January 1987	+2.0			+3.0	+3.0				
8 January 1990									
13 September 1992							-3.7		
17 September 1992							-7.0		-5.0
22 November 1992								-6.0	-6.0
10 January 1993						-10.0			
13 May 1993								-6.5	-8.0

Source: Eurostat.

FIGURE 2.8   GDP price deflator, 1961–90

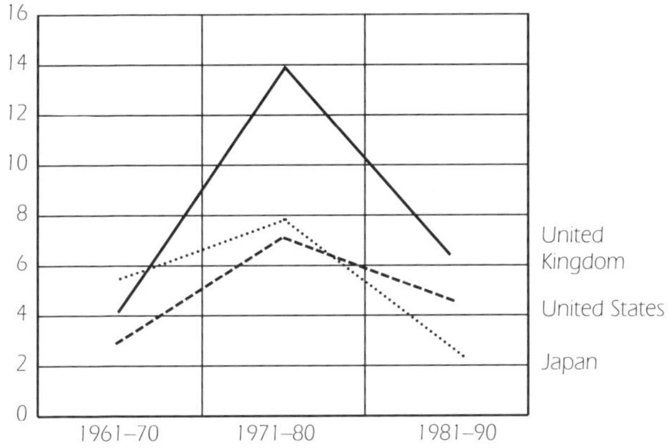

Source: data from European Commission.

Single European Act and plans for a truly single market to be completed by the end of 1992. Influential analyses argued that the single market would be a major boon for the European economy and allow it to compete better in the international economy. A functional logic also dictated that in order to take full advantage of a single market, Europe would also require a single currency as a further step to remove all potential barriers to trade. Thus the economic argument of a single currency contributing to trade added an important component to the debate over the utility of monetary union. The Commission's *One Market, One Money* report (1990: 36) outlined the economic advantages of monetary union, arguing that a single currency differs from a fixed exchange rate in six areas: lower transaction costs, greater price transparency, economies of scale for financial instruments, greater credibility, greater visibility which sends important signals to markets and other actors as to the importance of price stability, and the creation of a 'more balanced international monetary regime'.

   The political impetus for monetary union emanated from the French government. European monetary cooperation had long been seen as a way to counteract the influence of the dollar. In 1984 Roland Dumas, then minister for European Affairs, wrote the Dumas Memorandum in which he argued that the EMS could serve as a mechanism to reconstruct the international monetary system so as to shift power between the dollar, yen and the ECU. A stronger role for the ECU in private markets would allow for the defence of European exchange rates against the fluctuations of the dollar, and eventually it could become both a European and international currency. In November 1985 French negotiators lobbied for the inclusion of monetary policy in the Treaty of Rome, but the idea was rebuffed by the German delegation (Dyson and Featherstone 1999: 152–5).

The French continued to press their case for the strengthening of the EMS. Buoyed by the success of international monetary cooperation in the Louvre Accord of 1987, French finance minister Balladur argued that the international system required greater objectivity, automaticity and symmetry, referring to the need for a fixed exchange rate system along the lines of the Gold Standard, for central banks to be obliged to prop up flagging exchange rates and for such obligations to be extended to both weaker and stronger currencies (*Le Monde*, 24 February 1988, cited in Dyson and Featherstone 1999: 160). Balladur also floated the idea of a European central bank to his colleagues in 1988 (*Le Monde*, 8 January 1988). Indeed, given the expected completion of the internal market in 1993 and the concomitant removal of capital controls, the contemporary EMS threatened to be overwhelmed.

The French plea for monetary integration was followed by an Italian memorandum (Amato 1988) which, like the French memorandum, criticized the strong German currency and its structural external surplus. In addition to arguing for widening the EMS's fluctuation bands, the Amato memorandum expressed reluctance to agree to the proposal on capital control liberalization without safeguards being built in, including 'a recycling mechanism which could borrow funds on the market and reallocate them in such a way as to compensate the inflow and outflow of capital' (cited in Gros and Thygesen 1998: 397).

Surprisingly, the Italian and French memoranda provided Germany with a window of opportunity to reframe the debate, as the institutional implications of monetary integration were not defined in either (Gros and Thygesen 1998: 397). Genscher's rejoinder, 'A European currency area and a European central bank', proposed a single currency and central bank as an 'economically necessary completion of the European internal market' (cited in Gros and Thygesen 1998: 937). Surprisingly, he even suggested that at the June European Council meeting in Hanover a group of experts be appointed to submit a report. Finance minister Gerhard Stoltenberg soon afterwards submitted his own memorandum to Ecofin on 15 March (Stoltenberg 1988). In it he noted the importance of price stability and independence for a European central bank. It detailed the interim phase between when monetary union would be agreed upon and implemented, arguing for the need for independent national central banks that prioritized price stability. It also objected to the French and Italian claims of the need to address the asymmetric features of existing monetary cooperation in Europe. However, the *sine qua non* of monetary union for Germany would be full capital liberalization (Gros and Thygesen 1998: 399).

At the 1988 Hanover European Council, the Member States agreed that:

> in adopting the Single Act, the Member States confirmed the objective of progressive realization of Economic and Monetary Union. They therefore decided to examine at the European Council meeting in Madrid in June 1989 the means of achieving this Union. To that end they decided to entrust to a Committee the task of studying and proposing concrete stages leading towards this Union. The Committee will be chaired by Mr Jacques DELORS, President of the European Commission.

Delors was charged with devising a plan for monetary union in Europe, so he convened the national central bank governors from the Community along with another member of the Commission and 'three personalities', Niels Thygesen (Professor of Economics, Copenhagen), Alexandre Lamfalussy (Director-General of the Bank for International Settlements in Basel and Professor of Monetary Economics at the Catholic University of Louvain-la-Neuve), and Miguel Boyer (President of Banco Exterior de España). Delors requested that the central bank governors be involved in order to form a consensus among them and avoid criticism regarding the technical aspect. Delors noted the surprise that greeted this suggestion, as it was likely that he had been expected to form a committee composed of figures appointed by the governments themselves, possibly the finance ministers (Delors 2004). The result were submitted on 12 April 1989, and like its predecessor, the Werner

Report of 1970 planned for EMU to occur in three stages. Unlike the Werner Report, however, no new institutions would be created in order to coordinate economic policy. The three stages of the Delors Report were:

1. Stage One: Increased cooperation between central banks with relation to monetary policy, removal of obstacles to financial integration, monitoring of national economic policies, coordination of budgetary policy;
2. Stage Two: Preparatory stage for the final phase of EMU, establishment of the ESCB and progressive transfer of monetary policy to European institutions, narrowing of margins of fluctuation within exchange rate mechanism;
3. Stage Three: Fixing of exchange rates between national currencies and their replacement by a single European currency, responsibility for monetary policy would be transferred to the ESCB.

(source: Commission, http://ec.europa.eu/economy_finance/euro/origins/origins_4_en.htm)

Shortly after the submission of the Delors Report, Europe's political geography changed dramatically with the fall of the Berlin Wall in November 1989 (discussed further in the next chapter). This gave new urgency to European cooperation The French had long viewed monetary integration as an important part of its foreign policy, and 'German unification offered an historic window of opportunity to accelerate EMU' (Dyson and Featherstone 1999: 196).

The European Council had adopted the Delors Report in June 1989 in Madrid. The First Stage would be launched in July 1990. Shortly thereafter the French presidency convened a high-level group of officials from national finance and foreign affairs ministries in order to prepare for the intergovernmental conference. At the end of October the Guigou Report was submitted (High Level Group 1989), which was quickly countered by the UK Treasury's publication of an alternative strategy for monetary union. In December 1989 the Strasbourg European Council decided to arrange an intergovernmental conference on EMU before the end of 1990, with a parallel conference on European Political Union (agreed upon at the 1990 Dublin European Council). From 1990–91 the Maastricht Treaty was negotiated, which formalized plans for monetary union.

Theoretical considerations

Ideas

Changing ideas on the relationship between governments and markets were reflected in the strategies pursued by governments during Bretton Woods and afterwards. As economic circumstances changed, new ideas arose and policies adapted. During the postwar period a system of embedded liberalism (Ruggie 1982) was created. While at the international level liberal economic ideas advocating free trade predominated, at the domestic level governments constructed a strong welfare state that would compensate the losers of globalization. Thus governments were able to combine the best elements of the classical Gold Standard (fixed exchange rates and the resulting stability and trade-enhancing effects) while avoiding the negative political ramifications of such policies that governments experienced in the 1920s and 1930s. According to the Mundell–Fleming conditions (Fleming 1962, Mundell 1960), a government can only enjoy two of the following three at any one time: a fixed exchange rate, capital mobility and monetary sovereignty. Under the Bretton Woods system, states had limited capital mobility (as governments had implemented controls in order to restrict their movement) and adhered to fixed exchange rates while governments were able to retain monetary sovereignty.

Over time rising capital mobility eroded the utility of capital controls, and governments had to adapt. During the 1980s a stability culture in Europe developed (Dyson 1994, McNamara 1998, 1999). The success of the German Bundesbank in taming inflation and the strong economic growth that seemed to result from its policies encouraged other governments to follow its example. Central bankers in particular can be considered to have formed a type of epistemic community in Europe advocating German-style monetary policy (Verdun 1999). German policy advocated a strong currency and price stability to sustain the country's international competitiveness and thus its economic strength. A strong currency dampens inflationary pressures, and investors have greater confidence in the currency's future value. This creates a virtuous circle of growth and stability. 'Competitive disinflation', a term coined by Jean-Baptiste de Foucault, became the economic rationale for basing monetary policy around a strong and stable currency. This contrasted with the inflation–crisis–devaluation scenario faced by weaker currency countries during the early part of the EMS (Dyson and Featherstone

1999). The economic woes faced by the weaker currency countries during the early 1980s diverged sharply from the stronger currency countries like Germany. This evidence of successful policy provided Germany with even greater influence, which rested not only on its economic and political muscle, but also on the wide acceptance of German economic ideas (McNamara 1998).

Interests

The first set of interest-based theories look at monetary cooperation from a systemic perspective and the importance of the international context in which monetary integration took place. Rising capital mobility (Andrews and Willett 1997) had posed a conundrum for governments as far back as the 1960s, when it first threatened monetary cooperation under Bretton Woods. The situation continued to develop over the ensuing decades. Indeed, the first phase of EMU began even before the Maastricht Treaty was signed. On 1 July 1990 the free movement of capital was established throughout Europe, along with intensified economic surveillance as states worked on convergence. This not only encouraged European states to follow more market-oriented policies, it was also acknowledging the power that mobile capital had already accrued and the difficulty in restraining it.

Capital mobility destabilized the fixed exchange rate system of the Bretton Woods system, and its rise and fall contributed to the development of the literature on hegemonic stability theory (Keohane 1980). Two strands arose, a benign version and a coercive one. In the benign version, the hegemon provides a public good to the international system. Thus one can look at the United States as providing international monetary stability, which benefits all participants. In the coercive version, the hegemon benefits disproportionately from the functioning of the system and has a vested interest in using its power to keep it in operation despite the costs accrued by the other participants. In this view the United States abused its dominant position in the international monetary system in exporting its inflation to other countries, destabilizing the system for the short-term gain of the US economy.

When the German mark became the de facto anchor of the EMS, some extrapolated from hegemonic stability theory to the German dominance theory, which posits a regional leadership role of Germany. The German mark was the anchor currency of the EMS, thus permitting Germany to operate with more independence than the other countries. As mentioned above, the 'n – 1' problem means that in a fixed exchange rate regime only one currency enjoys an independent monetary policy; the other currencies must adjust to it. Although Germany did not take an active leadership role in the EMS in the same way as the United States did during the Bretton Woods era, Germany alone set its own interest rates (which in turn became the floor for other interest rates set in Europe). This was problematic because the mark was often subject to different exchange rate pressures than the other European currencies. When the dollar weakened, for example, investors flocked to the mark and drove up its value against the dollar and the weaker European currencies. This wreaked havoc on European monetary stability, and gave rise to the various attempts at European monetary cooperation (Giavazzi and Giovannini 1989; Henning 1998).

Though the mark served as the anchor currency of the system, this does not mean that Germany served as the system's hegemon. Economists have found evidence of asymmetry using various economic measures (Kutan 1990, Wyplosz 1989), with Germany at times also being affected by other members' currency movements despite the general asymmetry (Fratianni and von Hagen 1990, Hafer and Kutan 1994, Weber 1991). Moreover, Germany's reluctance to assume this role as such makes the term 'hegemon' difficult. Political scientists have referred to Germany's 'leadership' (McNamara 1998) and 'standard-setting' (Kaelberer 2001), with other countries emulating the German model. This emulation resulted from Germany's relative economic success during the postwar period. Germany enjoyed strong growth, a healthy balance of payments ledger and low levels of inflation.

Germany was not the only country to play a leadership role in monetary integration. In fact, Germany did not seek leadership of European monetary cooperation but found itself at its centre by virtue of the strength of its economy and the influence of ideas on central bank independence. Monetary integration required a country to act as a leader and to push cooperation forward, something Germany could not be relied upon to do. Therefore the Franco-German engine was essential in promoting monetary cooperation (Chang 2002). The German foreign policy establishment viewed monetary cooperation favourably as a way to promote further integration, but Germany would serve as no more than a passive leader given the trepidation of its partners over more overt signs of German leadership and power. Further-more, as noted above, important actors like the Bundesbank eyed monetary cooperation warily because it could compromise German goals. Thus a monetary system revolving around German leadership would resemble the mark zone of the Snake, comprising Germany and smaller countries willing to follow its lead. German interest in monetary union should be viewed in light of its interest in getting its European partners to remove capital controls, but only in a way that would not threaten its price stability (Gros and Thygesen 1998).

Without France, the EMS would not have encouraged a Europe-wide membership, it would not have been linked to other issue areas, and it would not have served as an impetus for further integration. Although the French franc was a weaker currency during most of the 1980s, the French government never let it be forgotten that France traditionally served as one of the motors of European integration, and that it is the Franco–German axis around which the European Community revolves. Thus the French government could exert a moral authority during negotiations that only it and Germany possessed, since they held the power to make cooperation move forward (Chang 2002). If France dropped out of the EMS it would be no better than the Snake and ultimately would fail in its objectives of stabilizing exchange rates and promoting European integration.

While Germany and France were both broadly in favour of mone-tary integration, there were some important differences. Whereas Kohl wanted monetary integration to occur in tandem with progress on political union, Mitterrand prioritized the former and did not want to allow political union to impede its progress (Dyson and Featherstone 1999: 198). The French government thus promoted its own version of monetary integration, which contrasts with that of Germany (in the form of the Genscher and Stoltenberg memoranda).

The second issue concerns the asymmetric nature of monetary integration. Balladur had argued for greater symmetry in European monetary cooperation, an 'implicit criticism of German policy' (Gros and Thygesen 1998: 397). In addition to promoting power at the European level, monetary union was also part of France's broader geopolitical strategy. The rise of Mikhail Gorbachev to the post of general secretary of the Communist Party in the USSR renewed French concerns that Germany could turn its back on Europe in exchange for unification. Mitterrand therefore used monetary integration as part of post-1986 French efforts to bind Germany more closely to Europe (Dyson and Featherstone 1999: 166).

Similarly the Italian proposal for monetary integration also criticized the asymmetry, in addition to its lack of attention to economic growth. The Amato memorandum blamed Germany's 'fundamentally undervalued' currency and its external surplus for the removal of 'growth potential from other nations'. The sections on an escape clause for the directive on capital liberalization and the enlarging of the EMS fluctuation bands also clearly point to Italian interests (Gros and Thygesen 1998: 396–7).

Given the momentum that had been accumulating, with proposals coming from numerous Member States, it was advantageous for the central banking community (in the form of the Committee of Governors) to become involved in the project despite their misgivings about the idea of monetary union. Unlike during the EMS negotiations a decade earlier, they wanted to avoid being marginalized (Gros and Thygesen 1988: 400).

Governments defined interest in terms of not only relative power, but how a domestic audience would interpret government policy. For example, although the EMS countries negotiated realignments according to a consensus model, states came to the bargaining table with conflicting preferences. In both the Snake and the EMS, the burden of adjustment fell on the weaker currency countries. Governments viewed devaluation as an admission of failure (Mélitz 1988), a public indication of the government's inability to provide an economy that could sustain the exchange rate level. This explains why France periodically devalued alongside other countries in order to avoid being the sole 'problem country'; a general realignment (one involving several of the EMS countries) allowed governments to rationalize that a system-wide problem existed.

This also made politically significant the issue of the amount by which the strong currency country revalues its currency versus how much the weak currency country devalues. In economic terms this seems to be primarily cosmetic; whether Germany revalues 5 per cent and France devalues 10 per cent (or the reverse), the end result is a devaluation of 15 per cent for the franc relative to the mark. Politically, however, this issue involved blame-shifting for the cause of the imbalance (such as blaming overly tight German monetary policy instead of lax French policy) and avoiding the appearance of incompetence or irresponsible behaviour (Andrews 1993). Eliminating the need for publicly embarrassing devaluations was an important contributing factor to European monetary cooperation.

In addition to catering to the general public, governments also wanted to appease specific interests. Interest group theories also can help us understand the rising interest in monetary cooperation, and why some countries were keener than others during this period. In particular the rising power of mobile capital and internationally based business made both low inflation and stable exchange rate more important to governments desiring to curry favour and investment in their country (Frieden 1991).

Institutions

The most significant institution during this early period was the institutionalization of monetary cooperation, in particular the EMS. Why was the EMS successful? Economic theories stress the disciplinary role of the EMS and the credibility that it brought. In lieu of central bank independence (and more recently, supplementing it), the EMS participants chose to abdicate monetary policymaking decisions to the Bundesbank. The reasoning is similar to that for granting independence to the central bank: by 'tying your hands' to noninflationary targets set by the Bundesbank via international commitments, the promise not to inflate becomes more credible (Giavazzi and Pagano 1988). The international agreement, with its accompanying entanglements and reputation concerns, forms a bond that the governments offer markets: if the government reneges and forgoes the bond, presumably it will lose its accumulated credibility.

With European monetary union, the EMS countries were 'buying' Germany's credibility by handing over monetary policymaking to a central authority that has been explicitly modelled after the German Bundesbank. The advantage of this over continuing to delegate authority to the actual Bundesbank was that the governments had been forced to respond to Germany's shocks, rather than domestic shocks or even European shocks. The cost of responding to an asymmetric shock that hits the anchor currency became clear in the years after German unification. Blindly following German policy was difficult when that entailed raising interest rates during the middle of a recession.

There was also an institutional logic to monetary cooperation. Given that capital controls were to be abolished as part of the

1992 Single Market programme, the latter had a spillover effect on monetary cooperation. The French government in particular was cognizant that the changes would destabilize the existing EMS and required substantial reform, which helped prompt the European governments to seriously consider further monetary integration (Dyson and Featherstone 1999). For Germany, the spillover logic extended to political union. Both the Genscher Memorandum and a speech Kohl made to the European Parliament argued that spillover from the EMS and EMU could encourage European political unification (Dyson and Featherstone 1999: 273).

Domestic institutional prerogatives also played a role. The finance ministries, foreign ministries and central banks of each country were involved in negotiations for monetary union, in addition to the executive. In some instances different offices had different priorities. For example, in the German case the foreign ministry was keen on pursuing monetary union whereas the Bundesbank was more sceptical about the prospects of maintaining price stability on a European level. It was necessary to appease both the ordo-liberal and the security coalitions to get agreement within Germany before negotiations could be fruitful on the European level (Dyson and Featherstone 1999).

Finally German unification also presented actors with opportunities to reframe the debate. According to Dyson and Featherstone (1999: 262–3), Kohl had been approaching monetary integration from a negotiating stance forged by the ordo-liberal coalition, headed by Bundesbank vice-president Hans Tietmeyer. German unification 'offered to the chancellor a sudden opportunity to transform the terms of debate: to upgrade the significance of the foreign and security policy aspects of EMU'. Once German unification came on the table, the chancellery, foreign office, finance ministry and economics ministry promoted EMU, deeming the potential costs worth the expected electoral and diplomatic dividends (Kaltenthaler 1998: 70).

Conclusion

European monetary cooperation began as a reaction to US initiatives, both positive (in joining the Bretton Woods system) and negative (forming the Snake and EMS in response to the dollar's instability). Buoyed by the success of the EMS in stabilizing exchange rates, it then became a force for integration. While economic concerns regarding the impact of exchange rates on trade were important, there were also significant political ramifications to monetary cooperation. States assumed different roles (as leader versus follower) in these cooperative schemes, and enjoyed different benefits. The inherent asymmetry of monetary cooperation was soon revealed under both the Snake and the EMS, despite the attempts to make the latter more symmetrical. While the stability and credibility that the EMS offered were desirable, certain Member States soon sought to extend monetary cooperation to monetary union in an attempt to re-equilibrate the system.

Chapter 3

The birth of the euro and the Eurozone

While plans for monetary union got off to a quick start, implementing monetary union was a more arduous task. First the states needed to agree on the terms of monetary union, which would be outlined by the Maastricht Treaty. Old tensions between the monetarists and the economists flared, although an agreement was finally achieved. However, subsequent accords tried to rectify the imbalance that was reached, insofar as the Maastricht Treaty itself largely corresponds to German political demands at the expense of governments that would have preferred more political control and a greater official emphasis on economic growth (in particular the French government).

However the success of monetary union hinged not only on the introduction of the euro, but also on its implementation. The weakness of the euro during its early days, sluggish economic growth in the larger euro area economies, reform fatigue in the Member States, and the need to reform the Stability and Growth Pact all indicated the limits of monetary integration in curing Europe's economic ills. This chapter outlines the major events that followed the signing of the Maastricht Treaty up until the present day. It concludes with a consideration of economic and political theories that can explain the Eurozone's successes and failures during its first decade of operation. This chapter concentrates on theoretical considerations up until the launch of the euro in 1999; subsequent chapters cover theoretical developments since that time.

Negotiating and renegotiating monetary union

Buoyed by the success of the Single Market programme and the stability of the European Monetary System, various figures raised the issue of monetary union, including French prime minister Edouard Balladur, European Commission president Jacques

TABLE 3.1   *Chronology of monetary integration, 1990–98*

1990	Britain enters ERM; IGC in Rome.
1992	Maastricht Treaty signed.
1992–3	ERM crisis.
1994	Phase 2 of EMU: European Monetary Institute created.
1995	Enlargement: Austria, Finland and Sweden join the EU. Madrid European Council sets 1999 deadline for EMU, names the euro.
1996	Dublin European Council approves coins and notes, agrees on structure for ERM II. Italian lira re-enters ERM.
1997	Amsterdam European Council adopts resolution on Stability and Growth Pact and a resolution on Growth and Employment; resolution on ERM II. Luxembourg European Council passes a resolution on economic policy cooperation.
1998	EMU membership decided; ECB created; conversion rates fixed.

Delors, and German foreign minister Hans Dietrich Genscher. The pace of the debate accelerated rapidly after the fall of the Berlin Wall in 1989, and plans were drawn up as to how to proceed with monetary union. Of particular interest were the institutional configuration of EMU and the pace at which it would occur.

Rapid German unification (the Berlin Wall fell in November 1989, and in October of the following year the Federal Republic of Germany and the German Democratic Republic were unified) had produced a shock to the German economy and by extension to European integration. Increased internal demand and rising imports replaced the export-led growth which had acted as the engine of European economic growth for over a decade. As early as 1989 Bundesbank officials and policymakers called for a revaluation of the mark to accommodate the changing economic environment. Germany's European partners, in particular France, refused these requests on the grounds that devaluation would destroy the credibility gains acquired since 1987 and could damage prospects for monetary union.

The Elysée expressed its desire to the German Federal Chancellor's Office to speed up plans for the intergovernmental conference

(IGC) on EMU, to which Kohl's foreign policy advisor Joachim Bitterlich replied with a demand to speed up political union (Dyson and Featherstone 1999: 204). Kohl had argued for an IGC on EMU to begin in 1991, to be followed in 1992 by separate IGCs on institutional reform and political union, with the latter two forming a package that would be ratified in 1993. Mitterrand was concerned that Germany's interest in political union could slow down monetary union (Dyson and Featherstone 1999: 197). This issue would not be decided until the June 1990 Dublin European Council: the two IGCs would begin 13–24 December and their work be completed before the end of 1992, the date when the single market was due for completion.

The British wished to avoid monetary union and its accompanying loss of sovereignty. Thatcher had hoped that if Britain clearly stated its intention to not participate in monetary integration despite any measures taken by the other Member States, Germany (under pressure from the Bundesbank) would also opt out (Thatcher 1993: 720). As an alternative to the Delors Report's approach, Major even proposed a parallel currency (the hard ECU) that would be run by a new institution called the European Monetary Fund (EMF). The EMF would thus distribute hard ECUs in exchange for national monies, with the excess being repurchased by national central banks. The proposal for this evolutionary approach to monetary union went nowhere.

The German Bundesbank predictably found the prospect of monetary union a cause for concern, and went on the offensive in September 1990, arguing that it would require the fulfilment of a strict set of convergence criteria prior to EMU, in addition to the elimination of capital controls. Moreover, the Bundesbank rejected the idea of automatic starting dates which would override fulfilling the criteria, and demanded that the ECB be modelled on itself, committed to price stability and not obliged to support the government's economic policy (as the Bundesbank was) (Deutsche Bundesbank 1990). These were presented not as suggestions but rather as conditions for Bundesbank acquiescence to monetary union (Kaltenthaler 1998: 80).

French negotiators continued to press for a monetary union that more closely conformed to French ideas and interests. In October 1990 French lobbying for a political counterweight to the independent ECB was dubbed by Pierre Bérégovoy as '*gouvernement économique*' (Dyson and Featherstone 1999: 208). For the French, such a *gouvernement économique* would be useful in promoting coherence between monetary policy and budgetary and exchange rate policies, in addition to adding legitimacy to monetary union (necessary in light of an independent central bank). Such an idea was anathema to Germany, in particular the Bundesbank, as it would potentially threaten the new central bank's independence. French negotiators, on the other hand, were concerned about what they viewed as Germany's lack of concern for economic growth in pursuit of price stability. Nevertheless they knew that central bank independence would not be open for negotiation, and reasoned that having a seat on the board of an independent ECB was preferable to the status quo of following Bundesbank policy (Dyson and Featherstone 1999: 222–3).

The Thatcher government had been increasingly criticized for its Euroscepticism, which contributed to a number of prominent resignations in her cabinet, including notables such as Geoffrey Howe and Nigel Lawson. The economic arguments for remaining outside monetary union no longer held as much sway, and politically it began to look more like a liability than an asset as the pro-Europe faction in her party gained influence. Finally in October 1990 Thatcher brought the pound into the ERM in a wide band of 6 per cent, largely on the counsel of her new chancellor of the Exchequer, John Major. Some expressed pique at her unilateral decision, which did not include the participation of her European partners in deciding the exchange rate of the pound in the ERM (a rate generally agreed to be overvalued). Nevertheless the general reaction was rather positive. British participation was seen as bolstering the credibility of monetary integration, as it was one of Europe's largest and most international economies.

In December 1990 the IGC on EMU opened in Rome. The Delors Report (written largely by the Committee of Governors) was not substantially altered in terms of the creation of the European System of Central Banks (ESCB). Budgetary policy proved to be a trickier issue, although agreement was finally reached with upper limits for deficits and debts set at 3 per cent (of GDP) and 60 per cent respectively. Even more difficult was the discussion on the transition from Stage Two to Stage Three, which only recommended a gradual transfer of authority with no timetable. In the discussion, three opposing views emerged. The United Kingdom predictably preferred not to automatically pass to Stage Three, which required the addition of a separate protocol allowing it to opt out. Germany and the Netherlands stressed the need for the strict fulfilment of the convergence criteria prior to Stage Three, opposing automatic deadlines. The third view was offered by Italy and France, which assumed that convergence would occur rapidly after monetary union and should not restrict membership. Thus the Maastricht Treaty merged the latter two perspectives with the creation of the convergence criteria but the inclusion of Article 109j(4): 'If by the end of 1997 the date for the beginning of the third stage has not been set, the third stage shall start on 1 January 1999,' although membership is not automatic, since 'Before 1 July 1998, the Council ... shall, acting by a qualified majority ... confirm which member states fulfil the necessary conditions for the adoption of a single currency' (Gros and Thygesen 1998: 408–10).

The German-led group of countries is generally viewed as having won the battle over the institutional configuration of monetary union. The German delegation made EMU contingent on the fulfilment of the Maastricht Treaty convergence criteria. Focusing on nominal versus real convergence, the Maastricht Treaty demands convergence of inflation rates within 2 per cent of the average of the top three performers in the European Union, interest rates within 2 per cent of the three lowest in the European Union (not within the euro area), debt levels under 60 per cent of GDP, public deficits under 3 per cent of GDP, and stable exchange rates (defined as no devaluations within the ERM within the past two years). Moreover, conforming to the stability culture that had taken hold of Europe (and elsewhere), successful applicants were expected to have relinquished capital controls (actually part of the Single Market programme) and granted their central banks independence. These tough criteria were not only intended to ensure a high degree of economic convergence among the Member States, they were also expected to exclude a number of states that Germany feared would weaken the new currency's credibility.

In terms of the sequencing of EMU, the economist versus monetarist debate described in the previous chapter was resurrected. The Germans and the Dutch wanted economic convergence prior to monetary union. Indeed, Buiter (2006) noted that while Germany's stated objective for the convergence criteria relating to fiscal/financial matters was to ensure the successful operation of EMU, the unstated objective was to keep out weaker currency countries like Italy, Spain and Portugal. The Italians and the French, however, argued for a wider membership than the strict convergence criteria would likely allow, assuming that greater convergence would take place (and be easier) after EMU. The French government preferred as many participants as possible, not wanting EMU to be so dominated by German interests as previous exchange rate cooperation in Europe had been. In addition, the French government pushed for an automatic deadline for EMU to take place, regardless of how many countries fulfilled the criteria. There was a compromise: Germany got its convergence criteria, but the decision on who fulfilled the criteria would be a political one, and monetary union would begin on 1 January 1999 at the latest.

As plans for European integration continued apace, the Gulf War and the disintegration of Yugoslavia diverted the attention of leaders. EMU's high politics nature became apparent as France asked for a final fixed date for the beginning of Stage Three of monetary union in exchange for the recognition of Croatia and Slovenia, a German proposal (Dyson and Featherstone 1999: 216). Despite (and at times because of) political exigencies arising from the end of the Cold War, monetary integration progressed.

The 1992–93 ERM crisis

The Treaty on European Union was signed in Maastricht, the Netherlands, on 7 February 1992. Although it entailed numerous innovations in European integration (notably the three-pillar system and name change from European Community to European Union), the headliner was the agreement on monetary union. The ratification of the treaty required a referendum in several countries, a procedure that was expected to be nothing more than a formality. The French government was so confident of the ratification and popularity of the plan that it scheduled a referendum for September 1992 in order to create political momentum for the incumbent Socialist government prior to the spring 1993 parliamentary elections.

The ensuing currency crisis created shockwaves in Europe and beyond, as monetary union and the future of European integration suddenly came under question (Cobham 1994, Eichengreen and Wyplosz 1993, Harmon and Heisenberg 1993). The crisis began in Denmark. The government held a referendum on the Maastricht Treaty on 2 June 1992, and the Danes voted 'no'. Though Denmark has traditionally not been one of the strongest proponents of European integration, the outcome nevertheless stunned observers, as this small country had put the entire ratification process at risk. There was no contingency plan for the rejection of the Maastricht Treaty, so it was not clear if the Danish 'no' vote could derail it. And now that the monetary integration no longer looked certain, foreign exchange market actors began to rethink the way that they viewed the existing exchange rate arrangement under the ERM and the viability of the current exchange rates.

In the spring of 1992 we saw a rise in exchange market speculation against the Italian lira and the British pound, both of which experts agreed were overvalued. The relaxation of US monetary policy during the summer of 1992 exacerbated Europe's currency woes. As the dollar sank, the mark grew stronger and its EMS partners weaker. The Italian lira in particular was under constant attack during the summer of 1992. The situation came to a boil at the August 1992 Ecofin meeting, when the British and Italian representatives requested an interest rate reduction from Germany. The German delegation refused, given that the post-unification German economy had heated up and was under threat of inflation. The Bundesbank geared monetary policy towards German economic conditions, not European conditions. After this meeting failed to produce a change in German interest rates, market pressure against the lira and pound intensified.

Shortly thereafter German Bundesbank president Helmut Schlesinger was interviewed by the German publication *Handelsblatt*. After the interview, one of the reporters asked him about his position on the pressure against these currencies. While not making an official policy statement, the Bundesbank president's candour in replying that economic fundamentals likely merited realignment sent shockwaves through the financial market, and was interpreted as a lack of support by the German government for the British and Italian currencies. The psychological barrier against speculating against EMU-bound currencies had been broken, and massive pressure finally caused both the pound and the lira to leave the ERM (as devaluation was deemed by the governments to be insufficient to stem the pressure). The departure of the pound, in particular, was an acrimonious one. The British government complained loudly of the betrayal of its ERM partners and of the inherent defects of the system itself. This event hardened the always-present Euroscepticism found in Britain, and its participation in monetary union was put on hold indefinitely. Britain has not even joined the ERM II because of the 'fault lines' of the system.

'Black Wednesday' was just the beginning of a difficult period for Europe's currencies. In the wake of the British pound's expulsion from the ERM, attention was focused on the French franc, as opinion polls predicted a narrow margin of victory for the Maastricht Treaty referendum that would take place at the end of the month. The German government and central bank both went on the offensive to prevent the franc from falling victim to market speculation, publicly stating their support for the franc and the strong economic fundamentals that underpinned it. The franc was thus granted a temporary respite, although it once again suffered from speculation in the run-up to the legislative elections in the spring of 1993. Speculation against other currencies like the Irish punt, Spanish peseta and Portuguese escudo prompted numerous devaluations. Even countries not officially participating in the ERM such as Finland and Sweden found their currencies under attack. After unsuccessfully pressuring the Bundesbank to lower interest rates in July, the ERM bands were finally widened in August 1993 to 15 per cent in both directions. At the time analysts predicted that the widening of the bands amounted to a death knell for monetary integration. German chancellor Helmut Kohl acknowledged that the crisis had pushed back the start of EMU by one to two years (*Financial Times*, 10 August 1993), an estimation which seemed optimistic at the time. French prime minister Edouard Balladur also expressed his doubts about when EMU would begin. But the revised ERM proved to be resilient in the face of Member States' continued support for pushing forward with monetary integration.

Thus the ratification of the Maastricht Treaty continued, with the Danish 'no' vote being resolved through a second referendum which passed successfully in 1993. This referendum permitted the Danes to opt out of EMU indefinitely, thus making Denmark and the United Kingdom the only two countries in the European Union with a formal derogation on EMU (all other members are required to eventually adopt the euro). The European Union went forward with the plans for EMU with the creation of the European Monetary Institute (EMI) in 1994 as a precursor to the European Central Bank. This interim institution was charged with preparing for the changeover by coordinating monetary policies among the EU Member States and providing surveillance. Its headquarters was Frankfurt, Germany and it was presided over by Alexandre Lamfalussy, a Belgian who sat on the Delors Committee and had formerly served as general manager of the Bank for International

Settlements. The EMI's Council comprised the governors of the national central banks, which would prepare for the transition to EMU and the eventual transfer of authority to the European Central Bank once monetary union was begun.

Despite the implementation of institutional mechanisms for monetary union, it was difficult to remain optimistic about the starting date. In April 1994 none of the EU states had fulfilled the convergence criteria, not even Germany. In November of that year, ten states suffered from excessive deficits. Politicians such as Greek foreign minister Theodore Pangalos tabled a revision of the EMU calendar (*Les Echos*, 14 February 1994). Italian foreign minister Antonio Martino even suggested proceeding with EMU without the convergence criteria in order to maintain unity in Europe (Du Bois 1999: 398). Opinion polls also produced worrying results. While the unpopularity of the single currency in countries like the United Kingdom and Denmark was expected, similar results in Germany (*Bulletin Europe*, 28 July 1995) were potentially more troublesome. Nevertheless, at the June 1995 Cannes European Council, the year 1999 was confirmed as the starting date for EMU.

Meeting and maintaining the Maastricht Treaty convergence criteria

Governments across Europe enacted various reforms in order to meet the convergence criteria. However, the prospect of a government being less prudent with its fiscal policies in the wake of monetary union remained. In the short term a government had the prospect of being denied membership to monetary union to encourage debt reduction and balancing budgets. Once a country qualified for monetary union, however, it could run looser fiscal policy, dilute the credibility of the euro area as a whole, and threaten the entire region with higher inflation through spillover effects. In a worst-case scenario, it could be up to the ECB to rescue a fiscally insolvent Member State. Although the Maastricht Treaty explicitly excludes this possibility with its 'no bail-out clause', some analysts do not find this credible given the enormous political pressure that would be exerted to prevent the financial collapse of a euro area Member State.

The public scepticism towards monetary integration that had been demonstrated by the weak support in the French referendum (the '*petit oui*' in which the Treaty's proponents only obtained 50.5 per cent of the votes) and the negative result of the first Danish referendum had not abated. Specifically the German populace was concerned about the prospect of trading one of the strongest and most credible currencies in the world for a potentially weaker, unproven currency. In order to assuage these domestic fears, which had been increasing in Germany and were being exploited by the political opposition, German finance minister Theo Waigel proposed the creation of a Stability Pact in 1995. The pact would institute the Maastricht Treaty's fiscal criteria past the inception of monetary union. The French government, however, displayed little enthusiasm for yet another measure that would institutionalize further the stability consensus upon which monetary union was based, and the Jospin government pressed for a *gouvernement économique* which would act as a political counterweight to the

---

Box 3.1 ERM II

The European Council decided at its December 1996 meeting that the ERM II would replace the existing ERM beginning on 1 January 1999, at the beginning of monetary union and thus replacing the European Monetary System. Negotiations for the ERM II officially concluded in September 1998, and the ERM II was subsequently amended on 16 March 2006. Membership in the arrangement would be voluntary, although governments holding a derogation could join (as Denmark did).

Within the ERM II, a central rate would be established between the euro and the non-euro currency, with a fluctuation band of plus or minus 15 per cent around the central rate. A narrower fluctuation band could also be negotiated at the initiative of the non-Eurozone state, and such agreements are also supported by the automatic intervention and financing mechanisms discussed below. All interested participants, including the ECB, retained the right to initiate an exchange rate realignment. Any such decisions must be made by common accord among the Eurozone Member States, the ECB, and the central bank governors of the non-Eurozone states, subsequent to consulting the Economic and Financial Committee.

$\longrightarrow$

Bundesbank. The Italians also tried to enlist the Spanish to block the German proposal (Du Bois 1999: 401).

As a compromise, the German government agreed to rename the policy the Stability and Growth Pact in order to acquiesce to French concerns that monetary union needed explicitly to account for growth in addition to price stability. Although this change was not seen as significant at the time, it would be invoked constantly almost a decade later during the debate on the reform of the SGP that passed in 2005. The other compromise was the creation of the Eurogroup in lieu of a *gouvernement économique*. This informal body is composed of the Ecofin members participating in EMU, and meets prior to Ecofin in order to discuss concerns common to euro area members.

These decisions were taken at the Dublin European Council in December 1996. In addition to setting the foundation for the SGP,

→

The ECB and the central banks of the affected currencies are obliged to keep one another informed about interventions in the foreign exchange market, either at the margins or coordinated intramarginal interventions. Any automatic interventions at the margin could be suspended if they were to conflict with the primary goal of price stability. In order to finance interventions, very short-term credit facilities are available for the ECB and the non-Eurozone country for both marginal and intramarginal interventions, with an initial maturity date of three months which can be automatically extended for a maximum of three months. However, the debtor central bank must not pass the ceiling laid down in its total indebtedness. If a debt is renewed automatically for three months, it is eligible to be renewed again for three more months upon the approval of the creditor central bank.

The ministers and governors of the central banks of the Member States not participating in the exchange-rate mechanism do not enjoy voting rights. Intervention at the margins is in principle automatic and unlimited, with very short-term financing available. However, the ECB and the central banks of the other participants can suspend intervention if this conflicts with the primary objective of maintaining price stability.

numerous other decisions were made relative to monetary union. Of particular interest was the creation of the ERM II (see Box 3.1), a matter made even more relevant by Italy's re-entry into the ERM just a month prior to the Council meeting.

In order to ensure successful convergence across the European Union, states underwent economic and monetary surveillance prior to EMU. The Commission submitted a recommendation to the Council, which then set broad guidelines for the Member States. The Commission then monitored the states and submitted reports to Ecofin, which could address recommendations to Member States that were in violation of the aforementioned guidelines. The states were expected to undertake triennial convergence programmes which the Commission assessed and the Council passed.

In 1994 all of the Member States save for Ireland and Luxembourg were found to be in breach of the deficit targets, with the average rate being double the recommended rate. The first deadline for monetary union in 1996 passed, as it was clear that the Maastricht Treaty's convergence criteria were unattainable for most of the European Union. In 1995 the Madrid European Council approved the new timetable for monetary union in 1999. By this time it was acknowledged that, ironically, even Germany might fall short of meeting the criteria. Nonetheless taking monetary union off the table was not viewed as a viable policy option, and states proceeded with the goal of EMU in 1999. Succeed they did, but not without a few one-off measures such as revaluing gold reserves and selling off state-owned assets in order to reduce budget deficits. In December 1997 only three countries (Finland, Luxembourg and Portugal) fulfilled all of the criteria (Du Bois 1999: 404). By 25 March 1998 the Commission declared that Belgium, Germany, Spain, France, Ireland, Italy, the Netherlands, Austria and Portugal also fulfilled the criteria, a move that was criticized two days later by the Bundesbank since Italy and Belgium had been approved despite their high debt levels (Du Bois 1999: 405).

In 1998 EU leaders met to determine the first member of EMU as well as the institutional business of selecting the new president of the ECB. This turned out to be a more contentious exercise than initially anticipated, as most Member States had already voiced their support for Wim Duisenberg of the Netherlands. At the last minute, however, French president Jacques Chirac put forward

French central banker Jean-Claude Trichet as a candidate. Although the economic credentials of neither Duisenberg nor Trichet were ever in question, the French government held firm in its preference for a French central bank president, particularly in light of the selection of Frankfurt, Germany (seat of the German Bundesbank) as the home of the new institution. A compromise was reached in which Duisenberg would stand for half a term and then be replaced by Trichet, an arrangement which was later renounced by the former.

Nevertheless, everything was now in place for the launch of the euro in 1999. The inaugural members included 11 of the 15 EU Member States. Both Britain and Denmark secured an opt-out from monetary union, and this derogation exempts them from mandatory participation in EMU. Neither Greece nor Sweden successfully fulfilled the criteria, although for the latter this was a deliberate strategy to enable it to remain outside the Eurozone. However, not all of the EU11 states had fulfilled the criteria either (see Table 3.2). In particular, Belgium and Italy were quite far from the debt target of 60 per cent of GDP. But the wording of the Treaty had an escape clause which allowed governments that were 'approaching' such levels to be accepted into monetary union, contingent on the approval of the European Council. Thus on 1 January 1999 European Monetary Union officially came into operation.

Launching monetary union

The early days of the euro were relatively uneventful. Perhaps the biggest problem was the decision of shopkeepers across Europe (but especially in countries like France and Italy) to take advantage of the changeover by rounding up prices. Although this only appeared as a small upward tick in overall inflation levels, in the minds of many Europeans the introduction of the euro is strongly associated with price hikes as milk, bread, coffee and haircuts, among other things, suddenly became more expensive.

The other remarkable aspect of the euro's early years was its weakness relative to the dollar (see Figure 3.1). On 4 January 1999, the euro traded at $1.17. In the face of productivity gains, economic growth and rising stock market returns in the United States, the euro began to depreciate steadily. While some governments (Germany, Belgium) welcomed the weakness of the euro, others (France) took a

TABLE 3.2 *Council Decision 98/317/EC of 3 May 1998 on Identification of the Member States Participating in the Third Stage of EMU*

	Central bank independence	Inflation	Excessive deficit	Exchange rate stability	Long-term interest rate	Government debt
Austria	Yes	1.1	No	Yes	5.6	63.8
Belgium	Yes	1.4	No	Yes	5.7	122.2
Finland	Yes	1.3	No	Yes	5.9	53.6
France	Yes	1.2	No	Yes	5.5	58.5
Germany	Yes	1.4	No	Yes	5.6	59.6
Greece	Yes	5.2	Yes	No	9.8	114
Ireland	Yes	1.2	No	Yes	6.2	63.6
Italy	Yes	1.8	No	Yes	6.7	118.1
Luxembourg	Yes	1.4	No	Yes	5.6	6.4
Netherlands	Yes	1.8	No	Yes	5.5	67
Portugal	Yes	1.8	No	Yes	6.2	56
Spain	Yes	1.8	No	Yes	6.3	65.3
Sweden	No	1.9	No	No	6.5	70

Source: http://europa.eu/scadplus/leg/en/lvb/l25037.htm
Information on government debt is for 1997, *source:* Eurostat.

TABLE 3.3 *Chronology of monetary integration, 1999–2009*

1999	EMU begins.
2000	Greece becomes 12th member of euro area. Lisbon Strategy launched. Danes reject the euro in a referendum.
2002	Introduction of euro coins and notes.
2003	SGP suspended. Swedish referendum rejects the euro.
2004	Enlargement: ten new states join the European Union.
2005	Reform of Lisbon Strategy and SGP.
2007	Slovenia becomes 13th member of euro area. Enlargement: Bulgaria and Romania join the European Union.
2008	Cyprus and Malta join the euro area.
2009	Slovakia joins the euro area.

more defensive posture. Even the central banking community was divided on the issues of whether or not this was a worrying trend, and whether the Eurozone should take action (Henning 2007: 321–22). By January 2000 the euro dipped below parity, and the Eurozone became more active in its public support of the currency. By September foreign exchange intervention had begun, first with its G7 partners and in November unilaterally (Henning 2007).

FIGURE 3.1   Dollar–euro exchange rate, 1999–2004

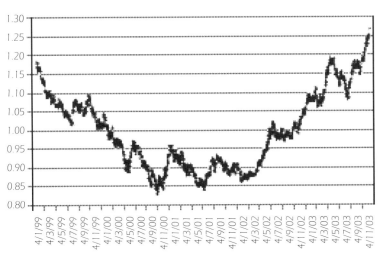

Source: European Central Bank.

The euro's introduction occurred at an economically auspicious time, with strong growth throughout the region (see Table 3.4). However, instead of saving during good times (as envisaged by the SGP), the European governments by and large took advantage of this favourable economic climate to reduce taxes and provide relief to an electorate that was acknowledged to suffer from 'reform fatigue' in the aftermath of qualifying for EMU (Buiter 2006).

With EMU under way, the European Union turned its attention towards becoming more competitive economically. In March 2000 the Lisbon Agenda was launched, with the goal of creating 'the world's most competitive, knowledge-based economy'. The use of soft law was expanded and the open method of coordination presented the European Union with both a challenge and an opportunity. On the one hand, a system of cooperation without any penalties for noncompliance could lead to a lot of empty promises with no results. On the other hand, it offered an opportunity to expand the European Union's reach into new policy areas. The goals of the Lisbon Agenda were ambitious, and required serious reforms on the part of many Member States. However, in the wake of qualifying for the Maastricht Treaty criteria, many governments found it difficult to justify further reforms to the domestic populace.

By early 2002 this reform fatigue presented a problem for Portugal, and more importantly for Germany, as both were nearing the deficit limits set by the SGP. As the originator of the pact, undergoing the excessive deficit procedure (EDP) that acted as an

TABLE 3.4   *Eurozone growth rates, 1999–2001*

	1999	2000	2001
Austria	3.3	3.4	0.8
Belgium	3.1	3.9	1
Finland	3.4	5	1
France	3.3	4.1	2.1
Germany	2	3.2	1.2
Ireland	10.7	9.2	6.2
Italy	1.9	3.6	1.8
Luxembourg	8.4	8.4	2.5
Netherlands	4	3.5	1.4
Portugal	3.9	3.9	2
Spain	4.7	5	3.5

official reprimand against a country's fiscal policies would have been politically embarrassing during an election year. Thus both Portugal and Germany escaped official censure so as not to hurt the German government's re-election prospects (and censuring Portugal without censuring Germany would have been too obviously politically biased).

In 2003 several other countries joined the ranks of Portugal and Germany in suffering from excessive deficits. In November 2003 the Ecofin Council voted to hold the pact in abeyance rather than punish Germany and France, a move which caused the Commission to bring the case before the European Court of Justice (ECJ). In July 2004 the ECJ ruled that while the Commission could not compel the Council to act on its recommendations, the Council nonetheless must take action and cannot suspend procedures. Momentum for SGP reform grew, and in the spring of 2005 the pact was reformed. On the one hand, the pact was made more flexible in order to accommodate economic exigencies that made adhering to the pact difficult in the short-term but would be beneficial for the economy in the long run. No list of such policies was drawn up, but among those cited as most likely candidates were pension reform, programmes that would encourage research and development, and policies that promote European integration.

In 2005 the Lisbon Agenda was also reformed and became known as Lisbon 2. The process was streamlined and refocused so as to concentrate on economic growth. While not disavowing the importance of social policy or the many other policies that fell under the rubric of the original Lisbon Agenda, it was acknowledged that they had been ineffective and the European Union was still a long way from achieving its goal. Wim Kok had chaired an inquiry into the Lisbon Agenda and its effects, coming to the conclusion that its all-encompassing nature was harmful rather than helpful. Instead of creating synergies between different issue areas, the Lisbon Agenda became meaningless. Thus by refocusing on economic growth, the hope was that other policy priorities could later follow from this and build on its success. However, stronger economic growth was needed in order to pay for these other priorities, hence the orientation.

On 1 January 2007 Slovenia became the 13th member of the Eurozone. The previous spring the application of Lithuania had been denied since it had higher inflation than that required by the Maastricht convergence criteria. Lithuanian officials, among others, pointed out that the criterion on inflation was based on the levels of the three countries within the European Union that had the lowest inflation. However, had the criterion been based on the levels of the three countries within the Eurozone, Lithuania's rates would have been acceptable. Nevertheless the European Union decided on a strict application of the convergence criteria, in contrast to the original launch of the Eurozone in 1999 when Belgium and Italy far exceeded the reference levels. In 2008 Malta and Cyprus joined Slovenia among the ranks of the Eurozone, and once again the number of countries within the Eurozone exceeds the number of countries on the outside. In 2009 the addition of Slovakia brought the number of Eurozone members to 16.

In the second half of 2008 the subprime financial crisis that had originated in the United States in the summer of 2007 hit Europe. Initial attempts at a European response were rejected in favour of national plans, as several Member States adopted unilateral measures to protect their financial systems, including the partial nationalization of some banks and providing deposit guarantees. On 7 October EU finance ministers made a disappointing announcement that EU-level action would be limited to a guarantee by each of the Member States of savings of up to €50,000 for one year (though some countries were ready to guarantee up to €100,000). According to reports, Germany and the United Kingdom (the European Union's largest financial market centres) hesitated to adopt more specific actions at the level of the European Union (*Financial Times*, 7 October 2008).

The continued market instability prompted stronger action on the part of first central banks and finally Member State governments. On 12 October an extraordinary meeting between the heads of state and government of the Eurozone countries was held at the behest of the French presidency. The countries pledged to support the Eurozone financial sectors, including state guarantees on inter-bank lending and the recapitalization of banks. This plan was based largely on the United Kingdom's £400 billion bailout plan. The ECB also announced it would accept a larger range of collateral from banks, including assets with a credit rating as low as BBB– (previously the threshold had been A–). The Eurozone braced itself for its first recession amid questions over whether the current governance structure would be adequate for dealing with a global financial crisis.

Theoretical considerations

Ideas

After the signing of the Maastricht Treaty, economic ideas and political interests shifted rapidly. Markets had treated the currencies as if they were already fixed since the late 1980s, ignoring signs of the weakening economies of Britain and Italy until the events in the spring of 1992 which triggered a wave of speculative attacks that would last over a year. The economics field does not have a singular agreed formula regarding exchange rate determination. Indeed, an exchange rate that many consider overvalued can exist for a long time without the rate being changed or the currency suffering from speculation. A prominent theory involved the existence of multiple equilibria, meaning that a single set of economic conditions can support a number of viable exchange rate levels (Obstfeld 1986). In a fixed exchange rate system what is going to determine the switch from one exchange rate to another depends on market expectations regarding future economic conditions. If market actors believe that future economic conditions will differ from current ones, exchange market pressure will arise for the government to realign the currency to a new level which corresponds with market actors' expectations. Thus a self-fulfilling attack could occur if markets believed that economic policies and therefore economic conditions would change in the future, even in the absence of an actual policy change. Some have gone so far as to argue that the exchange rate is normally disconnected from economic fundamentals and one must look elsewhere to understand exchange rate volatility (de Grauwe and Grimaldi 2006).

What of the move to monetary union? Although the economic rationale exists for a single currency based on trade effects, the economic case for monetary union was not unambiguous. According to the leading economic theory pertaining to a single currency, optimum currency area theory, the European economies did not possess the characteristics that would make giving up national currencies advantageous (Eichengreen 1992b). When sacrificing a national currency, a government gives up an important tool of economic adjustment. This becomes particularly important when the currency area faces an economic shock which affects regions differently. For example, the United States is generally taken to be an optimum currency area. If a hurricane hit Florida and caused massive damage, its economy would no longer be similar to other states that were unaffected by the hurricane. However, the United States has other adjustment mechanisms which make it possible for Florida to continue to follow a single monetary policy. The federal government could declare Florida to be in a state of emergency and disburse funds to alleviate the damage. In response to rising unemployment that might occur, many workers in Florida would be willing to move to where jobs are more readily available. This example points to two traits that the United States enjoys as an optimum currency area that Europe does not: a system of fiscal transfers and labour mobility. These factors offset the loss of a single currency as a mechanism of adjustment. In the absence of these, however, European economies would find it much more difficult to adjust to economic shocks, and one could see the persistence of economic disparities in their wake. The ERM zone had experienced an asymmetric shock, German unification, and Europe did not have the instruments available under optimum currency area theory to adjust. Given the incompatibility of a single interest rate that would suit all of the ERM economies, the relatively weak mobility of European labour, and absence of fiscal transfers, the only mechanism for adjustment that remained was the exchange rate. This adjustment, however, was only undertaken under extreme foreign exchange market pressure.

The above analysis is based on what have been referred to as Mundell I assumptions (de Grauwe 2006, McKinnon 2004), following Mundell's writings from 1961 on the subject. Mundell I assumes a Keynesian worldview in which price and wage rigidity can be balanced through active monetary policy and thus stabilize the economy. However, according to later work done (1973), aka Mundell II, monetary union would not result in the loss of the exchange rate as a policy tool because it was no longer useful as such. This follows from monetarist ideas which view active monetary policy as a cause of instability rather than a solution. The exchange rate is thus no longer considered an effective tool for adjustment, as the central bank should be concentrating on price stability and not trying to fight market forces. Instead, monetary union was beneficial because the exchange rate, rather than a policy tool, had become an important source of asymmetric shocks. In a world of widespread capital mobility, exchange rates attracted destabilizing speculative attacks such as that seen in 1992–93. Thus thinking had shifted away from the optimum currency area theory based on Mundell I and towards that of

Mundell II, with the exchange rate no longer able to stabilize economic conditions. In fact, they were more likely to be a destabilizing factor. However, de Grauwe (2006) notes that as some euro area countries have suffered competitiveness losses since the introduction of the new currency, Mundell I ideas are coming back into fashion.

But according to Wyplosz (2006: 216), European politicians paid no heed to the debates of academic economies. Optimum currency area did not play an important role in the formation of the Maastricht Treaty; indeed, its emphasis on price stability rather than on output and employment is 'monetary union's original sin'. Rather than economic rationale, political ideas and motivations were primary when it came to making the case for monetary union.

An important political idea driving monetary integration during this time was that it was part of European political union. Despite some disagreement within Germany on the terms of monetary union, 'at a deeper level, was a broader, shared "normative" belief about the importance of European unification for Germany' (Dyson and Featherstone 1999: 266).

Interests

What advantages would result from a single currency? We can consider European-level interests versus country-level interests. At the European level, a single currency held the prospect of allowing Europe to have more autonomy from the United States. The dollar's volatility continued to cause problems for European economies in the 1980s, with high-profile foreign exchange intervention being undertaken by the major central banks (the United States, Germany, United Kingdom, France and Japan) in order to prevent the dollar's rise (the Plaza accord of 1985) and then to stop its descent (the Louvre accord of 1987). This argument is an extension of the one made in the 1970s regarding the return to exchange rate cooperation, the desire to create a zone of monetary stability that would insulate the European economies from the dollar's movements. The French, for example, had expressed the need for a 'political roof' for EMU. The new post-Cold War realities of a united Germany and single superpower required binding the former to Europe and balancing the latter, as Pierre Bérégovoy argued in a presentation to the Council of Ministers on 5 December 1990 (Dyson and Featherstone 1999: 223). Moreover, the

Europeans could also take a leading role in the international monetary arena in which the United States had been dominant for the last few decades. In international economic fora like the IMF and the World Bank, the European economies clearly acted as a junior partner to the United States despite their combined economic weight which could rival that of the dollar. Finally, a single currency also carried seignorage benefits which further gave European economies greater autonomy.

The structural condition of rising capital mobility gave markets greater power and made it increasingly difficult for governments to control capital flows and therefore maintain exchange rate parities. Thus a consensus emerged among major actors that capital mobility was at best desirable (following on the movement towards market liberalization in the 1980s) but at the very least unavoidable and difficult to control. This created a confluence of both powerful economic interests and a prevailing economic orthodoxy (Goodman 1992, Gros and Thygesen 1998, Henning 1998, McNamara 1998) which became institutionalized as part of the Maastricht Treaty (in so far as states are required to liberalize capital movements). Numerous interests stood to gain from this move to monetary union, in particular financial interests and other groups (like businesses with considerable international economic transactions – see Moravcsik 1998). Financial actors supported the cementing of the stability culture in monetary union, and a single currency was expected to bring considerable trade benefits. The expected losers were those that would not benefit from the exchange rate stability promised by a single currency and would feel more acutely the loss of monetary policy, specifically the exchange rate, as a policy instrument (Frieden 1998).

Greater autonomy was also sought by individual European states so as to emerge from German monetary dominance. Since the beginning of the decade all ERM participants needed to follow the monetary policy of the Bundesbank so as to avoid capital flight and their exchange rate from depreciating. For example, if the Bundesbank were to raise its interest rates, all of the ERM participants would follow in lockstep within minutes. If the Bundesbank raised its rates and a country refused to follow suit, capital would leave that economy and go to Germany's, which was now offering higher interest rates and thus a better return on investment. Germany generally enjoyed lower interest rates than its neighbours because of its superior economic credibility. Indeed, other economies paid an interest rate premium over and above that of Germany in order to keep capital from fleeing into Germany's more stable economic environment. Fixing their currency to the mark offered advantages such as the aforementioned lower interest rates enjoyed by ERM states. However, when the Bundesbank made monetary policy it did so with only the German economy in mind, not the European Community as a whole or the region comprised of ERM participants. This had the potential to cause substantial problems should the needs of the German economy differ greatly from those of its ERM partners, a situation that happened in the wake of Germany's unification in 1990. Thus the creation of a single European currency held the promise of greater monetary sovereignty as a European central bank would need to take into account the needs of all the participants and not just Germany. The other states would have a seat at the table that they did not enjoy when the Bundesbank made monetary policy for Germany and de facto for all of the ERM members (Chang 2003, Dyson and Featherstone 1999, Grieco 1995, McNamara and Jones 1996).

The advantages for Germany in joining monetary union were ambiguous (Moravcsik 1998, Heisenberg 2005). Germany was the only country in the ERM that had considerable monetary autonomy. Moreover it had successfully exported its stability culture to other EC states. What advantage would accrue to the country that held the anchor currency of the ERM? In particular, the German consensus on the importance of price stability had spread, but many continued to doubt the level of commitment of other European economies. EMU held the threat of requiring Germany to one day bail out one of its EMU partners so as to prevent spillover of a financial crisis into another state. Germany thus proceeded cautiously during the initial period of negotiation for monetary union.

In 1989, however, the sudden fall of the Berlin Wall changed the debate entirely. The German government under Helmut Kohl took advantage of this historic moment, with Kohl as the man who unified Europe (monetarily) as well as Germany. In turn, his European partners were eager to bind a united Germany more closely to Europe. Monetary integration thus fuelled greater political integration in Europe, and this political imperative outweighed the economic concerns of the advisability of such a move (Andrews 1993, Baun 1996, Garrett 1993). Indeed, German foreign policy elites played an important role in negotiating the Maastricht Treaty as part of the overall objective of alleviating the security dilemma that Germany has had with its neighbours, in particular France, through institutional means (Kaltenthaler 2002). Some have even argued that monetary union was the price that Germany paid for its unification (Kaltenthaler 1998: 79), although the plans for EMU had preceded the fall of the wall.

Despite these interests which were allied in favour of monetary integration, it was not a foregone conclusion. In particular the participation of Germany was critical for EMU to get off the ground, and as the country with the most to lose it zealously guarded its interests from forces that could undermine the hard-won credibility of the mark and the Bundesbank's monetary policy. Institutionally, the German government fought for (and won) an independent central bank which was modelled after the Bundes-bank and would privilege price stability over all other goals (Heisenberg 1998, Kaltenthaler 1998, Loedel 1999). While the ERM participants had delegated monetary policy to an independent central bank years earlier (albeit not their own), central bank independence was not yet a widely accepted practice. Many central banks, including those in France, Italy and the United Kingdom, had historically been dependent on the government and were required to support its policies (Goodman 1992). Supporting the government's economic policies would only be a secondary priority for the ECB, although only to the extent to which it did not threaten price stability. Such an institutional configuration essentially pitted those concerned about the credibility of the central bank with those that argued for the need for institutions to follow the democratically expressed wishes of citizens (thereby following government instructions). Although the French government agreed to the principle of an independent central bank readily enough, it lobbied hard for a *gouvernement économique* which could act as a political counterweight to the ECB. This issue would not be settled even well after the signing of the Maastricht Treaty.

Institutions

The most important institutional arguments during this period relate to institutions that were created to support EMU. As they are dealt with extensively in the next two chapters, I shall only highlight some essential points here. The independence of the ECB reflected the preferences of countries like Germany and the Netherlands, but it quickly became an important actor in its own right. It has a significant role to play internally (in setting European monetary policy) as well as externally (in representing the Eurozone, along with Member States, in some international fora). While central bank independence had been successfully used in other countries (like Germany), having such a powerful supranational institution was a new experience, and the ECB needed to deal with numerous concerns regarding its transparency, accountability and legitimacy.

The creation of a powerful supranational institution like the ECB contrasts with the relatively weak role given to the Commission. Mitterrand early on had deemed EMU 'too important to be left to EC finance ministers. The European Council rather than the Commission was the appropriate centre for political direction of EMU' (Dyson and Featherstone 1999: 194). Similarly French negotiators had also declined to grant the European Parliament co-decision on monetary union. Thus monetary union had a decidedly more intergovernmentalist overtone, although the French failed to persuade others to make the ECB accountable to national parliaments and the EP (Dyson and Featherstone 1999: 237).

The SGP was also the result of a political compromise between French and German interests. It was based on the same economic rationale as the Maastricht Treaty convergence criteria, but its weak implementation indicated an erosion of the consensus and support enjoyed by the treaty. Despite numerous criticisms of the treaty and the SGP, the institutionalization of their criteria means that both current and future Member States must respect them, lest they risk censure. Thus these institutions have created path dependence (Pierson 2000) which continues to impact the Eurozone.

Domestic institutions and internal politics also played an important role. Although the Bundesbank had staked out a rather strong position in relation to the scheduling of monetary union not taking precedence over the fulfilment of the convergence criteria, the German foreign office and chancellery were able to soften what had been a very strict economist position into a somewhat monetarist one. The German government did not want to miss the chance to hasten European integration despite the misgivings of the Bundesbank and finance ministry (Kaltenthaler 1998: 82–3).

Conclusion

The birth of the Eurozone in 1999 constitutes a small miracle given the tumultuous decade that preceded it. Indeed, the resilience of the

European Union in the face of setbacks like the 1992–93, post-Maastricht debates over the content of monetary union, clashes over political symbols like the nationality of the first ECB president, and the composition of the first group of Eurozone countries was impressive. However, although some countries posted a strong economic performance during the early years of the euro area, others were disappointed by the weakness of the euro relative to the dollar and the generally sluggish economic growth of the Eurozone as a whole.

While much of the rationale given for monetary union is of a technocratic nature so as to justify the use of policies that ostensibly try to remove politics from monetary policy, in fact politics never left. The economic arguments for monetary integration are widely contested, and numerous economists and central bankers have stressed the political nature of monetary cooperation in Europe. Political factors have both motivated the creation of the euro and hampered the effective implementation of numerous euro area policies.

Chapter 4

The institutions and decision processes of monetary union

EMU has presented a major challenge to the Eurozone states. Monetary policy has been delegated to the European Central Bank (ECB), which sets interest rates for the entire euro area. While interest rate policy had largely been delegated to the Bundesbank during the EMS period, the complete delegation of monetary policy and the loss of the exchange rate as an adjustment tool still exacted a price from certain Member States. Even Germany, whose large economy plays a major factor in the ECB's decision making, has had to deal with sub-optimal interest rates since the euro's inception. Moreover, sharing a currency has also led to greater economic policy coordination, due to supposed greater spillover effects between participating economies. Governments have been loath to delegate even more power after creating such an independent central bank, however, and most economic policy coordination has been done under the auspices of soft law, which has proven to be less than completely effective. Finally, as a fledgling currency area, the Eurozone must still prove its independence and credibility to markets while maintaining its legitimacy. This chapter addresses these issues by examining economic governance in the Eurozone. The first part looks at the basic architecture of monetary union (the monetary and economic pillars), followed by the key actors and institutions involved in Eurozone governance and the roles that they play. The chapter concludes with a consideration of the major theoretical issues associated with the governance of the Eurozone.

Architecture

The Sapir Report (2003: 3) described the governance system as:

A patchwork of different arrangements for managing economic policies in the EU .... Four basic approaches have been adopted:

delegation, commitment, coordination and autonomy of national policies. Not only are there different approaches, but also many different instruments are used to execute policy, ranging from hard collective rules to milder instruments of persuasion and soft procedures for cooperation and dialogue. The picture that emerges is one of confusion and tension – confusion created by the complexity of the system and diversity of the roles performed, tension in the gap between goals and means.

Table 4.1 reflects the complexity of the EU economic governance system, which is characterized by different forms of coordination ranging from delegation to autonomy. EMU is not a union in the sense of a single policy but rather the coordination of economic policies within a relatively loose framework. In some policies (like monetary policy) a single policy does exist for all of the participating members. In other policies Member States are encouraged to take into account recommendations when forming national policy, though repercussions are minimal if they fail to respect them. Thus EMU is based on two pillars, monetary policy and economic policies. The monetary pillar is governed by the European System of Central Banks (ESCB), comprised of the national central banks of the Member States along with the ECB, and it corresponds to the 'delegation' described by Sapir. Its federal structure is reminiscent of the Bundesbank, upon which it was based. The Eurozone's monetary policy is set by the ECB and executed by the ESCB. It thus decides on the interest rate for all of the participating states and makes its decisions with the primary objective of achieving price stability. Though it made no revisions to the ECB's statutes, the Lisbon Treaty neglected to give the ECB a special status apart from institutions like the European Parliament (EP) despite its inclusion in the Constitutional Treaty. In a letter dated 9 August 2007, ECB President Trichet wrote to Manuel Lobo Antunes, the Portuguese Europe minister (then holding the rotating presidency), 'Because of its specific institutional features, the ECB needs to be differentiated from the union's institutions,' referring to the need to keep the bank free from political pressure (*Financial Times*, 11 August 2007). This argument was ultimately rejected, although the independence of the ECB was never in question.

The move to monetary union was also supposed to consolidate the gains made in the stabilization of the exchange rate. As far as intra-EU affairs is concerned, EMU left intact the Exchange Rate

TABLE 4.1 *A schematic representation of the EU governance regimes*

	Micro	Macro
Delegation	CAP Trade (goods) Competition (most) Product market rules Regional development (some) R&D (EU)	Monetary policy (for Eurozone)
Commitment	VAT State aids Greenhouse emissions control	Fiscal policy (Art. 104) (for Eurozone)
Coordination	Labour markets Financial supervision Service and utility markets Regional development	Fiscal policy (Art. 99)
Autonomy	Direct taxation National public spending Education Welfare R&D (national)	

Source: Sapir et al. (2003: 77).

Mechanism II (see Table 4.2) in order to provide incumbent Eurozone members with the institutional support to fix their exchange rate against the euro.

Regarding the euro's external exchange rate, the issue becomes a bit trickier. Does this fall under monetary policy (thus controlled by the ECB) or economic policy (leaving the prerogative with the Member States)? Responsibility for this was deliberately left vague, given the lack of consensus between Member States on the best institutional model to adopt. Different nation states have chosen various divisions of labour between the central bank and the finance ministry, with some countries (like the United States) giving primacy to the finance ministry, and others (such as Germany)

TABLE 4.2   *ERM II membership*

Member State (national currency)	Central rate (EUR 1)	Fluctuation band
Denmark (krone)	7.46038	+/- 2.25%
Estonia (kroon)	15.6466	+/- 15%
Lithuania (litas)	3.45280	+/- 15%
Latvia (lats)	0.702804	+/- 15%

Source: European Commission.

favouring the central bank. No agreement existed among the Member States, unlike the broad consensus on central bank independence. Which body controls the exchange rate in the Eurozone is therefore ambiguous in the Maastricht Treaty, and the division of labour was tested early on.

In 1999 German finance minister Oskar Lafontaine and French finance minister Dominique Strauss-Kahn (*not* in coordination with other Member States) advanced the idea of a target zone between the euro, the dollar and other currencies, an idea to which the ECB was 'unreservedly hostile' (Henning 2007: 320). Thus in 1999 the major actors in exchange rate policy (Eurosystem, Eurogroup, finance ministries, central banks) negotiated institutional prerogatives regarding foreign exchange operations. Article 111, paragraph 1 in the Treaty on European Union (Maastricht Treaty, TEU) gave the authority to commit to formal exchange rate agreements (such as pegging the euro to another currency) to the Council, which can also give the ECB 'general orientations' for the exchange rate. Despite this legal framework, the negotiators did not draw heavily on Article 111 during their discussions, as it did not give much direction on the issue of foreign exchange operations under a flexible exchange rate system (Henning 2007: 324). Ultimately it was decided that the ECB would take the lead in issues dealing with foreign exchange intervention. However, the chairman of the Economic and Financial Committee (EFC) would communicate with the US Treasury when it came to planning the details of joint interventions, as the Eurozone's G7 partners prefer to deal with elected politicians. Finally, the ECB president would act as spokesperson for the Eurozone with financial markets (Henning 2007).

Given the importance of trade to the Eurozone, the exchange

rate will no doubt continue to be a relevant topic in the future. The French president Sarkozy has made numerous references to the euro's exchange rate, indicating that he would prefer more active management. Sarkozy argues that politicians (rather than unelected central bankers) should assume responsibility for the exchange rate; this is the case in the United States and even pre-euro Germany. In addition, the exchange rate should be used as a policy tool in order to enhance the economy's competitiveness (*Financial Times*, 1 July 2007). German chancellor Angela Merkel, however, expressed her distaste for an activist exchange rate policy.

The issue of exchange rate responsibilities highlights a major problem in the EU governance structure, namely the ambiguity of responsibility. EU-level actors (like the ECB and the Commission) enjoy different levels of power and responsibility according to the specific issue area, but even within a specific policy it may not be clear which actor has priority when disagreement ensues. Even when an actor clearly has a legally recognized institutional prerog-ative, other actors have tried to infringe upon or influence decision making (such as when Member States exhort the ECB to lower interest rates). Finally, Member States have guarded their remain-ing policymaking capacities, and the potential for clashes with supranational institutions like the ECB is a perennial feature of EMU governance.

The economic pillar has been subject to more revision since 1992. New agreements have been added and old agreements altered in order to better reflect the changing interests of the Member States. While some aspects of the economic pillar (such as the internal market) already existed, some policies were developed concurrently with the monetary pillar (like the Broad Economic Policy Guidelines (BEPG), whose legal basis is in Article 99 of the TEU) while others were developed after monetary union began (such as the Lisbon Agenda). Linsenmann and Wessels (2006: 115) commented on the 'almost continuous revision of, and amend-ments to, the existing rules of Euro social governance and the introduction of new procedures'. Ardy et al. (2006) counted eight economic coordination mechanisms: Ecofin and the Eurogroup, the Stability and Growth Pact (SGP) and Cologne processes (macroeconomics), the Luxembourg and Cardiff processes and Lisbon (microeconomic) and the BEPG.

Control over the second pillar remains largely with national governments. Although EMU participants are expected to treat such policies as a matter of common concern because of the spillover potential to other Member States, many economic policies are only loosely coordinated at best. For example, the SGP sets objectives for Member States in achieving budgetary discipline, although the precise policies followed are up to the individual governments. The Member States need to keep their deficit levels under 3 per cent of GDP, lest the Commission report their violation and recommend to the Council that a warning be issued. If the Member State fails to correct the situation, then the excessive deficit procedure (EDP) is enacted and eventually sanctions are levied. The 2005 reform made the SGP less rigid by allowing the time between diagnosis of a violation and punishment to be lengthened, and now Member States can avoid censure by making a case for the economic merits of policy decisions that contributed to the high deficits. Although the likelihood of serious action being taken against a Member State has therefore diminished, the SGP still comprises a major element of EMU economic policy and has the backing of 'hard law' (albeit one that has not been used and will likely not be).

Much of the economic pillar is composed of policies using soft law. For example, under the Lisbon Agenda the European Union sets broad guidelines for governments to follow in order to make the European Union the world's most competitive economy by improving its competitiveness, but the policy programmes are designed and implemented by the Member States themselves. Should a government fail to respect its obligations, there would be no consequences, as it operates according to soft law, specifically the employment of the open method of coordination (OMC). The OMC is a form of soft law in which ideas are exchanged between Member States in order to persuade one another and learn from each other's best practices, with benchmarking and peer pressure used to encourage compliance. Its dubious track record led to its reformulation in 2005 with a focus on jobs and growth (with other objectives like social policy and environmental policy taking a back seat). Lisbon 2's Integrated Guidelines are more detailed and coherent than in Lisbon 1, when a myriad of different guidelines existed for various policies. According to some observers, Lisbon 2 also contains more constraints than its predecessors. However, others have noted that the flaws that prevented the original Lisbon Agenda from being effective are still in place (Federal Trust 2005).

Other economic policies that support monetary union (competition policy, internal market policies) are taken at the European level and operate more along the lines of the traditional Community method which demands the greater involvement of institutions like the Commission and the Parliament. The trend towards soft law stands in contrast to the Community method, as the former is more intergovernmental and infringes considerably less on state sovereignty (Kohler-Koch 1999, Linsenmann et al. 2007). But progress in this area has also been uneven. The internal market has still not been completed, and an essential component of it, the liberalization of services, was far weaker than originally envisioned. Nevertheless a trend in favour of softer forms of economic coordination seems to have emerged (Meyer et al. 2007).

Some have faulted this imbalanced structure with making Eurozone policy prone to inconsistency. A report by the Federal Trust (2005) charged that the existing system contains multiple sources of fiscal policy, requires greater intellectual and administrative support at an EU-level, lacks the capacity to improve the euro area's economic performance and contributes to the euro's unpopularity, as positive economic outcomes are attributed to national policies whereas negative ones are blamed on the euro. This combined with post-EMU reform fatigue has made it difficult for the Eurozone to fully reap the benefits of integration, as much more work remains.

EMU's major actors

The first institution under consideration is the ECB. When the ECB took over monetary policy of the Eurozone, it assumed the functions previously undertaken by the national central banks, which henceforth formed part of the ESCB. The ECB is one of the most independent central banks in the world, having been modelled on Germany's Bundesbank. According to Article 108 EC, the ECB cannot 'seek or take instructions from Community institutions or bodies, from any government of a Member State or from any other body'.

In fact, the ECB was granted even more independence than its predecessor, the Bundesbank. For example, the Bundesbank was required to support the economic policies of the German government under the threat of the revocation of its independence by a simple act of parliament. However the ECB's primary mandate is maintaining price stability in the Eurozone, and supporting the Member States' economic policies is only a secondary objective. Furthermore its independence can only be revoked through a treaty revision, which would require a unanimous vote of all the Member

States and the ratification of all the national parliaments. Thus changing the ECB's mandate or independent status is far more difficult than it would have been to change the Bundesbank's, and this independence has shielded it from government pressure.

Indeed, the ECB has been criticized for not doing enough to support Member State policies and perhaps going too far in its pursuit of price stability. Inflation was the bane of European economies in the 1980s, but was no longer a headline economic issue in the more recent era of slow growth and high unemployment in certain Eurozone economies. The ECB follows the tenets of the sound money paradigm and its belief that price stability is imperative to market credibility, attracting investment and ultimately engendering stronger economic growth in the economy. However some Member States have viewed the Bank's tendencies as excessive and inhibiting economic growth.

The European Council plays a critical role in forming broader economic policy within the European Union. It defines the political guidelines for the European Union, advancing integration into new issue areas as well as consolidating cooperation in existing ones. Major decisions, such as the creation of the ECB, the formation of the SGP and the launching of the Lisbon Strategy, all had to pass through the European Council. It thus handles decisions that either add to European legislation or change existing legislation (as opposed to proposals by the Commission, which implement decisions already taken by the Council). In order to make institutional changes (such as amending the treaties), an Intergovernmental Conference (IGC) must be called at the initiative of a Member State or the Commission (and approved by a simple majority of the Council of Ministers). Government representatives, along with the Commission, conduct the preparatory work for the IGC, with the European Parliament acting as an observer and engaging in discussions with the General Affairs Council. The European Council then makes any final decisions regarding treaty changes (Europa Scadplus nd).

The intergovernmental body that deals with economic and monetary issue on a more regular basis is the Economics and Financial Affairs Council (Ecofin). This group is composed of the economics and finance ministers of all the EU Member States, both inside and outside the Eurozone. Ecofin's responsibilities include economic policy coordination, economic surveillance, financial market activity, budgetary and fiscal policy monitoring, all aspects dealing with the euro, the movement of capital and the European

Union's economic relations with non-Member countries. Ecofin also participates in meetings of the European Council when matters under its jurisdiction come under discussion (such as the decision to reform the SGP). The President of the Ecofin Council has the right to attend meetings of the ECB's Governing Council, but does not enjoy voting rights and does not normally utilize this prerogative anyway (Ardy et al. 2006: 69).

Ecofin has the legal authority to make decisions on behalf of the Member States (unlike the Eurogroup). The bulk of its decisions are made by qualified majority vote, although the preference is generally to find a consensus (Heisenberg 2005). In addition, fiscal matters require unanimity. For example, Ecofin's ratification was needed for the excessive deficits procedure to commence under the SGP. When Ecofin deliberates on matters concerning the euro and EMU, non-Eurozone countries do not vote (Europa Scadplus nd).

A subset of Ecofin is the Eurogroup. Composed of the Ecofin ministers of countries participating in the Eurozone, the Eurogroup is an informal body which meets prior to Ecofin in order to discuss matters of common concern to those sharing the single currency. French negotiators originally conceived the Eurogroup as a political counterweight to the ECB. As the German government offered its ideas for the creation of a Stability Pact in order to ensure the continued adherence to sound money principles after monetary union began, French officials expressed concern over the domination of the pursuit of price stability over all other goals. Moreover, the French government does not have the same history of central bank independence as Germany. Indeed, the Bank of France remained dependent on the French Treasury until its independence was needed in order to fulfil the Maastricht Treaty convergence criteria. The German government refused to consent to a *gouvernement économique* which might threaten the independence of the ECB. The compromise was the Eurogroup, which has no formal mandate and no outside technical assistance, putting it at a disadvantage against the ECB. The French, however, have not given up on the idea of a *gouvernement économique*, as French president Nicolas Sarkozy has repeatedly made reference to the need for one.

The Eurogroup comprises the finance minister and one senior official or deputy minister from each Eurozone state. Other participants who have been invited to contribute to its deliberations include the director general of DG ECFIN, the commissioner for Economic and Financial Affairs, the Commission president (on occasion), the president and vice president of the ECB, the president and secretary of the Economic and Financial Committee, and the director-general of the Social and Economic Affairs Directorate of the Council's General Secretariat (Puetter 2004). Since January 2005 the Eurogroup has had a fixed presidency of two years. Its first president was Jean-Claude Juncker of Luxembourg. The vice-president of the Eurogroup, however, will continue to rotate and will be the acting Ecofin president (provided he/she comes from a Eurozone country).

In contrast to Ecofin, in which numerous other officials and ambassadors attend meetings, the Eurogroup is kept deliberately small, allowing for discussion and debate. In Ecofin meetings, on the other hand, the large number of participants can preclude debate and members tend to rely more on prepared notes and speeches, making it more difficult to truly exchange ideas and engage in policy learning (Puetter 2004, 2006). The Eurogroup does not have the power to take formal decisions (that right is reserved for Ecofin). It also has no permanent staff. Thus far it has worked to create a consensus among its participants on EU policy in order to operate more cohesively within Ecofin, as opposed to considering broader economic issues that impact the euro area (Federal Trust 2005). Only Eurozone members may vote on issues dealing with the exchange rate, making the Eurogroup a de facto substitute for Ecofin despite its informal status. The ECB, however, must be consulted in the above instances (Henning 2007: 318).

The Eurogroup has been subject to 'creeping institutionalization' in the Lisbon Treaty, which contains enabling clauses which are functionally equivalent to Article 99 for Eurozone coordination (Chapter 3A) (Begg 2008: 11). In addition, Article 115a states that only Eurozone countries can participate in Council votes on budgetary surveillance and economic policy guidelines. Article 116 also clarifies that non-Eurozone members of the European Union will not participate in some areas, such as in the nomination of the executive board of the ECB. The treaty thus gives the Eurogroup formal status, although it still does not have the power to take decisions and remains dependent on peer pressure for influence (Begg 2008).

Expert committees play a supporting role for Member States in governing the Eurozone. The Economic and Financial Committee (EFC) is the successor of the Monetary Committee, which was set up by the Treaty of Rome (Article 102(2)), with its powers augmented in the Maastricht Treaty. On 1 January 1999, the Monetary Committee was transformed into the EFC. The EFC is comprised of representatives from the finance ministries (normally senior officials with responsibility for EMU affairs, although sometimes they have the status of a deputy finance minister or secretary of state), the Commission and the ECB. The officials from finance ministries and central banks are there as experts rather than national representatives (Ardy et al. 2006: 73).

Its functions are as follows: issue its opinion to the Council or the Commission (it can also do so on its own initiative); monitor Member States' financial positions; provide preparatory work for Ecofin and Eurogroup meetings; and analyse capital movements and balance of payments situations on an annual basis. The chair of the EFC also attends Ecofin meetings. In addition, the EFC drafts the speech given on behalf of the European Union by the finance minister of the country holding the presidency at the spring and annual meetings of the IMF (Smaghi 2004: 235).

No permanent working groups exist within the EFC, although after the European Union expanded to 25 members the EFC divided into two different groups in order to ensure efficiency. The full committee which includes officials from national central banks convenes in order to consider issues like the general state of the economy, financial stability and the International Monetary Fund (IMF). The national central banks are excluded when other matters are under discussion (Begg 2008: 13).When it comes to financial services, the EFC meets in a separate formation using information provided mainly by DG ECFIN and DG Internal Market (Angeloni 2008: 23).

Like its predecessor, the EFC has a reputation for secrecy at the national level, operating without the input of other ministries that could help articulate a national position. In addition, no minutes are taken in EFC meetings. This is because of the delicate nature of the matters that are under discussion and the important consequences of any leaks for market activities. The EFC members are more open amongst themselves, and they prefer to operate according to consensus (Puetter 2004, Jacobsson and Vifell 2007). Indeed, they are obliged to 'be guided, in their performance of their duties, by the general interests of the Community' (*Official Journal of the European Union*, 2003, L 158/59). There are signs, however, that the EFC's meetings have become more political and that national politics plays an increasingly important role in deliberations. In particular divisions have occurred between big states and small states (Linsenmann et al. 2007), a tendency which was also present in its predecessor, the Monetary Committee (Verdun 2000). Such developments are important to note, as EFC members not only discuss technocratic details but also express their policy preferences and contribute to the debate on the appropriateness of policies like the SGP (Puetter 2007: 27).

Other preparatory bodies are the Committee of Permanent Representatives (COREPER), the Economic Policy Committee (EPC) and the Eurogroup Working Party. COREPER assists in the preparation of Ecofin's agenda. COREPER members are ambassadors, as opposed to the EFC members who prepare Eurogroup meetings, who tend to have more technocratic training. The EPC conducts economic analyses and offers advice on 'more fundamental policy challenges' (Puetter 2007: 27). Begun in 1974, the EPC is composed of experts at the level of senior civil servants and is substantially larger than the EFC. They work towards the coordination of national economic policies, particularly structural policies and those dealing with the Cardiff process. The EPC goes over the national reports in order to devise guidelines for the Member States (Hodson and Maher 2001). One of its primary functions is contributing to the construction of the BEPGs, giving the Commission important information upon which it bases its recommendation. In addition, the EPC participates in debates on structural reform, in particular the surveillance mechanisms described by the Lisbon Agenda. It also considers other policies like those pertaining to creating jobs and environmental policies. Their debates tend to be less political than those of the EFC (Puetter 2007: 27–8). The perspective of the EPC tends to be broader and of a more long-term nature in comparison with the EFC because of its broad remit. The breadth of its responsibilities also means that at times tension can arise regarding which issues fall within its jurisdiction and which are the responsibility of other committees (Ardy et al. 2006: 74–5).

In 2003 Ecofin adopted statutes affecting the expert committees in preparation for the 2004 enlargement. These statutes can subsequently be amended by the Council (unlike Treaty changes) but nevertheless indicate the importance attached to the functioning of these committees and how their small size has been an asset. The number of members per delegation was cut in half. Regarding the EFC, national central bankers were removed from the committee, only participating occasionally when their expertise is needed. Only two EPC delegates per country are now sent (previously it was four), and once again the central bankers were removed (Puetter 2007: 32). Table 4.3 outlines the role that these committees, Ecofin and the Eurogroup play in economic policymaking in the European Union.

The European Parliament maintains the right to be informed of the ECB's actions and regularly hears reports from the EU Presidency, the Commission, the ECB president and the Eurogroup president. The Parliament also debates these reports and can hold hearings, but its role remains largely consultative. The trend over the years has been to gradually increase the Parliament's powers in order to buttress the European Union's claim to democratic legitimacy, and this may include an expanded role for the EP as monetary integration progresses. But currently the Parliament's role remains relatively ambiguous. Struggling to emerge from accusations that it is little more than a talking shop, the Economic and Monetary Affairs Committee of the EP could conceivably play an important role in increasing public awareness of the ECB's policies and pressuring it to justify its actions, thereby creating greater transparency and greater accountability (Chang 2002). The EP is the only directly elected institution in the European Union, giving it claims to democratic legitimacy and authority, at least in theory.

For example, the president of the ECB regularly answers questions posed by the committee, much like the chairman of the Federal Reserve in the United States appears before Congress. In the US context, these hearings attract great interest, as they signal how the Fed views the economy and what future policies might be. In the European context, these hearings do not attract as much attention from the financial press, making their outcomes less relevant to markets and the public. In addition, there are no real consequences to these hearings, as the Parliament holds no authority or sanctioning mechanism against the ECB. This has led some to argue that the EP needs to be able to 'both bark and bite' (Buiter 1999: 181). The issue of media attention has been discussed within the committee itself, and various strategies are being considered to increase public awareness of their activities (interview with member of Economic and Monetary Affairs Committee of the European Parliament, Strasbourg, June 2001).

Aside from its relationship with the ECB, the Parliament's role in EMU is limited to being informed. The Council president

TABLE 4.3 *Standard procedures for decision making on economic policy coordination*

Institutional characteristics	Standardized procedure: official Council meeting	Minister plus one	Expert discussion	
Institution/group	ECOFIN	Eurogroup	EFC	EPC
Task	Formal decision making, policy review	Policy review	Policy review, provision of expertise, draft decisions	Policy review, provision of expertise, forward-looking studies and work on indicators
Membership EU-15, until May 2004	15 ministers plus national delegations (up to 120 people)	12 ministers	30 national representatives	60 national representatives
EU-25, after May 2004	25 ministers plus national delegations	12 ministers	25 national representatives	50 national representatives
EU-27, after January 2007	27 ministers plus national delegations	15 ministers as of January 2008	27 national representatives	54 national representatives

Source: Puetter (2007:30), updated by author.

informs the Parliament of the BEPGs, and the Commission and Council president also inform the Parliament upon the completion of multilateral surveys. Moreover, once a Member State receives a recommendation from the Council, the Parliament's Economic and Monetary Affairs Committee can invite the Council president to appear before it. However, neither the macroeconomic dialogue nor the SGP reform involve the Parliament, with the latter seeking the involvement of national parliaments instead (Ardy et al. 2006). The Parliament has an informal Lisbon Coordinating Committee, but it lacks the influence of its sectoral committees. It has had trouble influencing structural reforms, in part because its committee structure does not correspond well to the areas covered by the Integrated Guidelines (Begg 2008: 13).

Similarly, the Commission's role is relatively constrained, as it does not enjoy its normal role of sole agenda setter within the context of monetary policy. Rather its primary role is surveillance, with Eurostat and DG ECFIN sharing responsibility. While the Maastricht Treaty did not specify an agency in regards to the surveillance function, by 1995 Eurostat had established itself as the leading agency overseeing applicant countries (Savage 2005: 51). DG ECFIN, however, handles SGP surveillance because of its forecasting capacity (Savage 2005: 53–5).

The Commission monitors Member State economic policies and performance as part of the BEPGs (part of the Lisbon 2 Integrated Guidelines) and the SGP. If Member State policy and/or economic conditions deviate from the objectives set by Ecofin, it is up to the Commission to issue a recommendation. However, Ecofin is not obliged to follow the Commission's recommendation, it remains a political decision. When Ecofin decided to suspend the SGP in November 2003 so as to avoid acting upon the Commission's recommendation to open up the excessive deficit procedure against France and Germany, the Commission took the case to the European Court of Justice (ECJ). The ECJ ruled that Ecofin must take a decision on the Commission's recommendation, although it did not have to go along with its recommendations. Under the BEPGs and Lisbon 1, the Commission also had a muted role, though it was strengthened under Lisbon 2. The Lisbon Treaty strengthens the Commission's powers, enabling it to issue warnings to Member States over inflation, pay hikes and reform measures (or the lack thereof), in addition to its ability to warn states over deficits. The

Commission has argued that its ability to use early warning should be used more frequently (Commission 2008).

In general the Commission tends to play a more passive role than normal. Although it attends most meetings of the Council and the aforementioned committees, giving important administrative and technical assistance, its roles of agenda setter, information provider and gatekeeper tend to be usurped by the EFC. Nevertheless its data plays a significant role in the assessment of budget deficits and national stability programmes. Moreover its opinions form the basis of the BEPGs. Finally, despite its inability to issue sanction or recommendations, the Commission can still make its views known in the form of open letters to Ecofin (Ardy et al. 2006: 77).

Accountability and governance

The method of accountability between the major actors is clearly stated in the Treaty in some instances, whereas in others the actors have played an active role in building up a system of accountability. When it comes to the ECB, care has been taken to prevent undue political influence on its decisions, although numerous mechanisms exist for the Commission and Member States to engage in a dialogue with the ECB (although the latter is never obliged to follow suggestions). Article 113 EC states that a member of the Commission and the president of the Council are allowed to attend ECB Governing Council meetings and may submit items to be considered, although they do not have voting privileges. In turn, the ECB president may also attend Council meetings when relevant issues relating to the ESCB and its duties arise. The ECB also has the right to be consulted should national or community-level bodies draft legislation that would impact the monetary realm (EC Article 105(4)).

The ECB's nominal accountability is to the European Parliament. It is required to issue quarterly reports, and the relevant EP committee can request the presence of the ECB president or executive board member. Moreover, the ECB president regularly appears before the EP to answer questions, much like the chair of the Federal Reserve appears before the US Congress. However, the EP has no sanctioning mechanism over the ECB, unlike in the United States. The ECB's system of accountability is therefore relatively weak. It tried to extend it even further by attempting to make itself exempt from the jurisdiction of the European Anti-Fraud Office

(OLAF) by creating an internal anti-fraud unit. The ECB considered itself out of the jurisdiction of OLAF, given it is not part of the European Union's institutional apparatus and enjoys its own budget that is separate from that of the European Union. However, the ECJ ruled that the ECB is not the sole independent institution of the European Union and that its 'independence does not have the consequence of separating it entirely from the European Community and exempting it from every rule of Community law' (Case C-11/00, Commission v. ECB, 2003 ECR I-7147, para. 64). The ECB is also subject to the rulings of the ECJ, and is controlled by the Court of Auditors.

The relationship that is debated most frequently is perhaps the one between the Eurogroup and the ECB. As an informal body, the Eurogroup does not enjoy formal powers. However, as the government representatives in the economic and financial realms, they have a de facto influence in the management of European economic and monetary affairs. Moreover they have a claim as the representatives of their respective national electorates, and certain members have evoked this role/obligation to carry out the wishes of the domestic populace.

Some members of the Eurogroup have tried to influence ECB policies through two different mechanisms. First, public statements have been made to the financial press regarding the level of interest rates, pressuring the ECB to weaken monetary policy so as to permit stronger economic growth. This has not proven to be a successful strategy. If anything, the ECB hardens its stance so as not to give even the appearance of being influenced by such statements. However, there have been some exceptions. In 1999, for example, the Finnish presidency pressured the ECB to publish its economic forecasts. Although members of the Executive Council originally opposed such a measure, the ECB finally agreed in November 1999 (*Financial Times*, 18 November 1999).

Second, there have been calls on the part of government representatives for more contact between the Eurogroup and the ECB. Such proposals have existed for a long time in an effort to secure a monetary policy that adequately takes into account the diverse economic and political needs of the Eurozone countries. Early in the euro's history, the then-Eurogroup president (Belgian finance minister Didier Reynders) fostered his vision of a dialogue between the ECB and Eurogroup which would not compromise the ECB's independence but would still account for political power. This prompted a warning from Bundesbank officials that such interference could jeopardize monetary stability (*International Herald Tribune*, 5 February 2001). Academic observers generally have sided with the ECB on such conflicts; for example, Alesina et al. (2001: 13) wrote, 'our judgment is that the potential benefits of these formal meetings are less than the risks they entail'. Nevertheless political pressure has continued, with Sarkozy even visiting the Eurogroup in 2007.

In 2006 Eurogroup president Jean-Claude Juncker and EU Monetary Affairs commissioner Joaquin Almunia wrote to ECB president Jean-Claude Trichet to request more informal contact in order 'to foster a common understanding of the key policy challenges facing the euro area' (*Financial Times*, 7 June 2006), a request to which the latter neglected to respond directly. Trichet dismissed the need for further Eurogroup consultation, stating, 'I'm Mr. Euro, there is no doubt. We issue the currency and, if I might add, there is my signature on the notes' (*Financial Times*, 9 June 2006). This was interpreted as another signal from the ECB that it would not allow its independence to be compromised, even through actions that might only hint at such influence. Juncker responded by noting, 'I'm the first in line with responsibility for economic and fiscal issues in the Eurozone' (*FT Deutschland*, 16 June 2006), trying to defend his own role as well as the importance of the finance ministers more generally.

This exchange reached an impasse and died down, but it generally illustrates the lack of success national governments have had in trying to press their views and influence ECB decisions. For example, in autumn 2005 certain Eurogroup states tried to dissuade the ECB from raising interest rates (*Financial Times*, 30 November 2005), but to no avail (rates were raised a quarter of percentage point in December). In 2006 Eurogroup members pleaded with the ECB not to raise interest rates in light of the relatively high exchange rate and the still fragile upturn in the growth rate (*Le Monde*, 6 July 2006). Interest rates continued to rise in August, with further increases later in the year and continuing into the next.

Although both parties later emphasized the spirit of cooperation that defines their relationship, a blame-shifting tendency has developed which does little to improve the credibility and reputation of either institution. Both are quick to highlight their responsibilities and to note the limitations of their own institutions. For example,

Trichet responded to queries regarding slow growth in the Eurozone by rebuking the Member States, saying, 'A necessary increase in growth potential assumes the active implementation of structural reforms...the problem lies entirely with putting it into effect,' with the 'lack of flexibility' in European labour markets presenting a particularly vexing issue (*Agence France Presse*, 31 March 2006).

The ECB's relationship with the Member States becomes even more complicated when one considers the latter's inability to speak with a single voice, despite the existence of the Eurogroup and its appointment of a chairman with a longer term (two years). In September 2000, for example, German chancellor Gerhard Schröder commented that the weak euro should be welcomed as it boosted exports. A week earlier, however, German finance minister Hans Eichel and French finance minister Laurent Fabius had attempted to boost the euro's value by emphasizing the Eurozone's strong economic fundamentals (*Guardian*, 6 September 2000), and a communiqué issued by the Eurogroup from Versailles stated, 'A strong euro is in the interest of the Euro area' (Eurogroup Communiqué Versailles, 8 September 2000).

Such coordination problems were not limited to the early years of the Eurozone. In the summer of 2005 politicians from Italy, Germany and France were demanding more cooperation from the ECB to stimulate growth, whereas the Austrian finance minister shifted the blame back to the Member States: 'What is important is not that monetary policy and fiscal policy should be agreed more closely but that the financial policies of the individual countries themselves should be better co-ordinated' (*Financial Times*, 18 July 2005). During the summer 2006 debate over interest rate hikes, Spanish finance minister Pedro Solbes expressed his apprehension over the euro's exchange rate with the dollar (*Le Monde*, 7 June 2006), as did French finance minister Thierry Breton (*Financial Times*, 11 June 2005). Austrian finance minister Karl-Heinz Grasser contradicted these assessments, claiming that ministers were 'not very concerned' about it (*Financial Times*, 9 June 2006).

In addition, governments within the Eurogroup continue to make major economic policy decisions without the input of their Eurogroup counterparts. Germany's government under Angela Merkel decided to increase its VAT starting from 2007 without taking into account the reservations of countries like France and Belgium, which were concerned about the impact this would have on Eurozone growth (*Le Monde*, 6 June 2006). Moreover, national budgets are prepared and submitted to national parliaments via different procedures at different times.

Problems of assessing the Eurozone and holding it accountable do not only concern EU institutions and Member States. Given the divergence in economic performance and strategy among the Member States, the lack of differentiation between them by market actors is rather surprising. Monetary union led to a convergence in bond spreads in the Eurozone, weakening the market discipline of more fiscally profligate countries. In order to restore such discipline without negatively affecting more economically sound countries (which an interest rate hike would do), the ECB publicly warned banks that it would no longer accept as collateral the sovereign debt of countries with a rating of less than A– from one of the major ratings agencies (*Financial Times*, 8 November 2005). According to Erik Nielsen, chief European economist at Goldman Sachs, 'it is a huge development...as it will induce markets to discriminate more between government bonds based on their rating and the debt situation of Euroland countries' (*Financial Times*, 10 November 2005).

This need not have affected any of the Eurozone countries in the short-term, as all were within range. Nevertheless, the impact was felt almost immediately by some of the weaker economies of the Eurozone. For example, after the ECB's announcement, investors demanded from Portugal (rated three to four notches above the ECB's minimum level at the time) a yield spread of 11 basis points above comparable AAA-rated German government bonds on its new five-year bond issue, whereas prior to the announcement, it had offered 10 basis points. Some investors nonetheless pulled their orders (*Financial Times*, 9 November 2005).

The cohesiveness of the Eurogroup was tested severely in autumn 2008 when European financial markets came under attack. The initial lack of a European response was caused by the weak institutional structure of the European Union and Eurozone for dealing with such threats. EU financial market coordination is still underdeveloped considering the importance of this sector. The increasingly international nature of finance makes this problematic. In 2004, for example, a quarter of the assets of the top 30 European banks were outside their home market, subject to 'nearly 50 different institutions [that] had cross-border and cross-sectoral features capable of complicating emergency management' (Pauly 2008: 6).

At the EU level there are several mechanisms and institutions in place to deal with financial market regulation. The Treaty basis for financial cooperation in the European Union rests on the single market (which covers financial services), and the duties of the ESCB regarding the prudential supervision of credit institutions, safeguarding financial stability, and ensuring well-functioning payment and securities settlement systems in the Eurozone. Thus cooperation on financial issues primarily occurs through Member State cooperation with some functions delegated to the ECB.

Financial market integration in the European Union has taken place through the Financial Services Action Plan (FSAP), a wide-ranging programme of legislation covering nearly all components of the financial sector. The institutional arm of the FSAP is the Lamfalussy framework, which is made up of four levels. Level 1 consists of Community legislation (directives and regulations) under the co-decision procedure. Level 2 deals with Community legislation that the Commission adopts outlining technical details for the principles approved in Level 1 under the comitology procedure. Level 3 contains national securities regulators who ensure that the Community legislation is carried out. Level 4 is the Commission ensuring that Member States comply with Community legislation. Thus representatives from the Member States, Commission, European Parliament, ECB, and national banking and regulating authorities all participate in the Lamfalussy process.

National authorities still govern national financial systems. Only national governments have the capacity to bail out banks; the European Union has neither the financial resources nor the legal competence. Despite the rising internationalization of financial market activity, financial regulation and supervision continue to exhibit a strong national bias, with national administrations and some sectors of the financial industry reluctant to transfer policy-making authority to the European Union (Angeloni 2008).

The role of the ECB is relatively constrained. It can provide additional liquidity, as it did in 2007 and 2008 in response to the crisis, but it does not have the same resources at its disposal as the US Federal Reserve, for example. Indeed, ECB president Jean-Claude Trichet noted that Europe must choose a strategy that 'is appropriate for us' because the European Union and Eurozone are structured differently (*Le Figaro*, 30 September 2008). Nevertheless the ECB has been involved in European financial market integration. For example, the ESCB has created a Banking Supervision Committee

(BSC) which is made up of representatives from national central banks and national banking supervisors. The BSC provides a forum for discussion on issues related to banking and financial stability. This is the only role delegated to the ECB in ensuring financial stability, aside from its open-market operations (Véron 2007).

Thus 'the prudential framework for pan-European banks has become a maze of national authorities (51 are members of Committee of European Banking Supervisors alone), EU-level committees (no fewer than nine) and bilateral arrangements' (Véron 2007: 4). Where responsibility for policy is ambiguous, it is difficult to hold specific actors accountable (Verdun 1999). Indeed, EMU has exacted uneven costs and benefits across the Eurozone, and it is unclear who should be held responsible, although publicly the ECB has been handed much of the blame. With the election of French president Nicolas Sarkozy in 2007, the Eurozone governance question will no doubt remain on the table. The next section examines suggestions on how best to reform Eurozone governance.

Reforming the Eurozone's governance system

European governance has been sharply criticized during the first decade of monetary union. Stylized models have demonstrated the danger of such differences, in that when different actors have different views, it leads to an excess of policy activism in an attempt to generate different economic conditions by pushing economic variables in different directions. This affects the economic outcomes in relation to output, inflation, budget deficits and interest rates (Falboni et al. 2007).

The governance structure has also had a weak track record in identifying problems in advance. For example, it did not identify the policies followed by Italy and Portugal in 1999 that led to price hikes in non-traded goods, leading to excessive real exchange rate appreciation and harming their competitiveness (Pisani-Ferry 2006). In addition, the high inflation of Slovenia (approaching 7 per cent in 2008) so soon after its accession to the Eurogroup also indicates room for improvement. Pisani-Ferry et al. (2008) emphasize the need for greater clarity in monetary governance for the following reasons:

- political (in which citizens and governments know both what EMU can and cannot do)

- economic (so as to improve economic performance)
- for the sake of enlargement (as some rules are not appropriate for the newer Member States (Pisani-Ferry 2008: 3).

In particular, numerous elements are new to European cooperation and deviate from traditional methods of coordination, making EMU governance even more complex than the multilayered structure already indicates.

Thus the reform of the Eurozone governance system has occupied both official and unofficial actors. The Lisbon Treaty considered the issue of the European Union's economic governance but left it largely unchanged. In light of the tenth anniversary of the euro, the Commission issued its analysis and emphasized the importance of improving the coherence of the Eurozone's external representation (Commission 2008). Politicians also have been active in the debate on the future of the Eurozone's governance. French president Nicolas Sarkozy has kept alive the argument that the Eurozone would benefit from a *gouvernement économique* and that the euro's exchange rate should be managed. Former Belgian prime minister Guy Verhofstadt suggested that the Eurozone governments should try to pursue further integration in other areas (Federal Trust 2006). Further institutionalizing cooperation between the euro area countries, in particular strengthening their economic governance, would help alleviate the perceived democratic deficit, allowing the Eurozone to be more effective and thus provide better economic results for EU citizens.

Academics and Eurozone observers have made numerous suggestions regarding how to best reform the Eurozone's governance. Some issues that have arisen include:

- Augment its administrative capacity.
- Make better use of it as a forum to discuss economic policy coordination, in particular to rationalize national processes in economic and budgetary matters so that national traditions do not interfere with the functioning of the Eurozone.
- Make larger strides in the creation of an ideational consensus within the group regarding optimal monetary and economic policy, which includes which types of policy instruments are the most effective.
- Strengthen the Eurogroup into a body that could make fiscal policy recommendations to Member States (Smaghi 2004,

Federal Trust 2006, Linsenmann et al. 2007, Jacquet and Pisani-Ferry 2000).

Considering all of these official and unofficial suggestions for the reform of the Eurozone governance structure will be a long-term process. It is not simply a matter of altering specific institutional rules and regulations. Many details regarding Eurozone governance were left unspecified in the Maastricht Treaty because of their contentious nature. Although a consensus had developed that enabled ceding sovereignty to the independent central bank, this consensus was pragmatic in that it fulfilled other Member State goals as well (McNamara 2006). Indeed, progress in economic and monetary integration rested with the ability to appeal to a wide range of actors that had different interests in integration (Jabko 2006). However, governments refused to further lock themselves into policy commitments and preferred looser forms of cooperation in order to retain as much room for manoeuvre as possible. Although this has led to suboptimal policies in the Eurozone, such second-best solutions appear to be the only politically feasible ones unless governments are able to enlarge the aforementioned pragmatic consensus to include additional issue areas. The French presidency of the European Union tried to use the financial crisis as a rationale for creating its long-desired economic government (Sarkozy 2008), but this idea received a cool reception from Germany.

Theoretical considerations

The case for economic policy coordination is ambiguous. On the one hand, economic policy coordination prevents states from freeriding off the fiscal restraint of their neighbours, as monetary union spreads the cost of fiscal profligacy across Member States (Ardy et al. 2006). Moreover there is concern that fiscal policy remains consistent with monetary policy (Sargent and Wallace 1981), particularly given that the latter is decentralized and risks bailouts (Eichengreen and Wyplosz 1998). On the other hand, policy coordination could lead to political pressure on the ECB, potentially leading to an inconsistent policy mix if the ECB succumbs to political pressure and its credibility becomes threatened. Alesina et al. (2001) and Issing (2002) have emphasized the importance of national economic policies, arguing that if these remain healthy and sound coordination would be unnecessary. The Werner Report had envisaged a more centralized system for economic policy, in contrast to the Delors Report which called for national policy coordination. Ardy et al. (2006: 104) have characterized the choice of coordination as one that 'balances competing aims rather than being the most economically efficient'. The strength of the pillars is quite uneven in favour of the monetary pillar. Monetary policy is completely centralized, run by the ECB, while economic policy is mainly decentralized. Why would this be the case?

Ideas

When monetary union had come up in the context of the Werner Report and the Delors Report, fiscal coordination was envisaged to be much stronger, either taken at the Community level (Werner Report) or at least subject to binding rules and procedures (Delors Report). Pisani-Ferry (2006) explains the difference in terms of the different rationales used for the different accords. Economic theories were used to justify decisions rather than serve as a foundation for the decisions made. Indeed, academic contributions to monetary union were quite limited (Pisani-Ferry 2006: 829). For example, academic arguments regarding the SGP (seen as unnecessary given the no bail-out clause in the Maastricht Treaty) as superfluous did not play an important role in policy debates. Similarly, Pisani-Ferry argues that the economic basis of the BEPGs were rather weak. In general, economic analysis does not support the need for the second pillar of economic cooperation, although it has evolved over time.

The main points of tension in the governance of the Eurozone rest in economic debates over price stability versus economic growth, and political arguments of credibility versus legitimacy. On the one hand, a belief in the importance of price stability and the use of an independent central bank to pursue credibly policies that would engender it has become a central tenet of the economics profession. Indeed, the ECB, like the Bundesbank before it, has been hawkish in its fight against inflation and against any encroachments on its independence. However, whereas the Bundesbank had been supported strongly by the German government, the ECB has faced criticism from governments, in particular the French government. The Bundesbank had occasionally clashed with the German government over some issues (such as German monetary union and EMU), but normally it could count on the support of the government, all of which supported price stability. While the sound money paradigm enjoys widespread support in central banking circles around the world, politicians have shown differing degrees of commitment to it. When it coincided with their political objectives, its necessity was often invoked. Thus for example the Italian government used the need to follow such policies in order to remain influential within the European Community and be part of the first wave of monetary union. Similarly the French government extolled its virtues as a way of re-establishing French economic competitiveness internationally in the wake of the economic crisis of the 1970s and early 1980s.

However, currently the sound money paradigm is paid lip service but many have publicly questioned its utility and whether the European Union has gone too far in its pursuit. From an economic perspective they may have a point. Indeed, inflation had ceased to be a major problem for most countries since the 1990s, if not earlier. While high levels of inflation would be damaging to an economy, 2 per cent is historically quite low and the economic benefits of keeping it so low are not clear-cut (Kirshner 1999). Despite the upturn in inflation in 2008, the more threatening economic menace is unemployment, and politicians argue that the pursuit of the price stability has hampered efforts to improve growth and thus lower unemployment. According to conventional economic wisdom, however, such a trade-off between growth and employment does not exist. Indeed, policy activism should be discouraged because of the dynamic inconsistency that would arise as a result of market expectations, thus making an independent central bank (or delegating) the best solution (Kydland and Prescott 1977, Barro and Gordon 1983, Rogoff 1985). However, a paradox exists in the ECB's strategy of trying to shape market expectations, which 'is the opposite of that required by the hand-tying model, where the markets form expectations so efficiently that the authorities cannot manipulate them' (Schelkle 2006: 677).

Interests

Now that inflation no longer seems to be such a strong threat and governments are hungry for a win to give to the domestic populace after so many years of reform trying to qualify for monetary union, politicians are questioning the ECB's policies and encouraging the ECB to focus more on economic growth. Indeed, if Posen's (1998) observation that an independent central bank is more likely to be too strict rather than too lenient so as to earn a reputation for being inflation averse is true, this could have negative effects on growth and unemployment. Furthermore, monetary integration created both winners and losers within countries (Frieden 1991, 1998). The problems that the European Union has had with compliance reflect the multiplicity of interests at play and the governments' attempts to satisfy their demands enough to ensure re-election (Schelke 2006).

In addressing reform fatigue, it is difficult to overstate the role that elections play. Since EMU began in 1999 we have seen the return of political business cycles in the national Eurozone economies, indicating that politicians are once again ceding to pressure to give voters a feeling of prosperity prior to elections (Buti and van den Noord 2004). This has had the effect of governments evading Eurozone obligations prior to national elections, such as was the case of Portugal in 2001 and Germany in 2002, contributing to their subsequent problems in adhering to the SGP (Linsenmann and Wessels 2006).

The complexity of EMU governance can also be traced back to the different interests of France and Germany. The ambiguity surrounding exchange rate management, for example, reflects French preferences for managing the exchange rate conflicting with Germany's tradition of a stable currency. The result is a sharing of duties between the ECB and Ecofin, a compromise which confuses responsibility and corresponds to neither country's preferences (Begg 2008).

Finally another potential divide can be seen between the interests of the smaller Member States and the larger ones. Liberal intergovernmentalism argues that integration is driven by the larger states. Indeed, the events in October 2008 largely corresponded to this prediction. Sarkozy had called a meeting of the four largest EU economies (France, Germany, Italy and the United Kingdom) to discuss a coordinated response to the crisis. This move caused some tension within the European Union, with representatives from Spain, Belgium and other EU countries that were not invited to the meeting reportedly unhappy with their exclusion (*Financial Times*, 3 October 2008). While the conclusions were later supported by the other Member States, some concern had been expressed about what kind of a precedent such action could set. Sarkozy defended this meeting before the European Parliament and argued that this had been done 'in the service' of the other states (Sarkozy 2008).

Institutions

The current disagreement among policymakers (for example, the ECB and certain Member State governments) regarding the optimal monetary policy to follow thus presents EMU with problems of accountability. Monetary union has repeatedly faced charges that it is insufficiently accountable, a situation that perhaps would best be rectified through greater political integration, which would allow for fiscal transfers and depoliticize asymmetric shocks (de Grauwe 2006). Despite its claims to devising policy for the entire Eurozone, monetary policy is still nationally oriented in the sense that its governance structure inevitably returns to a nationally oriented system; even in the ECB most posts are delegated according to the nationality of the holder (Schelkle 2006). The financial crisis that erupted in Europe in 2008 saw some backlash against EMU's structure. The European Parliament in particular was very pointed in its remarks that the Commission had not done enough during the crisis, leading Commission officials to defend their actions (or lack thereof) by pointing out the limits of the Commission's competence in this area, with Barroso saying, 'We need to be pragmatic and not announce projects that will be refused by the Member States' (*Le Monde,* 15 October 2008).

Questions of Eurozone governance therefore must consider the multiple layers that work together. At the supranational level there is the ECB. Ecofin and the Eurogroup operate under an intergovernmental framework. However, the finance ministers hold different responsibilities in their respective domestic contexts, making it difficult to form a cohesive body at the level of the Eurogroup given that some finance ministers do not have commensurate authority at the national level for what was being sought for the Eurogroup (Henning 2007: 324). In addition, bodies like Ecofin and the Eurogroup are composed of finance ministers. Oftentimes national policy reforms supporting economic and monetary cooperation require the participation of other ministries like labour, employment and social ministries (Begg 2008). Efforts at rationalizing governance such as the Lisbon 2 reforms indicate that the Member States are amenable to European-level coordination, but the real issue at stake is the extent to which they can implement these policies at the domestic level (Linsenmann and Wessels 2006: 116).

In fact, Dyson (2000) argues the ECB and national governments do not form a traditional principal–agent relationship in which the nation states can be considered the principals and the ECB the agent, as the ECB wields too much independent authority. The ECB not only enjoys veto power over exchange rate policies that concern the euro, it also determines how to interpret its mandate of price stability in quantitative terms. Dyson writes, 'It was not given an inflation target by Euro-Zone governments, and it was not required to negotiate such a target. This right biased the Euro-Zone to operate in an ECB-centric manner' (2000: 16). Moreover, 'the ECB was deliberately created by governments so that it would evade such control and be able to set and pursue its own preferences' (2000: 110).

In addition, traditional oversight mechanisms (McCubbins and Schwartz 1984) are either nonexistent or subverted in favour of the agents rather than the principals. For example, police patrols and fire alarms are alternative mechanisms for principals to ensure that agents comply with their demands and implement their preferences. Police patrol oversights are centralized, active and direct mechanisms versus the more decentralized fire alarm oversights which are undertaken by a wider variety of actors to monitor the actions of the principals. The interesting twist in this situation is that it is the Member States rather than the ECB that are monitored by police patrols under EMU. The surveillance programme of the SGP consists of the Member States submitting stability and growth convergence programmes to the Council and the Commission. Based on a recommendation by the Commission, the Council adopts an opinion of the programmes under consideration and can invite the Member State to revise objectionable material. Updates of the programme are submitted annually, thus setting up an early warning system for states vulnerable to exceeding their deficit limits.

The ambiguous nature of responsibility and accountability, however, effectively makes these issues a shared concern for national governments and the ECB alike. Just as national governments cannot entirely shift the blame for undesirable economic outcomes, the ECB must realize that its privileged institutional position rests on a relatively precarious basis of political support. The Member States acquiesced to Germany's demands for ECB independence, but other governments may still undermine this now that the goal of monetary union has been reached. Backlash against the stability-oriented culture of the European Union has been brewing, and if monetary union does not deliver the expected economic (and political) benefits that its adherents promised, the ECB would be hard pressed to justify its policies. Buiter (1999) argues that one of the primary challenges facing the ECB is that monetary integration is proceeding at a faster pace than general public acceptance for European integration, as EMU's institutions are not embedded within society (Verdun and Christiansen 2001: 278) and are therefore prone to greater criticism. The issue of responsibility is further complicated by the fact that the ECB, Council and Commission can have different views on the economy cycle, which lead them to push different policies (Balboni et al. 2007).

Perhaps a better model than a principal–agent relationship would be one of collective responsibility. Just as an entire government will rise or fall based on the success of its policies (rather than blaming individual ministries), discerning whether the central bank or national governments would be damaged more by the failure of monetary union may be a moot point. Both undoubtedly have a large stake in the long-term success of EMU despite disagreements on the precise form that it should take. Thus the ECB and the national governments are likely to restrain one another's actions and to try to anticipate the other's reaction to policy initiatives. While the ECB has a distinct advantage in that it can speak as a unified voice more effectively than the Member States, even within the context of the Eurogroup, this situation could change over time. Such rivalries and turf wars aside, neither group would benefit from EMU's failure (Chang 2002).

In addition to issues of accountability, we must also consider the efficacy of the current governance structure. France has continually sought the creation of a *gouvernement économique* in order to accommodate its desire to retain some sovereignty in macroeconomic policy and allow some scope for government intervention in the economy (Howarth 2007). The 2008 financial crisis renewed France's efforts to create a *gouvernement économique* as well as construct a new group, the heads of state and government of the Eurozone, arguing that the Eurogroup (of finance ministers) was not up to the task of managing such a large-scale crisis, and that only the heads of state and government had the required authority and legitimacy (Sarkozy 2008). Germany once again indicated a contrary viewpoint on the subject (*Frankfurter Allgemeine Zeitung*, 5 November 2008)

Therefore the institutionalization of EMU has generated a complex governance structure that most analysts find inadequate, and the addition of new institutions may hurt rather than help. For example, the Committee of European Banking Supervisors was created in 2004 to bring together European banking supervisors and agencies. Although bilateral and multilateral 'memorandums of understanding' were created regarding information sharing, it has been argued that such instruments make governance even more complex and thus less accountable (Véron 2007). As Pauly (2008: 11) writes:

> In the absence of a pan-European arbiter, who coordinates the coordinators at the moment of crisis, especially when those coordinators are not all similarly structured, similarly mandated by national governments, and most importantly, similarly trusted by finance ministries?... When and if it is forged, it will likely remain necessary to obscure it – because of the complex and decentralized nature of the European Union, because the strongest member-states are wary of assuming the full costs of bailing out weaker members, and because of shared perceptions of the related need to limit moral hazards confronting both market actors and member-states.

A domestic institutional explanation of the extent to which a government can manipulate inflation expectations is the extent to which wage bargaining is centrally coordinated (Calmfors et al. 1988, Hall and Franzese 1998). However, although the bargaining structure is important, additional factors like employment and growth will also affect economic indicators, making it more difficult to enact the correct policy mix (Driffill 2006). Such elements include employment taxes, demand shocks, price shocks, and changes in the money supply and in real interest rates, all of which would impact unemployment. Blanchard (2006), on the other hand, places little emphasis on collective bargaining and the coordination of wages, preferring to focus on real and nominal wage rigidity, labour market flows and economic shocks.

Conclusion

Research done on EMU governance demonstrates how politicized monetary integration has been. While a consensus has formed on the importance of price stability, governments have shown varying levels of commitment to it as a priority. Indeed, although the ECB has been able to define price stability as 2 per cent and below in the medium term, Member States have not always been willing to support this definition when it has interfered with other policy objectives. Domestic political considerations like institutions and elections impact how the respective governments view the optimal economic and monetary policy to pursue. The ambiguity of the Treaty in certain instances was not accidental, as achieving a consensus is difficult. However, the European Union's predilection for consensus indicates that a longer-term learning process may be necessary before any major institutional changes occur at the EU level, in so far as economic policy coordination is concerned. Although an economic rationale may exist for greater coordination (and even this is contested among academic economists), political logic demands more compromise and the continuation of a more loosely structured system of economic policy coordination in the foreseeable future.

Chapter 5

Centralizing monetary policy cooperation: the European Central Bank

The most visible symbol of monetary union (aside from the euro itself) is the European Central Bank (ECB). Located in Frankfurt, the city of the bank upon which it was modelled (the German Bundesbank), the ECB sets monetary policy for the second largest international currency. It is one of the most independent central banks in the world, and the ECB has zealously guarded its independence from any signs of political interference. This chapter outlines the ECB's development, describes its institutional capacity, and provides an economic and political rationale for its structure. The final part of the chapter considers the controversies that continue to surround the ECB.

The road (back) to Frankfurt

Achieving monetary union required the political support of the German government, which in turn necessitated the support of the Bundesbank. The Bundesbank was relatively unique in Europe in terms of its independence. Most of its counterparts were obligated to follow government policies, which at times led to economically undesirable outcomes. For example, the Bank of Italy was required to purchase any remaining Treasury bonds in government auctions, which had a debilitating effect on government finances as its debt levels grew. The divorce between the Bank of Italy and the government in 1981 was a significant step in the rehabilitation of the Italian economy in the 1980s and 1990s. Across Europe, central bank staff were increasingly viewed as politically neutral technocrats who could look after the long-term needs of the economy better than politicians motivated by short-term electoral concerns.

Nowhere was the influence of the central bank more pronounced than in Germany. However, much of the Bundesbank's influence in Germany was indirect, relying on its reputation and on public support rather than its legal powers (Marsh 1992). It operated within a federal system in which important actors like regional governments, social partners and the finance ministry also had a substantial impact on economic and monetary policy, making the Bundesbank's influence dependent on these other actors (Duckenfield 1999). Moreover, the bank was legally obligated to back the government's overall economic policies. The limits of the Bundesbank's influence were evident during Germany's unification. Bundesbank president Karl Otto Pöhl was quoted as saying in 1991, 'I had been talking myself blue in the face for eighteen months …. Everything I said was ignored' (Marsh 1992: 41), as the German government resisted the bank's sceptical analysis of the economic situation at the time and operated according to much more optimistic economic expectations.

Monetary union without Germany would have been unacceptable, and Germany would not have been able to convince the German electorate to give up the mark without being able to credibly assure them that the new currency would be as good as the old one. Central bank independence was non-negotiable for the Germany delegation and was viewed as necessary by other European countries in order to ensure market credibility. Although a broad consensus existed in Europe regarding the sound money paradigm and the importance of central bank independence (Dyson 2000, McNamara 1998), countries exhibited varying degrees of commitment to it. Even during the negotiations for monetary union, divergent preferences between countries complicated discussions, with the major issues being the prioritization of growth versus price stability, central bank independence versus a government-dominated monetary policy, and monetary union as a goal in itself versus a step towards political union (Chang 2002).

On 19 September 1990 the Bundesbank contributed to the debate in issuing a statement, arguing that monetary union must continue the Bundesbank's efforts against inflation through the abolition of capital controls, a set of strict convergence criteria, and a central bank which strongly resembled the Bundesbank (Kaltenthaler 1998: 80). Other European central bank governors, who had largely accepted that monetary union would be predicated on the German model, backed these ideas. The Bundesbank officially supported the government's efforts regarding monetary integration, as it is a political decision, although it expressed concern over the manner in which it was being pursued. In the same statement, it referred to monetary union as an 'irrevocable community of solidarity which, on the basis of experience, needs a far-reaching commitment in the form of a comprehensive political union for it to be permanent'.

The type of political union that actually ensued was relatively weak. Traditional 'high politics' issues such as a foreign policy and judicial and police cooperation became EU matters, but only under an intergovernmental framework, thus limiting the amount of policy harmonization and coordination. Nevertheless during the 1990s plans for the ECB proceeded without any major obstacles. The European Monetary Institute (EMI) was created on 1 January 1994 as part of Stage II of EMU, serving as an institution that guided the transition to monetary union by providing surveillance and through the coordination of national monetary policies. While national governments remained in charge of monetary policy, the EMI's task was to strengthen cooperation between central banks in order to assist monetary policy coordination. In addition, the EMI also created the organization and logistical groundwork for the European System of Central Banks which would take over monetary policy during Stage III of EMU. This institution replaced the EC Committee of Central Bank Governors; Belgian Alexandre Lamfalussy was named president. As director of the Bank for International Settlements, he was a familiar figure to the parties involved, and his appointment was well received.

The president of the new ECB would not have such an easy time of it. In principle, most of the Member States (except for France and Italy) had agreed upon Dutch central banker and EMI president Wim Duisenberg as the first president of the ECB. In November 1997, however, just six months before the final decision was to be made, the French nominated their own candidate, Jean-Claude Trichet. French president Jacques Chirac sought this position for a French central banker to temper the Germany-influenced institutional structure of the ECB, which would also be located in Frankfurt (*Financial Times*, 2 December 1998). Although Duisenberg is not German, the Dutch have closely followed German monetary and exchange rate policy for years and the Netherlands was the closest member of the mark zone to Germany. The conflict became heated as both sides stood by their choices. In May 1998 a compromise was brokered in which Duisenberg would assume the presidency of the ECB, but would 'voluntarily' step down midway through his term, allowing Trichet to helm the bank for the remainder of the term. Rumours also floated that this was part of a package deal which would give a German, Horst

Köhler, the presidency of the European Bank for Reconstruction and Development (EBRD) (*La Libération*, 2 May 1998). Köhler did become the EBRD's president, but it became unclear whether or not Chirac had actually achieved his concession. After the compromise was made, the German press and various German politicians repeatedly expressed their dissatisfaction. Finance minister Theo Waigel even publicly confirmed that there was nothing to legally block Duisenberg from refusing to step down during his term (*Financial Times*, 5 May 1998). And in an interview with a French newspaper, Duisenberg himself stated that he would not step down (*Le Monde*, 30 December 1998). He continued to refuse to confirm when he would relinquish the presidency, even as officials (including central bankers and finance ministers) repeatedly requested a clarification in advance of the launch of euro notes in January 2002.

On 8 February 2002, Duisenberg agreed to step aside, citing his age and making his retirement date of 9 July 2003 coincide with his birthday (he turned 68). His tenure as ECB president had been criticized, in particular the bank's communication strategy. His messages were at times misleading, such as after the terrorist attack of 11 September 2001 when he said that a sharp interest rate reduction would provoke a panic, only to cut rates a few days later. Analysts had attributed some of these communication difficulties to the fact that as the former president of the central bank of a small country, he was inexperienced in the subtle nuances of market signalling. Over time, however, he gained credibility.

The retirement of Duisenberg and accession of Trichet to the post were complicated by the latter's involvement in a French banking scandal which needed to be resolved before he could assume the presidency. He was acquitted of charges of wrongdoing in June 2003. On 1 November 2003 Trichet became the ECB's second president.

Structure of the ECB

The European System of Central Banks (ESCB) was created on 1 June 1998 as a result of the Statute of the European System of Central Banks and of the European Central Bank. The ESCB is composed of the ECB and the national central banks (NCBs) of all EU states (including non-Eurozone members), as per Article 107.1 of the Treaty. The Eurosystem is composed of the ECB and the NCBs of the Eurozone members. The ECB has three main decision-making bodies: the Executive Board, the Governing Council and the General

Council. The Executive Board is a six-member body composed of a president, a vice-president and four other members from the monetary and banking fields. The European Council (after consulting the European Parliament) recommends the members of the Executive Board. The executive board holds weekly meetings (on Tuesdays). Either the ECB president or the vice-president presides over the Governing Council, the Executive Board and the General Council meetings. In addition, the president may also attend Eurogroup meetings as well as take part in EU Council meetings that are relevant to the tasks of the ECB. The Executive Board prepares the Governing Council's meetings, implements the monetary policy set by the Governing Council via the NCBs, handles day-to-day operations of the ECB and carries out tasks delegated to it by the Governing Council, such as regulatory powers.

The Governing Council is made up of the Executive Board of the ECB and the national central bank (NCB) governors of Eurozone countries. The Governing Council must meet a minimum of ten times each year, as per the Statute of the ESCB. Normally the Governing Council meets twice a month, on the first and third Thursday. The EU Council president and a representative from the Commission attend these meetings (although neither has voting privileges). The Governing Council operates on a one-person-one-vote principle, with majority decision making on all issues except financial matters (where votes are weighted in accordance to the share of each NCB in the ECB's subscribed capital). The president has the power to cast the deciding vote when there is a tie. The primary duties of the Governing Council are setting interest rates for the Eurozone and ensuring the smooth performance of the Eurosystem's tasks. The Governing Council focuses on the entire euro area rather than country developments. The voting system in the Governing Council indicates that national central banks hold a majority over the Executive Board, although in practice it is the latter that dominates ECB decision making (Allsopp and Artis 2003: 11).

The General Council consists of the ECB's president and vice-president and the NCB governors for all EU Member States. Non-voting participants of General Council meetings include the other Executive Board members, the EU Council president and a representative from the Commission. Normally the General Council meets every three months when called by the president or a minimum of three members. Its primary task is to report on non-Eurozone countries' progress in reaching the convergence

TABLE 5.1 *The decision-making bodies of the ECB*

Executive Board	Governing Council	General Council
President	President	President
Vice-president	Vice-president	Vice-president
Four other members of the Executive Board	Four other members of the Executive Board	
	Governors of the euro area NCBs	Governors of all EU NCBs

Source: ECB (2004: 10).

criteria and to advise these countries on how to prepare for Euro-zone membership.

The ECB took over from its predecessor, the European Monetary Institute, in June 1998. On 1 January 1999 the ECB took control of monetary policy for the Eurozone, composed of the 11 EU Member States that joined the first wave of monetary union. In 2001 Greece became the 12th member of the Eurozone, and Slovenia became the 13th member and first member of the 2004 enlargement countries to adopt the euro. Malta and Cyprus brought the number up to 15 on 1 January 2008, with Slovakia's 2009 accession raising it to 16.

The enlargement of the Eurozone poses numerous challenges for the voting system of the ECB. The Treaty of Nice inserted an enabling clause, Article 10.6, into the Statute of the ESCB/ECB which allowed the European Council to amend Article 10.2 of the Statute on voting rules within the ECB, with both the European Parliament and the Commission providing an Opinion on the Recommendation. In February 2003 the ECB proposed a solution of rotation, which was accepted by the Council in March 2003 and went into effect in May 2004.

The ECB's rotation system was designed according to the following guiding principles:

- 'one member, one vote' and *ad personam* participation in which all Governing Council members continued to attend meetings and all votes cast by NCB governors with voting rights would continue to be weighted equally

- representativeness
- transparency
- consistency.

The new governing structure caps the number of national central bank governors with voting rights at 15 and is implemented in three stages. When the number of governors exceeds 15, the governors are allocated into two groups, according to the country's GDP (which comprises five-sixths of the country's ranking) and the total aggregated balance sheets of its monetary financial institutions (TABS–MFIs) in order to recognize the importance of the size of a country's financial sector on decisions made by the ECB (Table 5.2). The five governors of the first group share four voting rights, and the governors of the second group share 11. The ECB's Governing Council may delay the rotation system until the Eurozone group reaches 18 in order to ensure that no governor within any group will enjoy voting frequency of 100 per cent. When the number of Eurozone countries reaches 22, they divide into three groups in which the first group shares four voting rights, the second group composed of half of the total number of governors enjoys eight voting rights, and the third group is assigned three voting rights (Table 5.3). When the Eurozone reaches 27 members, the voting frequency of the first group will be 80 per cent, the second group 57 per cent and the third group 38 per cent. The composition of the groups will be adjusted whenever the aggregate GDP is adjusted according to Article 29.3 of the Statute, with the data for shares in the TABS–MFIs calculated at the same time. Alternatively, an increase in the number of national central bank governors due to enlargement could also trigger an adjustment of group composition (ECB 2003).

The European Parliament issued a non-binding rejection of the ECB's rotation solution, and the Commission issued a positive opinion, although it criticized the lack of a population measure. Confusion over the rotation's frequency, the allocation of voting rights to governors within each group, the clarity and transparency in relation to markets and the general public, and when the rotation system would begin were also noted (Commission Opinion, 2 February 2003). Other criticisms include a lack of appropriate regional representation and the failure to improve the efficiency of the ECB's decision-making process (Gros 2003, Horn 2003).

The ECB defended the rotation system and its economic criteria, arguing that as:

TABLE 5.2 *Governing Council rotation in two groups*

No. of governors	16	17	18	19	20	21	22+
Group 1 No. of votes/no. of governors	5/5	5/5	5/5	4/5	4/5	4/5	Moves to
Voting frequency	100%	100%	100%	80%	80%	80%	3 groups
Group 2 No. of votes/no. of governors	10/11	10/12	10/13	11/14	11/15	11/16	
Voting frequency	91%	83%	77%	79%	73%	69%	
Sum of voting weights	15	15	15	15	15	15	

Source: www.ecb.int.

TABLE 5.3 *Governing Council rotation in three groups*

No. of governors	22	23	24	25	26	27
Group 1 No. of votes/no. of governors	4/5	4/5	4/5	4/5	4/5	4/5
Voting frequency	80%	80%	80%	80%	80%	80%
Group 2 No. of votes/no. of governors	8/11	8/12	8/12	8/13	8/13	8/14
Voting frequency	73%	67%	67%	62%	62%	57%
Group 3 No. of votes/no. of governors	3/6	3/6	3/7	3/7	3/8	3/8
Voting frequency	50%	53%	43%	43%	38%	38%
Sum of voting weights	15	15	15	15	15	15

Source: www.ecb.int.

TABLE 5.4 *Possible distribution of countries into ECB voting groups*

	Euro-28	Euro25 (without BG, RO and TUR)	Euro22 (without UK, SW and DK)
Group 1	Germany	Germany	Germany
	United Kingdom	United Kingdom	France
	France	France	Italy
	Italy	Italy	Spain
	Spain	Spain	Netherlands
Group 2	Netherlands	Netherlands	Belgium
	Belgium	Belgium	Austria
	Sweden	Sweden	Ireland
	Austria	Austria	Poland
	Denmark	Denmark	Portugal
	Ireland	Ireland	Greece
	Poland	Poland	Luxembourg
	Portugal	Portugal	Finland
	Turkey	Greece	Czech Republic
	Greece	Luxembourg	Hungary
	Luxembourg	Finland	Slovak Republic
	Finland	Czech Republic	
	Czech Republic	Hungary	
	Hungary		
Group 3	Romania	Slovak Republic	Slovenia
	Slovak Republic	Slovenia	Lithuania
	Slovenia	Lithuania	Cyprus
	Bulgaria	Cyprus	Latvia
	Lithuania	Latvia	Estonia
	Cyprus	Estonia	Malta
	Latvia	Malta	
	Estonia		
	Malta		

Source: Gros (2003).

the ECB is an economic and not a political body, the use of the population criterion appeared as inappropriate ... moreover, the financial criterion, in contrast to GDP or population, is not purely national, but reflects the effective contribution of the various central banks to the Eurosystem.

A similar calculation hierarchy exists in the Federal Reserve System in which the presidents of the New York and Chicago Federal Reserve Banks have permanent voting rights and a 50 per cent voting right in the Federal Open Market Committee (FOMC), recognizing their role as financial centres, compared with 33 per cent voting rights for other regional governors (Mersch 2003). Nevertheless, while the rotation system may preserve the principle of 'one person, one vote', it damages its spirit and will make it more difficult for smaller countries to voice national and regional concerns at the European and international level.

Operations of the ECB

The ECB is one of the most independent central banks in the world. Neither the ECB nor its constituent national central banks can seek or receive orders from any political body, whether it is the European Community, national governments or any other body. In turn, neither Member State governments nor Community institutions are to attempt to exert influence on the ECB, as per Article 108 of the Treaty. In order to ensure its independence, the appointment procedures ensure long terms of office for Governing Council members. Executive Board members can only sit for one term of eight years. National central bank governors enjoy five-year terms.

According to the Treaty (article 105.1):

> the primary objective of the ESCB shall be to maintain price stability ... [and] without prejudice to the objective of price stability, the ESCB shall support the general economic policies in the Community with a view to contributing to the achievement of the objectives of the Community as laid down in Article 2,

those objectives being a high level of employment and sustainable, non-inflationary growth. The ECB's main tasks (Article 105.2) include defining and implementing monetary policy, conducting operations in foreign exchange markets, managing the Eurozone's foreign reserves, and overseeing its payment system.

The ECB's monetary policy targets price stability, 'a year-on-year increase in the Harmonized Index of Consumer Prices (HICP) for the euro area of below 2 per cent', as a medium-term objective (ECB 2006). In October 1998 the ECB had originally announced that price stability would be defined as an annual HICP increase of 'below 2 per cent', which was amended in May 2003 to be 'close to 2 per cent'. However Pisani-Ferry et al. (2008: 25) have noted that the Eurozone has overshot this reference value for most of the period without any apparent reaction from the ECB.

The ECB also conducts economic and monetary analyses to determine its monetary policy strategy. In order to achieve its objectives, the ECB has adopted a two-pillar strategy. The first pillar looks at monetary aggregates, in particular using the M3 as a 'reference value'. The second pillar considers other economic and financial indicators. Economists criticized ECB policy for its emphasis on the latter (Gros 2001, de Grauwe 2002, Cecchetti and O'Sullivan 2003, Gerlach 2004). In contrast to inflation targeting, monetary targeting is less transparent, and most central banks had already ceased to target the money supply by the time the ECB went into operation. However the ECB initially chose to follow the Bundesbank's monetary strategy so as to establish its credibility with financial markets. Following a 2003 internal review, the ECB modified its pillar system. The renamed economic analysis pillar looks at short to medium-term non-monetary indicators. The second pillar, monetary analysis, considers medium to longer-term objectives focusing on monetary aggregates, notably the M3. The press release of 8 May 2003 indicated that monetary aggregate analyses would be less prominent than they had been in the past (see also Wyplosz 2006). Nevertheless, if the two pillars indicate different outlooks, it is not clear what the ECB's response would be (Pisani-Ferry et al. 2008).

In order to guide short-term interest rates, the ECB uses open market operations, standing facilities and reserve requirements. Its open market operations comprise:

- transactions with a one-week frequency that also mature in one week (to provide regular liquidity)
- transactions with a monthly frequency that mature in three months

- fine-tuning operations that are used 'to smooth the effects of interest rates of unexpected liquidity imbalances'
- reverse transactions, outright transactions, and debt certificates that the Eurosystem uses for structural operations (ECB 2006: 22).

Standing facilities include a marginal lending facility and a deposit facility, used by credit institutions 'to obtain overnight liquidity from national central banks against eligible assets' and 'to make overnight deposits with the national central banks in the Eurosystem' (ECB 2006: 22). The minimum reserve requirement refers to the Eurosystem's requirement that credit institutions keep a minimum amount of reserves in national central bank accounts so as to keep money market interest rates stable and to ensure that a structural liquidity deficit exists (and can be manipulated) in the Eurozone's banking system (ECB 2006).

To fulfil its role of overseeing the Eurozone's payment system, the Eurosystem uses TARGET (Trans-European Automated Real-time Gross Settlement Express Transfer), a real-time gross settlement (RTGS) system for central bank operations and interbank transfers using large sums of euros in addition to other euro payments. Euros are processed and settled in real time. It is composed of national RTGS systems and the ECB payment mechanism, which are linked to one another. TARGET can be used for all euro transactions between and within Eurozone countries and other EU states for interbank and customer payments. Although non-Eurozone Member States can participate in TARGET, they are not obliged to do so (ECB 2006: 26–7).

The ECB and its critics

Most criticism of the ECB focuses on its independence (which some consider excessive) and the related issue of its accountability. What does the ECB's independence mean in practice? Independence can refer to instrumental independence as well as goal independence. Goal independence indicates the bank's ability to set monetary policy objectives, such as low inflation or a certain level of employment. Instrumental independence means that the central bank can choose the mechanism/policies through which to achieve its goal. Another type of independence is a bank's political independence (Loedel 2002), its ability to make decisions without political pressure from other actors. In the case of the ECB, its most likely source of political pressure would be the Eurogroup, although its role has thus far not lived up to some expectations.

The ECB benefits from both goal and instrumental independence. Although its mandate in the Maastricht Treaty specifies that it must pursue price stability, the ECB was able to set the definition of price stability (targeting 2 per cent in the medium term) while also deciding how to achieve it (via the two pillar system described above). This independence makes it vulnerable to charges of worsening the European Union's democratic deficit, especially during economically difficult periods (Begg and Green 1998: 134). Indeed, the ECB's institutional structure represents a significant 'departure from the norms of political accountability' (Elgie 1998: 54), which does exacerbate concerns over the democratic deficit. Thus some have called the attainment of political legitimacy the ECB's 'ultimate challenge' (Favero et al. 2000). Although a treaty set its primary objective, its goal independence makes its policy choices politically relevant and subject to debate. The tenuous political accountability chain between the electorates' preferences and the ECB's policy decisions makes assessing the legitimacy of the latter's choices difficult (Favero et al. 2000).

At the extreme, the ECB's control of monetary policy could be viewed as not just the delegation of authority but its abdication (Freeman 2002). Thus the ECB's imposition of the sound money paradigm can in fact be a 'mismatch' between its preferences and those of the median voter (Muscatelli 1998). Rather than an undesirable by-product of a political system dominated by short-term electoral concerns, political business cycles can be viewed as the expression of legitimate dispersion of preferences within society, one the ECB attempts to eliminate through its policies.

Others have argued that the ECB's independence represents no threat to the European Union's legitimacy, and that its powers still fall within accepted boundaries already established within Europe (Moravcsik 2002). Macroeconomic policy is not something that normally reflects the electorate's preferences in a manner that can be measured directly (Jones 2002), thus the ECB poses no significant threat to the European Union's legitimacy.

The ECB's mandate is the pursuit of price stability, but it is also required to support the Community's economic policies in a manner that does not jeopardize the former. It is debatable whether the ECB does that to the fullest extent possible. According to

Christa Randzio of the European Parliament's Economic and Monetary Affairs Committee, the ECB has not gone far enough in this regard (Elgie 2002). Others, however, have argued that the ECB has, in fact, shifted its emphasis towards economic growth and reducing unemployment (Talani 2005). Despite the ECB's independence it still finds itself part of a complex system of coordination which derives power from different sources (Howarth and Loedel 2003).

A related criticism of the ECB is its relative lack of accountability. From a managerial perspective, the ECB is accountable to the Court of Auditors as well as the EU anti-fraud office (OLAF). The ECB had argued that the latter poses a threat to its independence, but the Court ruled differently on this matter. Its attempt to gain special status in the Lisbon Treaty also failed. Given the need to protect its independence, many forms of democratic oversight are unfeasible, lest they threaten the bank's credibility. Hence transparency has been touted as indispensable in the bank's quest for legitimacy (Issing et al. 2001) and helps the private sector set its inflation expectations (Cruijsen and Demertzis 2007). According to Eijffinger et al. (1998), monetary policy can be considered transparent if its preferences are certain. This makes its actions more predictable by reducing forecast errors and enhances the credibility of monetary policy. A survey by de Haan et al. (2004) showed that financial markets were, in fact, able to anticipate most of the ECB's policy decisions. Others have argued that the ECB's strategy 'seems better designed to conceal strategy than to help the public understand it' (Favero et al. 2000), and have noted the upward trend in medium and long-term inflation expectations for the Eurozone and a concomitant erosion of ECB credibility, perhaps suggesting the need for greater transparency (Geraats 2008).

Another element of transparency considers *ex ante* versus *ex post* transparency. *Ex ante* transparency refers to transparency in how the bank expects to achieve its stated goals. The ECB was criticized, for example, for not publishing its forecasts of inflation and output, which would have enhanced *ex ante* transparency (it later conceded and since December 2000 publishes inflation projections in its *Monthly Bulletin*). The ECB refuses to publish the minutes of its meetings so as to prevent political pressure on national central bank governors lest the national governments have a way to monitor their voting (Buiter 1999). In defence of this practice, some (de Haan and Eijffinger 2000, Issing et al. 2001) argue that the prevailing sense of collective responsibility rendered publishing minutes and voting records of limited utility.

Instead, the ECB is *ex post* transparent, in that it is judged by its ability to meet its stated mandate of price stability (Issing et al. 2001: 133), as was the Bundesbank (Favero et al. 2000). In contrast, the Bank of England's operating procedures place greater emphasis on *ex ante* transparency, meaning that it explains how it will reach its stated goals through its policy decisions. Thus, members of the Governing Council operate under a principle of collective responsibility, unlike the Bank of England's Monetary Policy Committee, whose members are accountable as individuals. In order to promote transparency, the ECB publishes a *Quarterly Bulletin, Monthly Bulletin,* a consolidated *Weekly Financial Statement*, and an *Annual Report* which is addressed to the Commission, the Council and the European Parliament.

The ECB has argued that its accountability is to the general European public and the officials that they elect. Thus it has cultivated a relationship with the European Parliament's Committee on Economic and Monetary Affairs, with the ECB president appearing before it several times a year in order to answer questions. The ECB conducts an 'open dialogue' with all of the relevant actors in EU politics (Issing et al. 2001: 138–9). However, these mechanisms can best be described as falling under the category of 'soft law' in that none of these dialogues can oblige the ECB to take action. Actors can try to influence the ECB and place public pressure, but the bank's independence ensures that it need not follow any recommendations. Thus the related issues of independence and accountability constantly run up against one another, a tension that is not likely to be resolved in the short term.

Theoretical considerations

Ideas

In order to understand why so much authority had been delegated to the ECB, we must consider the historical experience of the 1970s and 1980s. After the two oil shocks, many European economies suffered from stagnating economic growth and rising inflation, which came to be dubbed 'stagflation'. Germany, however, came out of this period relatively unscathed, and much credit was attributed to the policies of its central bank, the Bundesbank. Its policy of pursuing price stability, which stabilized expectations and promoted investment, created a virtuous circle which engendered economic growth.

This became part of the processes of 'policy learning' and 'policy emulation' that McNamara (1998) describes: policy makers learned that their previous economic policies had become increasingly ineffective during the changed international economic environment of the 1970s and 1980s and emulated Germany's example. This was the critical difference between the ill-fated Snake of the 1970s and the success of the European Monetary System in the 1980s: participating countries accepted Germany's informal domination of the latter and adjusted their policies accordingly. According to Mundell–Fleming's 'unholy trinity', countries must choose two out of the following three: monetary sovereignty, fixed exchange rates and capital mobility. As capital controls became less useful and the policy environment became increasingly prone towards liberalization, EMS countries gave up their monetary sovereignty in order to defend the fixed exchange rate system. In exchange, the EMS countries enjoyed greater exchange rate stability.

As the 'sound money paradigm' (Dyson 1994, 2000) became more prevalent throughout Europe, central bankers began to play a more important role. In June 1988 the Delors Committee was created in order to devise specific steps towards creating monetary union. Rather than a committee of politicians, Delors invited the governors of the national central banks along with academic economists so as to avoid later criticism regarding the economics of the plan (Delors 2004). The central bankers already had a history of cooperation in Europe, not only as part of the EMS but also in the context of the Committee of Governors. This group dates back to 1964, and by the late 1980s it had developed norms and informal governing mechanisms which would later be reflected in the ECB (Andrews 2003). This included a strong predilection for central bank independence, which was underscored by the domination of German Bundesbank president Karl Otto Pöhl of the Delors Committee (Kaelberer 2003). Its recommendations were sent to the European Council meeting in Madrid the following year, and many of them were adopted and became part of the Maastricht Treaty. A non-negotiable element for EMU among the central bankers, backed by the insistent lobbying of the Germans and the Dutch, was that the new ECB be independent.

The logic behind central bank independence rests with the need to combat the short-term interests of politicians to manipulate monetary policy for political gain. Developed by Kydland and Prescott (1977) and extended by Barro and Gordon (1983), a 'time inconsistency' problem arises in which governments try to improve the economy's level of production through higher levels of inflation. While in the short run higher inflation can purchase higher output levels, this can only work if the market does not expect it: that is, if the inflation comes as a surprise. If the market anticipates higher inflation, contracts will be renegotiated so as to incorporate these expectations into future prices. This leads to higher inflation without growth. Markets try to judge the preferences of the government, but often there is uncertainty because incentives exist for a government to renege on its commitment to price stability.

Empirical evidence seems to bear out a link between central bank independence and lower inflation (Cukierman et al. 1994). Some research exists that supports the theory that it also leads to economic growth. For example, De Long and Summers (1992) find a positive relation between central bank independence and GDP per worker in industrial countries. But central bank independence may not be the cause of price stability (Alesina 1988) and may be neither necessary nor sufficient for price stability (Collins and Giavazzi 1992).

However, as governments in both developed and developing economies began granting independence to their central banks in the 1980s and 1990s, economists increasingly questioned the relationship between central bank independence and economic outcomes. While many studies found a relationship between the political status of a central bank and levels of inflation, central bank independence was not necessarily the causal force. Economic growth did not necessarily follow, making the popularity of central bank independence questionable. Alesina and Summers' (1993) study of 16 OECD economies found that central bank independence 'has no measurable impact on real economic performance', as measured by growth, unemployment or *ex ante* real interest rates. Furthermore, there is no correlation between delegation to an independent central bank and countries with higher government debt, political instability or employment-motivated inflationary bias (de Haan and Hag 1995). Finally the results of such studies varied according to how variables were measured (Eijffinger and de Haan 1996), making their conclusions suspect.

In addition, central bank independence concerns the larger issues of legitimacy. Much of European integration rested on a permissive consensus which is no longer taken for granted. From the perspective of legitimacy and democratic theory, the independence of the ECB can be problematic. The ECB is even more independent than the Bundesbank, as it would take a treaty change requiring unanimity among all 27 EU Member States to change its statute. According to Begg and Green, the ECB's extreme independence will lead to a 'substantial and widely perceived democratic deficit which will undermine the credibility of European economic institutions when adverse economic circumstances arise' (1998: 134).

Interests

Central bank independence has been portrayed as an institutional mechanism that promotes certain policy choices that increase social welfare. However, the results are not politically neutral (Kirshner 2003). Central banks have constituents, operate within a politicized system like other self-interested institutions and must court support within the government and the general populace (Bowles and Whit 1994). The ECB's independence and subsequent policies came at a cost for certain segments of society (Berman and McNamara 1999).

The most obvious interest is the impact that Germany and its allies had played in pushing for an independent central bank. The German government and the Bundesbank had made it clear that Germany would not be part of EMU if the ECB were not granted independence and a set of convergence criteria met so as to ensure the strength of the successor currency. Similarly the French government had been promoting monetary union on behalf of those interests that preferred seeing delegation to a European institution rather than the de facto delegation to the Bundesbank (see the previous chapter for more details).

The appointment process of the ECB indicates the continued significance of national interests even after the Duisenberg–Trichet affair. The nationality of appointments is an accepted factor: a Spaniard was replaced by another Spaniard in 2004 and Italians were swapped in 2005 (Ardy et al. 2006).

Despite the attempt to cloak monetary policy and central bank independence as technocratic decisions that will result in better policy, the choices made by independent central banks are not politically neutral. In the short and medium term, ensuing policy tends to favour mobile capital and financial interests (Posen 1993,

Berman and McNamara 1999). The support of the financial community has always been an important resource for central banks to stave off threats to their independence (Goodman 1992). Kirshner (1999) compared inflation to a 'Trojan horse' which would promote the interests of certain segments of society at the expense of others.

Institutions

Much has been written on how an institution like an independent central bank can affect policy outcomes. Institutional fixes from the EMS to the ECB have been credited for the greater credibility of European monetary policy. Was the fixed exchange rate system of the ERM accomplishing the same objectives as an independent central bank? Academic work on the subject finds that under certain conditions, central bank independence and fixed exchange rates can act as substitutes for one another (Clark 2002). However, one might be more suitable than the other, given political considerations. For example, both Keefer and Stasavage (2002) and Hallerberg (2002) consider the impact of multiple veto players on the effectiveness of central bank independence versus exchange rate pegs, although they reach different conclusions. Factors such as tying the hands of future governments (which may possess different policy preferences), the policymaking capabilities of the government in power, electoral opportunism and the partisanship of the government can all play a role in why monetary policymaking is delegated and which type of institution is used (Bernhard et al. 2002).

Central bank independence could also play a role in more disciplined fiscal policy, as an independent central bank is less likely to accommodate loose fiscal policy and would react by tightening monetary policy (Banaian et al. 1983, Burdekin and Laney 1988). In the case of Italy, for example, freeing the Bank of Italy from its obligation to buy unsold public debt at Treasury auctions led to a reduction in its debt monetization (Tabellini 1987). This relationship is not clear-cut, however, as other studies have not found a relationship between monetary and fiscal discipline (Grilli et al. 1991).

The success of central bank independence may be conditioned on the wage bargaining system. According to Hall and Franzese (1998), central bank independence can lead to higher unemployment rates in systems with uncoordinated wage bargaining, as the signals sent between the bank and the bargainers are less clear than in coordinated systems. However, Iversen (1998) finds that highly centralized systems will lead to higher unemployment because of the greater likelihood of conflict between the central bank and militant unions. Instead, an intermediately centralized bargaining system is best at ensuring that union behaviour does not become too militant in the face of an inflation-averse central bank, thus promoting lower unemployment.

Conclusion

The ECB faces a difficult challenge. While it has been delegated much discretion in setting monetary policy, it does so with neither the societal support nor historical influence of the German Bundesbank. Hence, it is prone to criticisms of illegitimacy at every turn. Its ability to hold down inflation (its primary objective) has been insufficient in generating public support for its mission. Instead critics have pointed to the Eurozone's disappointing economic performance and sluggish growth compared with the United States for much of its lifespan. In addition, it is forced to fight turf wars in order to protect its own independence as well as establish the credibility of the euro.

The ECB continues to pursue price stability despite pressure from governments to loosen monetary policy in order to promote greater economic growth. While the economic merits of such arguments are tenuous (as the long-term link between loose monetary policy and higher economic growth has been discredited), such statements retain political value. The ECB has countered criticism by pointing out the need for the Member States to undertake structural reforms, rightly arguing the limits of monetary policy in boosting economic growth. But the fact remains that the ECB is the most visible institutional symbol of monetary union, and governments had already undertaken substantial economic reforms in order to become members of the Eurozone. The news that this would be insufficient was unwelcome and politically unpopular, leading to questions regarding the efficacy of the ECB and thus its legitimacy and accountability. In fact, domestic political rules and institutions are critical in explaining a government's adherence to the sound money principles and its willingness and ability to undertake the needed economic reforms to complement the single currency. Although such blame shifting is ultimately counterproductive, the ECB will continue to be a lightning rod for criticism.

Chapter 6

Decentralizing economic policy cooperation: the Stability and Growth Pact and the Lisbon Strategy

The delegation of interest rate policy to the European Central Bank (ECB) was the most dramatic step in the monetary integration process. However, in order for EMU to succeed, supplementary policies needed to be introduced in order to support it. Monetary union was never viewed as an end in itself; both spillover effects leading towards monetary union (such as the single market) and the spillover effects expected to arise from monetary union (political integration and undertaking structural reforms) make an understanding of economic policy cooperation necessary in order to judge the success of EMU. Monetary policy does not exist in a vacuum, and the wrong policy mix between ECB decisions and Member State policies could negate any positive effects or even worsen economic conditions in both a Member State and the Eurozone as a whole. Conversely, a positive synergy could also be created in which economic and monetary policy support one another.

Unlike the centralization of monetary policymaking in the ECB, economic policies were coordinated in the numerous frameworks in which the Member States retained control over policy. While the Stability and Growth Pact (SGP) used hard law and held the possibility of sanctioning Member States, the coordination systems deployed the open method of coordination (OMC) as an alternative to the traditional Community method. This chapter considers each of these policy coordination mechanisms in turn, placing them within their historical context, providing economic and political rationales for their introduction and development, and explaining their functioning.

The Stability and Growth Pact

As domestic support for monetary integration waned because of the unexpectedly high costs of unification and fear over losing the mark to the untested currency, German finance minister Theo Waigel proposed a Stability Pact (Heipertz and Verdun 2005). The concern was that after states reached the criteria for monetary union, fiscal rectitude would wane. The ensuing inflation would generate higher interest rates and possibly would require a bailout on the part of fellow Eurozone members. Therefore the Stability Pact would encourage states to pursue balanced budgets, lest they risk sanctioning. Acceptance of this was necessary in order to guarantee the continued participation of Germany in monetary union, although the French government extracted some concessions during the negotiations. The sanctions would not be automatic (they must be decided by the Council), an employment chapter would be included in the Amsterdam Treaty, the Eurogroup was created (Heipertz and Verdun 2004: 989), and the Stability Pact was renamed the Stability and Growth Pact, thus emphasizing objectives other than price stability (Chang 2002, Heipertz and Verdun 2004). Although this addition was not considered significant at the time, it later proved to be useful during the subsequent reform of the SGP, as reformers pointed to the dual objectives of the pact and argued that it privileged stability over growth and thus needed reform. The SGP was officially adopted at the Amsterdam European Council in June 1997, committing Member States to a uniform medium-term budgetary objective of 'close to balance or in surplus'.

The original pact contained a preventive arm (Regulation (EC) No. 1466/97) and a punitive arm (Regulation (EC) No. 1467/97). The preventive arm involved the surveillance of Member States' budgetary situations and the coordination of economic policies. The Council can issue an early warning to a Member State in danger of incurring an excessive deficit (see Table 6.1 for the warnings issued). The punitive arm institutionalized the Maastricht Treaty's deficit criterion in perpetuity by implementing the excessive deficit procedure (EDP) (Article 104 EC Treaty) when the deficit exceeds 3 per cent of GDP (see Table 6.2 for the EDPs launched).

The cycle ran accordingly: Member States within the Eurozone and those within the ERM II submitted their annual stability

TABLE 6.1 *Early warning procedures*

	Portugal	Germany	France	Italy
Commission Recommendation to the Council to address an early warning	30 January 2002	30 January 2002	19 November 2002	28 April 2002
Council Recommendation with a view to giving early warning in order to prevent the occurrence of an excessive deficit			21 January 2003	
Council Decision to close an early warning procedure	12 February 2002	12 February 2002		5 July 2004

Source: http://ec.europa.eu/economy_finance/sg_pact_fiscal_policy/
fiscal_policy1075_en.htm

programmes, and those outside the Eurozone submitted 'convergence' programmes to the Council and the Commission. Deviating from the fiscal objectives could trigger the EDP. This process began when a Member State went over the 3 per cent limit, which the Commission then reported and made recommendations to the Council. The Council then determined whether there was an excessive deficit within four months of the reporting dates established in Regulation (EC) No. 3605/93. The Council then issued a recommendation, and the Member State would take action to rectify its deficit within six months and correct the deficit within a year of its identification, barring special circumstances such as a recession (a negative growth rate of 2 per cent). If the Member State did not comply, the Council could publicize its recommendations. Within a four-month period of taking the decision that the Member State had not implemented sufficient measures to correct its deficit, the Council could then penalize the Member State by requiring a non-interest-bearing deposit which converted into a fine after two

TABLE 6.2 *Excessive deficit procedures*

Country	Date of the Commission report (Article 104§3)	Council Decision on excessive deficits	Deadline for correction/ date closed
Hungary	12 May 2004	5 July 2004	2009
Portugal	22 June 2005	20 September 2005	Closed 3 June 2008
Italy	7 June 2005	28 July 2005	Closed 3 June 2008
Czech Republic	12 May 2004	5 July 2004	Closed 3 June 2008
Poland	12 May 2004	5 July 2004	Closed 8 July 2008
Slovakia	12 May 2004	5 July 2004	Closed 3 June 2008
Cyprus	12 May 2004		Closed 11 June 2006
Malta	12 May 2004		Closed 16 May 2007
United Kingdom	21 September 2005		Closed 12 September 2007
	11 June 2008	8 July 2008	Financial year 2009/10
Greece	19 May 2004		Closed 16 May 2006
Netherlands	28 April 2004		Closed 7 June 2005
Germany	19 November 2002		Closed 16 May 2007
France	2 April 2003		Closed 30 January 2007
Portugal	24 September 2002		Closed 11 May 2004

Source: http://ec.europa.eu/economy_finance/sg_pact_fiscal_policy/excessive_deficit9109_en.htm

years. The deposit would be composed of 0.2 per cent of GDP and one tenth of the difference between the deficit as a percentage of GDP in the year in which the deficit was judged excessive and the reference value of 3 per cent of GDP.

The euro launched in 1999 and was introduced as a physical currency in 2002. The SGP quickly become a point of contention. In February 2002 Ecofin ignored the Commission's recommendation to warn Germany about its budget deficit, which was approaching the 3 per cent threshold. This move was widely interpreted as political; German elections were scheduled for later that year, and it would have been awkward to chastize the government on an issue which it had previously championed so close to the election date. German Chancellor Schröder had begun an intensive lobbying campaign in 2001 to avoid such a warning, and ultimately Ecofin agreed. Portugal was also in breach of its deficit targets but escaped censure along with Germany, as it would have been politically difficult to chastize only one country when two were guilty of the same violation. However, by July it was clear that Portugal's budget deficit in 2001 exceeded previous figures and clearly went beyond the 3 per cent reference value. The Council instructed the Portuguese government in November to correct its budgetary situation.

The following year the Commission found France to have an excessive deficit, a decision with which the Council concurred. Germany was also found to have an excessive deficit in 2003, and by 2004 over half of the European Union had begun excessive deficit proceedings. Eurozone as well as non-Eurozone members fell foul of the SGP (the latter received warnings and recommendations to correct their deficits but were not fined).

In November 2003 the Council decided to suspend the EDP rather than act upon a Commission recommendation to begin proceedings against France and Germany. The Commission subsequently took the case to the European Court of Justice (Case C-27/04), requesting an annulment of the failure of the Council to adopt Commission recommendations to give notice to France and Germany regarding their excessive deficits, as well as an annulment of the Council's conclusions that contained the decision to suspend the excessive deficit procedure for France and Germany. The Court ruled in July 2004 that the Council was not obliged to adopt the Commission's recommendation given the inability to reach the required majority (thus in favour of the Council). However, the Council did not have the right to suspend the pact in its conclusions because it violated the Treaty's rules on how to hold the excessive deficit procedure in abeyance.

The Commission issued a communication (COM(2004)813) in December, in which it argued that while the budgetary situations in France and Germany still required vigilance, both countries were implementing measures that should rectify their excessive deficits by 2005 and no further action was necessary on the part of the Council. Thus all sides could claim some sort of victory from the crisis: the Commission was vindicated in that it forced a response from the Council, the Council had to act but did not have to adopt the Commission's recommendations, and ultimately France and Germany escaped excessive deficit proceedings.

Interestingly, none of these events produced much of a response from the financial markets, indicating that they take a longer-term view than the annual deadlines for the SGP (Leblond 2006) and perhaps even pointing to the irrelevance of the pact itself. Indeed, after the suspension of the EDP, some pronounced the pact dead (Begg and Schelkle 2004, Gros 2005, Leblond 2006), although this death could also have been viewed as the opportunity for its rebirth via reform (Begg and Schelkle 2004).

At the request of the Council, the Commission worked on proposals to reform the SGP, issuing a communication in September 2004 advocating improved economic governance and clarifying the pact's implementation (COM (2004) 581). In March 2005 the Ecofin Council agreed on measures that would improve the implementation of the pact, making it more flexible but hopefully increasing the likelihood that its strictures will be followed (see Table 6.3 for a summary of some of the major changes). In particular the Council identified five major areas for improvement:

- improve the economic rationale
- improve ownership by Member States
- save during good times to avoid pro-cyclical policies
- make better use of Council recommendations during periods of slow growth
- pay attention to budgetary surveillance regarding debt and sustainability.

To achieve these objectives, changes were made in both the preventive arm and the corrective arm. In the preventive arm, differentiated 'medium-term objectives' (MTOs) were introduced. Rather than stating that Member States must follow medium-term budgetary positions that are 'close to balance or in surplus', the revised pact gives each Member State its own MTO in which the economic characteristics of each country are considered. Although the 3 per cent deficit limit remains as a safety margin, other aspects like the debt-to-GDP ratio, potential growth rates and the budgetary impact of major structural reforms are considered. Acceptable conditions range from a medium-term deficit of 1 per cent for countries experiencing low debt along with the potential for high growth, to a deficit up to 3 per cent for countries facing high debt and low growth potential (Ardy et al. 2006). In order to achieve the MTOs, Member States are expected to devote 0.5 per cent of GDP per year towards adjustment, more during strong economic times and possibly less during weaker economic times (González-Páramo 2005). The Lisbon Treaty strengthens the SGP's surveillance procedure and enhances the role of the Commission. The Commission can issue 'warnings' under its own authority according to Article 99. Article 114 gives Eurozone countries the right to issue specific recommendations (Pisani-Ferry et al. 2008: 59).

Regarding the corrective arm of the SGP, the 'exceptional circumstances' clause has been revised. In the original SGP, a deficit exceeding 3 per cent of GDP might be acceptable provided that it was 'exceptional and temporary', which was defined as the result of a 'severe economic downturn'. The revised SGP has a less strict definition, as not only negative growth but also low growth can qualify. Possible 'relevant factors' that can be taken into account in judging an excessive deficit were not defined in the original SGP, but a rather long list of potential factors has been discussed for the revised pact.

The original SGP had a deadline of one year for the correction of an excessive deficit, barring 'special circumstances' which were undefined. The list in the revised SGP now provides a common understanding of special circumstances and requires minimum fiscal adjustment of 0.5 per cent of GDP per annum to correct. After the initial deadline has been fixed, revisions and extensions are also possible (González-Páramo 2005).

The ECB reacted with concern that weakening the pact could weaken the incentives of Member States to implement structural reforms and keep their fiscal houses in order (ECB press release, 21 March 2005). Later that year, the ECB announced that it would no longer accept collateral bonds from countries with less than a rating of A– from ratings agencies like Standard & Poor and

TABLE 6.3 *Comparing the old SGP with the new SGP*

	Old SGP	New SGP
Preventive arm Deficit and debt targets	3% of GDP, 60% of GDP	3% of GDP, 60% of GDP remain as reference
Medium-term budgetary objectives	Close to balance or in surplus	Gives each Member State its own MTO in which the economic characteristics of each country are considered; for Eurozone and ERM II members, should be between 1% of GDP and balance or surplus
Annual structural adjustment		For Eurozone and ERM II, annual improvement of 0.5%, depending on economic conditions. Major structural reforms can allow temporary deviation, such as: • potential growth • economic cycle • structural reforms (pensions, social security) • policies supporting R&D • medium-term budgetary efforts • fostering international solidarity • achieving European policy goals

(continued)

Moody's. The ECB lends cash on a short-term basis to banks through its weekly repurchase ('repo') agreements. It accepts as collateral government bonds. Since the euro was introduced in 1999, bond yields across the Eurozone had converged, making bonds from Eurozone countries substitutable for one another despite different economic conditions within the Member States. Without the disciplining effect of the markets, government incentives to reform had diminished, contributing to the budget

	Old SGP	New SGP
Corrective arm		
Annual structural adjustment		Always at least 0.5% of GDP
Suspension of EDP	Possible suspension for countries experiencing at least 0.75% negative annual GDP growth rate; automatic suspension in the case of 2% downturn	Non-application of EDP for countries experiencing negative growth or prolonged period of very low growth relative to potential
Time period for correcting excessive deficit	1 year	2 years
Extension of deadlines for EDP		Cases of 'unexpected and adverse economic events with major unfavourable budgetary effects occurring during the procedure'
Other relevant factors		If general government deficit close to reference value and excess is temporary, special consideration given to cost of pension reforms

deficits in many European countries. There had been an assumption among some market actors that the ECB would accept all Eurozone government bonds, contributing further to the compression of spreads (*Financial Times*, 10 November 2005). Although no Eurozone country was in danger of missing this cut-off, many viewed it as an effort by the ECB to encourage markets to differentiate between Eurozone economies more carefully, thus making freeriding by fiscally profligate countries more difficult.

A year after the reform, assessment of the SGP reform was mixed. The Commission declared the first year's experience to be 'rather positive' (Commission 2006a). On the one hand, the SGP's procedures were not quietly abandoned. Several countries were found to have excessive deficits (see Table 6.2), with no deviations from the 3 per cent rule. Perhaps more significantly, Ecofin issued a 'notice' to the German government (Council Decision, 14 March 2006) to take measures to correct its deficit, which was stronger wording than had been used in 2003. In 2007 the government deficit ratio of the European Union reached a 30-year low, reflecting both general economic recovery and an improved implementation of the SGP (van den Noord et al. 2008: 16).

On the other hand, it has been accused of not being rigorous, with the Council taking advantage of extending the pact's deadlines (González-Páramo 2006). Nevertheless fiscal positions generally appear more disciplined than previously, indicating that the reformed SGP may have restrained deficits after all. Since the SGP reform, all government deficits above 3 per cent led to the excessive deficit procedure (van den Noord et al. 2008: 16). More generally, the SGP has been credited with encouraging domestic stability pacts and making fiscal policy more coherent by providing governments with a common definition of acceptable levels of deficits and by strengthening the Ministry of Finance. The corrective arm seems to be credible and effective, although the preventive arm could be strengthened, as acknowledged by a Commission Communication (2007b) which suggested several proposals, such as:

- broadening the scope of the European Union's fiscal surveillance
- enhancing ownership of budgetary targets found in the stability and convergence programmes
- improving the reliability and credibility of the medium-term budgetary targets
- improving the monitoring of how budgetary plans are implemented.

Theoretical considerations

Ideas

The most important thing to note about ideas relating to the SGP is the lack of consensus regarding the economic merits of the pact, which in turn deprived it of some of the legitimacy enjoyed by other institutional features of EMU (like the independent ECB). It was questionable whether or not the SGP was an essential complement to the monetary policies based on the sound money paradigm. The economics literature had noted the possible links between monetary and fiscal policy and the dangers that could arise if the two diverged (Buiter et al. 1993, Beetsma and Bovenberg 1999, Buti et al. 2001). First, there is the problem of freeriding. If a state outside of monetary union runs a lax fiscal policy, the central bank can try to counter this by raising interest rates. However, within a monetary union the effects of the fiscal policy are diluted, and the central bank cannot target a single state for higher interest rates as punishment for loose fiscal policy. Hence states can freeride on the fiscal rectitude of partners in monetary union (Allsop and Vines 1996, Artis and Winkler 1998, 1999, Eijffinger and de Haan 2000). Specifically, there were concerns about countries like Italy diluting the credibility of the Eurozone (Dyson and Featherstone 1999: 532–3). Second, fiscal profligacy could put the banking system at risk if a debt crisis were to ensue. This would necessitate a bailout by the ECB, thus doing irreparable damage to its credibility. Although the ECB is not legally obliged to do this under the Maastricht Treaty, it could prove difficult for the bank to resist such pressure, hence the interest in the SGP.

The lack of consensus on the necessity of the SGP meant that it lacked widespread legitimacy, and had even famously been called 'stupid' by Romano Prodi (*Le Monde*, 17 October 2002). Among the criticisms of the pact are:

- EMU already lacks natural shock absorbers that politically integrated currency unions have, and countries need national fiscal policy (Obstfeld and Peri 1998, Obstfeld 1999), lest it lead to pressure for a bailout from the ECB (von Hagen and Eichengreen 1996).
- It uses arbitrary criteria for debt and deficits, which is ultimately more harmful (Begg 1991, Buiter and Grafe 2002).
- It focuses on deficits rather than debt (Bébassy-Quéré 2003).
- It is excessively rigid (Eichengreen and Wyplosz 1998).
- Imposing fines would worsen the economic situation of the concerned Member State (Eichengreen and Wyplosz 1998, Buiter et al. 1993).
- It could divert states from fulfilling more important economic reforms (Eichengreen and Wyplosz 1998).

- It does not differentiate between types of expenditures (Blanchard and Giavazzi 2004).
- The SGP is all stick and no carrot. It lacks rewards for fiscal prudence, only provides punishment (Bean 1998).
- It is too politicized – allowing the Council to take decisions makes sanctions unlikely.
- It is democratically illegitimate (Collignon 2004).
- There is no evidence that cross-border spillovers from fiscal policy are large enough to require internalization through supranational rules or institutions (Buiter 2006).
- It focuses too much on stability and not enough on growth (Ardy et al. 2006).

Some advocated scrapping the pact altogether (Arestis and Sawyer 2003, Enderlein 2004), while for others, strengthening the pact would have been the preferred option (Buti et al. 2003, de Haan et al. 2004b). Numerous reforms were suggested (Eichengreen and Wyplosz 1998, Buiter and Grafe 2002, Allsopp and Artis 2003, Buti et al. 2003, Artus et al. 2004, de Haan et al. 2004b, Buti et al. 2005). Overall, 'the theoretical debate [is] inconclusive, as both externality and credibility arguments can be reversed to yield opposite, and equally plausible conclusions' (Fitoussi and Saraceno 2002).

After the 2005 reform, some criticized the revised SGP as watering it down to the point of rendering it useless. Making more flexible a procedure that had already been less than constraining seemed to open the door to even looser fiscal policy (Feldstein 2005). Others emphasized the importance of 'ownership' of the pact (Annett et al. 2005, Buti 2006), arguing that governments will be less likely to criticize the pact in the future and more likely to abide by the new rules that they had a hand in reforming. According to this view, the problems were not with the principles underlying the pact but with the specific rules and their implementation.

Another strand of criticism posited that the SGP's previous flaws were still present, with two additional ones:

- The economics of the SGP are still questionable, as external constraints are placed on national fiscal autonomy in order to prevent spillovers that cannot necessarily be contained through debt and deficit management.

- The revised SGP deals with individual Member States rather than the Eurozone, impeding the creation of an appropriate fiscal–monetary policy mix (Buiter 2006: 688).

Those who were more sanguine about the future of the SGP argued for its continued utility in policymaking, in particular its importance in realizing the goals of the Lisbon Strategy (see below) (Marchat 2005). There was broad agreement, however, that more needed to be done on the national level in terms of structural reforms (Coeuré and Pisani-Ferry 2005).

The 2005 reform and the events leading up to it could be viewed as indicating the weakness of the consensus or possibly the beginning of a policy shift away from it (Clift 2006). Buti (2006) offers a table evaluating the new SGP from a political economy perspective, considering the reform from the viewpoint of those who view the pact as a smokescreen for its de facto dissolution (collusion) and those who see it as 'genuine' reform.

The alternative interpretations of the SGP are further indications of the indeterminate nature of the economic ideas behind it, and how political factors will play a critical component in which interpretation is believed or selected.

Interests

The interest-based theories of the SGP are based on intergovernmentalism and domestic political interests. From a political economy perspective, the saga of the SGP presents an interesting case. Economic reasons cannot fully explain why some countries adhered to the pact and others did not, as not all countries experiencing a cyclical downturn broke the Pact. Indeed, Finland, Ireland and the Netherlands all had stronger downturns than Portugal at the beginning of the decade (Feldmann 2003). Intergovernmental theories can therefore be used to explain the functioning of the SGP. The reform process had been dominated by larger Member States, which arguably had different economic interests and also possessed the political capacity to direct negotiations towards reform (rather than rigorously implementing the Pact) (Chang 2006).

Unlike small countries, large countries need not fear the political fallout that may follow a violation of the SGP. While a small country may pay a penalty in terms of a loss of reputation or influence within the European Union should it breach the Pact, concerns over their

TABLE 6.4 *The old and new SGP: two readings*

	Old SGP	New SGP: collusion	New SGP: genuine
Public visibility	High but fading	On the way to oblivion	Medium
Clear incentives	Blurred	Easy to get away with	Better rationale
Political ownership	Small Member States	High-deficit Member States (DE+FR+IT)	Germany and virtuous Member States
Constraining calendar	Close to balance a moving target	Medium-term objectives de facto never	MTO by the end of the Stability programme
Collegial culture	Acrimony prevailed	Mutual back-scratching	New collegiality based on trust

Source: Buti (2006).

reputation with other Member States or institutions weigh less heavily than domestic political imperatives (von Hagen 2002). Larger countries would also be less likely to suffer from any sanctions from fellow Member States, particularly if several countries violate the SGP. Larger countries innately possess influence, and if more than one country transgresses, it becomes even less likely that any punishment will be doled out (de Haan et al. 2004b).

Domestic political factors could be used to explain these governments' policy preferences. Heipertz and Verdun (2005) outline how political parties and national central banks in Germany and France played an important role in the creation of the SGP. The Bundesbank and the federal banking association initiated a public debate within Germany on stricter budgetary rules, fuelled by domestic discontent regarding giving up the national currency and spurred on by the opposition SPD party. This pressure spilled over into the ruling coalition, as their CSU partner opposed EMU and Bavarian prime minister Edmund Stoiber challenged Waigel for leadership of the CSU. Within

France, President Chirac was eager to demonstrate that EMU and the SGP could be used to spur growth and employment, as public frustration grew with the fiscal austerity needed to qualify for EMU.

By the time EMU was underway many experienced 'reform fatigue'. Some states even engaged in politically motivated spending, signalling a return to fiscal electoral cycles (Buti and Noord 2004). Fiscal policy on average is expansionary when output is above potential, but no cyclical bias in bad times can be detected, with the pro-cyclical bias primarily the result of increased expenditures (Turrini 2008).

No longer worried about qualifying for the Maastricht Treaty, not expecting rewards for good behaviour under the SGP, and with the general uncertainty surrounding the implementation of the SGP, Member States exhibited a surprising amount of flexibility in conducting their fiscal policies under monetary union. Having lost their monetary sovereignty and the possibility of devaluation under EMU, expansionary fiscal policy was used to pursue policy objectives that may not have been optimal for the Eurozone as a whole. Once again, elections and domestic institutions were decisive in shaping government preferences in budget policies. Donnelly (2005) explains how domestic political factors had shaped the various roles played by different countries in the SGP. Electoral competition and the weak state of the economy prompted the Schröder government to become more accepting of budget deficits than its predecessors. In France, the 2002 elections ended cohabitation in an atmosphere of discontent over weak growth and high unemployment, prompting finance minister Mer to agitate for changes in the SGP.

Institutions

Why did so many Eurozone members run into trouble so quickly? One problem could be the Eurozone's governance system, which allows for the politicization of decisions, particularly those made by the Council. Although impressive efforts had been made to qualify for monetary union under the Maastricht Treaty's convergence criteria, in some cases it still required a rather generous interpretation of the rules, as several countries were unable to reach the reference value for deficits. After the Commission recommended the abrogation of excessive deficit judgments of the Ecofin Council except for that of Greece, the European Monetary Institute

(EMI) expressed its concern about the sustainability of fiscal adjustment in the future Eurozone. Although the EMI did not actually question the Commission report, it did suggest the potential for future conflict between those responsible for monetary policy and those responsible for fiscal policy (Obstfeld 1999).

The reform of the pact also had implications for the relationship between Ecofin and the ECB. Already termed the 'policeman and judge' (Howarth and Loedel 2004) of the SGP, the ECB noted it was 'seriously concerned about the proposed changes to the Stability and Growth Pact' and that 'it must be avoided that changes ... undermine confidence in the fiscal framework' (ECB press release, 21 March 2005). The Bundesbank lamented that 'the new arrangements will crucially weaken the pact' (Deutsch Bundesbank press release, 21 March 2005).

Another institutional element of the original SGP is that it had been considered a case of hard law. It included sanctioning mechanisms, in contrast with other economic policy coordination policies which only issued recommendations. However, the line between hard law and soft law became blurred in the application of the original SGP, and its reform made it resemble soft law even more than hard law. It made the SGP more flexible but at the expense of the credibility of sanctioning (Hodson and Maher 2004).

Finally, domestic fiscal institutions could also impact a government's ability to follow a balanced fiscal policy. Research done on national fiscal institutions has distinguished between systems in which fiscal contracts are drawn and those in which fiscal power is delegated. In the fiscal contract/commitment model, the relevant political actors negotiate with one another at the start of the annual budget process, adhering to the multi-annual fiscal programme created by the government. Countries with such a system include Ireland, the Netherlands, Sweden, Denmark and Finland. Other countries delegate fiscal power to a strong finance minister, as is the case in France, Germany and Italy. In the 1990s, those countries that used a contract approach had been able to reduce debt more than those that delegate to a powerful finance minister (Hallerberg 2004, von Hagen et al. 2001). Thus budgetary institutions that have checks and balances appear to have an important effect on stemming fiscal pressure (Fabrizio and Mody 2006). Given that these institutions develop out of a specific political system (delegation from majoritarian systems, contract/commitment from consensual systems), it may not be possible to construct an effective EU-level fiscal framework (Hallerberg 2004).

Economic policy coordination: soft law and the open method of coordination

A key component of economic governance is surveillance under the Broad Economic Policy Guidelines (BEPG). The French had long supported economic surveillance as a means to both encourage economic policy coordination and promote EMU's 'political pole' (Dyson and Featherstone 1999: 215). Thus the Maastricht Treaty introduced the BEPG in Article 99(2). The first set of BEPGs was adopted in 1993 and contained rather general guidelines. They became more detailed over time, in particular after 1997 and the European Councils in Amsterdam and Luxembourg. In 1999 an additional section contained country-specific recommendations (as well as the Community-wide guidelines), and in 2000 the Commission submitted the first Implementation Report. The country-specific recommendations and monitoring of their implementation are now a regular part of the coordination cycle (Noord et al. 2008: 23). Since 2002 guidelines have been delivered every three years instead of annually, although surveillance still occurs annually, as do the Commission's updates to its recommendations. Table 6.5 summarizes the development of the BEPG.

At the spring European Council the guidelines are set for the European Union based on the priorities identified by the Presidency. The Commission monitors the economic conditions of the Member States and in April submits a recommendation to the Council, bearing in mind the Council's conclusions. Preparatory work for the Council is done by the Economic Policy Committee, the Economic and Financial Committee and the Ecofin Alternates, which go over the Commission's draft of the BEPG and makes changes that 'correct mistakes and water down criticisms' (Schäfer 2006: 77). The Council then accepts the BEPG and issues recommendations (based on a qualified majority vote, with a preference for consensus) to each Member State, which is expected to construct its economic policies in view of the Council's proposals. A report is given to the European Council, which formally adopts the BEPG in June. The Commission subsequently reports on the Member States' implementation of the recommendations in January.

The enhanced surveillance and coordination under the BEPG cover macroeconomic developments, exchange rates for the euro,

TABLE 6.5 *Development of broad economic policy guidelines (BEPG)*

Date Legal basis	Innovation
12 July 1999 Council recommendation	Describe policy mix of Eurozone as consisting of four elements: fiscal policy, monetary policy, wage bargaining, and 'a commitment from the Member States to press ahead with front-loaded, coherent and comprehensive reforms with a view to enhancing the adaptability and efficiency of product, capital and labour markets'
15 June 2001 Council recommendation	2001 BEPG make the first reference to the euro area in the country-specific guidelines (referring to budgetary policy, not structural policy)
25 June 2003 Council recommendation	2003-05 BEPG first recommendations specifically for the Eurozone relating to the policy mix, budgetary positions, inflation differences, external representation, and structural reforms
28 June 2005 Council recommendation	2005-08 Integrated Guidelines (merging BEPG and Employment Guidelines) include chapter on a 'dynamic and well-functioning euro area' encouraging 'better co-ordination of their economic and budgetary policies' along with a recommendation to continue structural reforms
2007 Update of Integrated Guidelines	Recommendations from the Council to the Eurozone Member States concerning budgetary consolidation, quality of public finances, competition in services and financial market integration, and labour market flexibility and wages

Source: Commission (2008: 139).

budgetary positions and policies, and structural policies (labour, product and services markets, and costs and price trends). The actual policy measures are determined by the Member States in accordance with the principle of subsidiarity. Nevertheless, the BEPG do offer guidelines for each country, and give the Council the right to specifically address Member States whose policies do not correspond to the BEPG.

In 2001 the effectiveness of the BEPG came into question when the Irish government chose to ignore a warning from the Commission in the context of the BEPG (Meyer 2004). According to the Commission report, Ireland's 2001 budget was inconsistent with the BEPG adopted the previous year, as the rapid growth of the economy combined with a planned tax cut threatened overheating and potentially had inflationary effects. According to the Commission release, 'budgetary plans are expansionary and pro-cyclical and therefore considered inconsistent with those [Broad Economic Policy] guidelines' (Europa rapid press release, 24 January 2001). The Commission thus invoked Article 99.4 of the Treaty on European Union (TEU) for the first time in order to issue a recommendation to end 'the inconsistency with the broad guidelines of the economic policies'. Ecofin adopted the recommendation against Ireland and supported the Commission's viewpoint of the 2001 Irish budget as expansionary, procyclical and inconsistent. Irish finance minister Charlie McCreevy refused to amend the budget, and the government adopted a 'communication strategy ... to win the economic argument and frame the issue as a matter of Irish national interest and sovereignty' (Meyer 2004: 821). Given the non-binding nature of the recommendations, no sanctions were ever envisioned, and Ireland did not appear to suffer from either the Commission and Council recommendations (the naming and shaming element) or its refusal to comply with them. Ireland's position was vindicated by both a report by the OECD which took a contrasting view from that of the Commission and by the upgrading of Ireland's long-term sovereign credit rating by Standard & Poor shortly thereafter (Hodson and Maher 2004).

The BEPG were followed by more policies that used loose coordination mechanisms. The weak economic state of the European Union in the early 1990s, combined with the spillover effects from monetary union, provided the impetus for an employment policy. Particularly on the side of the French, there had been concern about the emphasis of price stability in monetary union, and they were looking for opportunities to place a stronger emphasis on employment and economic growth as part of monetary integration. The process began with the 1993 publication of the Delors White Paper on *Growth, Competitiveness and Employment*. While the specific policies remained under the jurisdiction of Member States, the Commission would play a coordinating role by proposing new initiatives, providing data and analysis, and disseminating information in order to assist in the fight against unemployment.

The White Paper had no legal basis, but it inspired the subsequent European Council in Essen (1994) to tackle the unemployment problem more systematically. Despite pressure coming from various sources (including Delors, segments of the general population, and certain Member States) to undertake serious measures to alleviate the unemployment problem, countervailing pressure from those reluctant to delegate authority to the European Union led to the emergence of a solution based on soft law (Trubek and Mosher 2003). The Conclusions of the Presidency of the Essen European Council outlined five objectives with the ultimate goal of promoting employment, thus creating the 'Essen Strategy', which would:

- develop vocational training
- encourage productive investment via moderate wage policies, greater flexibility and the promotion of local initiatives that create new jobs
- reduce non-wage labour costs
- improve the functioning of labour markets
- target specific groups (young workers, long-term unemployed, women) and develop policies that would enhance their access to employment.

The Essen Strategy marked a departure from traditional employment-related policies in several ways. It was geared towards employment creation rather than employment protection (Rhodes 2005). This was more in keeping with the neoliberal economic policies that had gained favour in Europe over the past decade. In particular, monetary union would require more labour market flexibility in order to offset the loss of the exchange rate as a policy tool, as per optimum currency area theories. Moreover, the economic sacrifices required to satisfy the Maastricht Treaty convergence criteria meant that employment-improving policies to balance the austerity measures were welcome by governments (particularly social democratic governments) trying to keep the momentum towards monetary union on track (Notermans 2001). The Single Market programme and globalization already stoked fears of the dissolution of Europe's social model, and the European Union became its first line of defence (Trubek and Mosher 2003). This would, however, occur within a framework in which employment policy reinforces other policies, such as economic and social policy, so as to contribute to the construction of a coherent economic and social agenda in the European Union (Klosse 2005).

By 1996 the Employment and Labour Market Committee was charged with assisting the European Union to carry out these objectives. However, the Essen Strategy lacked a legal status. This situation was rectified by the 1997 Amsterdam Treaty (Articles 125–130 EC), which marked the next major step in the evolution of employment policy in the European Union and created the European Employment Strategy (EES) (Articles 125–130 EC). This created the legal basis for the Employment Committee (Article 130) and work done by the Commission in terms of research, analysis and the dissemination of information (Article 129).

On 20–21 November 1997 an Extraordinary European Council Meeting on Employment took place in Luxembourg. Anticipating the passage of the Amsterdam Treaty, measures were created to implement the employment chapter. These measures also were incorporated into the BEPG and included an annual report so as to form 'jointly set, verifiable, regularly updated targets' that Member States would strive to meet.

The EES had four components, Employment Guidelines, National Action Plans, a Joint Employment Report and Council Recommendations. Employment guidelines (distinct from the BEPG) would be created based on the results of the multilateral surveillance of economic policies, with the Commission drawing up common priorities for employment policies in the Member States. Respecting the principle of subsidiarity, the means by which states reached these goals would be determined by National Action Plans (NAPs) that the Member States would devise (based on a proposal from the Commission) from a multi-year perspective that aimed to conform to the four pillars of the EES: adaptability, entrepreneurship, equal opportunities and employability. A Joint Employment Report (drafted by the Commission and ratified by the Council) provided a summary of the NAPs and was used as the basis for the subsequent year's Guidelines. Finally the Council (by qualified majority), acting on a proposal by the Commission, had the ability to make non-binding recommendations on Member States' employment policies. Instead of harmonizing policy via directives, Member States used the process as an opportunity for the exchange of ideas and enabling a process of mutual learning by employing the business practices of benchmarking and best practice. Peer pressure (as opposed to fines) would be used to nudge recalcitrant states in the right direction.

In order to jump-start this plan, the European Investment Bank was instructed to release an extra ECU10 billion for small and medium-size businesses, new technology, new sectors and trans-European networks. In addition, a new budget heading was created (European employment initiative) in order to allow small and medium-size enterprises to create sustainable jobs (Presidency Conclusions of the Extraordinary European Council Meeting on Employment, Luxembourg 1997). A dialogue with social partners was also envisioned, which would provide information and feedback which would ultimately improve the efficacy of the strategy and enhance its democratic credentials by incorporating members of society.

In June 1998 the European Council met in Cardiff under the UK presidency. The objective was to address product, service, capital and labour markets and their impact on long-term public finances. Once again, the Council endorsed a system of benchmarking, surveillance, best practice and peer review in order to achieve its goals. The Council initiated an improved macroeconomic dialogue on economic reforms and prepared two reports. Cardiff I dealt with product and capital markets, and Cardiff II evaluated Member States' National Action Plans (NAPs) and their impact on employment. According to the latter, Member States needed to go further in structural reforms and to consider how these reforms interact with macroeconomic policies. Labour market reforms needed to be done in coordination with other reforms in different markets so as to form a coherent set of policies. This effort became known as the Cardiff Process. This did not result in policy guidelines but tried to promote reforms, which were used for BEPG Implementation Reports as well as by the Economic Policy Committee's work on economic reforms (van den Noord et al. 2008: 24).

In June 1999, the European Council met in Cologne and consolidated the existing EES by encouraging a macroeconomic policy dialogue between the Council, the Commission, the social partners and the ECB (dubbed the Cologne Process). Its main goals included sustainable and non-inflationary growth and a high level of employment (which would not interfere with the ECB's pursuit of price stability). Although it emphasized the Member States' continued commitments to the strictures of the SGP and the importance of a noninflationary monetary policy, it did channel public funds towards investment and job creation and advocated pay increases commensurate with productivity gains.

Lisbon Strategy

At the March 2000 European Council meeting the Lisbon Strategy was born. The purpose of the Lisbon Strategy was to create 'the most competitive and dynamic knowledge-based economy in the world, capable of sustainable economic growth with more and better jobs and greater social cohesion'. This would happen through a loose coordination of economic policies via benchmarking, target-setting and peer review, a process now broadly known as the open method of coordination (OMC). Hodson and Maher (2001) described the OMC as a 'heterarchical, decentred and dynamic process [that] supports and radicalizes the principle of subsidiarity, offers an alternative to treaty rules on enhanced co-operation, and addresses some of the legitimacy issues' (2001: 719). This contrasts with the Community method, which is distinguished by the agenda-setting power of the Commission, the predominant use of qualified majority voting in the Council, the participation of the European Parliament and the right of the Court of Justice to interpret Community laws (Wallace 2000: 28–9). Although these soft law mechanisms had existed and been implemented in the previously outlined initiatives on employment, the OMC would be extended to new issue areas such as social policy, R&D and macroeconomic policy, as well as maintaining its use in employment policy. The distinguishing feature of the OMC was that nation-states would retain the ability to make policy decisions, and legislation at the Community level was 'explicitly excluded' (Scharpf 2002). In 2001 sustainable development was added to the Lisbon Agenda's objectives at the Gothenburg summit. The Lisbon Strategy allowed for the adaptation and strengthening of the BEPG, as well as the Luxembourg, Cardiff and Cologne Processes to form a more comprehensive coordination system for economic governance.

The Lisbon Strategy thus rested on three pillars, economic, social and environmental (added in 2001, with the original Lisbon Strategy concentrating on competitiveness, jobs and social cohesion) (Europa Scadplus). This broadened its appeal to include those who viewed it as a first step towards greater integration in addition to those who were more sceptical, what Rhodes identified as 'the enduring double cleavage between the "federalists" and "subsidiarists" on the one hand, and between the socialists/social democrats and market liberals on the other' (2005: 290).

The original Lisbon Agenda employed a three-part strategy:

1. Promote a knowledge-based economy and society through policies that encouraged research and development, structural reforms that improved competitiveness and innovation, and the completion of the internal market.
2. Modernize the European social model, in particular targeting social exclusion.
3. Support a macroeconomic policy mix that would engender healthy and sustainable economic growth.

The strategy also employed some more concrete goals, such as:

1. Investing 3 per cent of GDP in research and development.
2. Promoting entrepreneurship by reducing bureaucratic obstacles.
3. Reaching an employment rate of 70 per cent overall, 60 per cent for women.

These objectives were envisioned to be reached by the year 2010. At the 2001 Stockholm European Council, additional goals were set: by 2005 an overall employment rate of 67 per cent and an employment rate of 57 per cent for women should be reached; by 2010 an employment rate of 50 per cent for older workers was envisioned.

In terms of research and innovation, the European Research Area was created in order to improve the coherence of research that took place within the European Union. European activity in R&D lags behind the United States and Japan, and the business world and academia do not collaborate as effectively as they could (Archibugi and Coco 2005). National systems for innovation differ substantially across Member States, and there is still an element of competition between states for resources, making collaboration more difficult (Prange and Kaiser 2005).

Social policy developed in tandem with employment policy (Kenner 2002, Rhodes 2005), and progress in this area has been halting. Social policy at the EU level differs substantially from that at the national level in terms of the purpose (supporting integration rather than redistribution), values (subsidiarity and a competitive form of solidarity as opposed to protection) and methods (dialogue-based and promoting social partnerships) (Daly 2006). The OMC's contribution to social policy was the creation of NAPs on poverty and social inclusion, which were examined by the Commission and the Council as part of the peer review process. It remained secondary to market-oriented policies, as social protection measures were viewed in light of how they potentially distort market forces and hamper competitiveness. Finally, it faced a collective action problem as the most powerful actors did not participating in the OMC (Daly 2006).

The use of the OMC has expanded rapidly into areas that have a treaty base (like the BEPG and the EES), areas that supplement the Lisbon Agenda (social protection and inclusion, pensions, health care), nascent areas (innovation and R&D, education, information society, environment, immigration, enterprise) as well as areas that have not been formally acknowledged (tax policy). While the Lisbon Agenda legitimized the OMC's expansion, it is still most used in the EES (Szyszczak 2006).

In 2000 a mid-term review of the procedures that had been begun since the Luxembourg process was undertaken. On the positive side, the Luxembourg process was seen to have created a common framework for structural reform, allowed the participation of a greater number of actors in the EES, and increased transparency and political accountability. The EU labour market had undergone substantial improvement since 1997, with 10 million new jobs being created (and 4 million fewer unemployed). However, differences remained between countries in terms of the performance of their labour markets, and in some cases the differences were worsening. Similarly, inconsistent progress was achieved on the four pillars of the EES, with the adaptability pillar suffering the most. This report was followed by an impact evaluation in 2002 carried out by the Commission and the Member States (Commission 2002), and at the 2002 Barcelona Council the economic and employment policy cycles were coordinated in order to render them more transparent and improve their visibility. Figure 6.1 outlines the new policy cycle.

The EES was further streamlined in 2003, as its primary objectives were refocused to full employment, improving quality and productivity at work, and strengthening social cohesion and

FIGURE 6.1 **Flow chart of the streamlined policy coordination cycle**

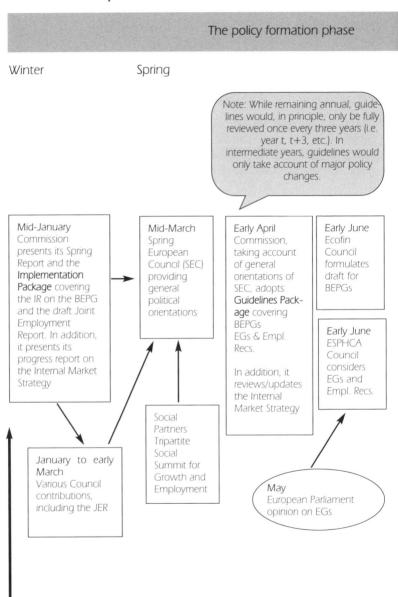

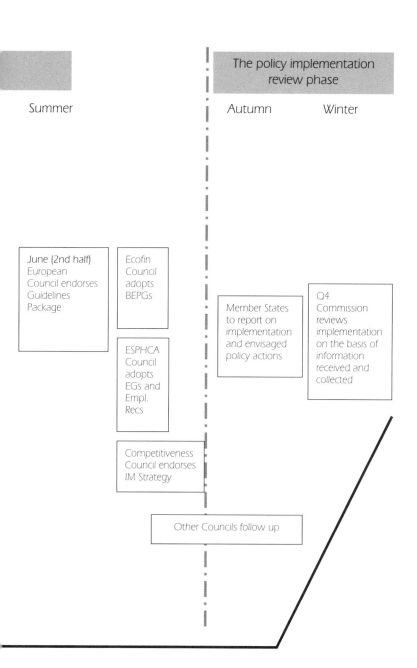

The policy implementation review phase

Summer

Autumn   Winter

June (2nd half)
European
Council endorses
Guidelines
Package

Ecofin
Council
adopts
BEPGs

Member States
to report on
implementation
and envisaged
policy actions

Q4
Commission
reviews
implementation
on the basis of
information
received and
collected

ESPHCA
Council
adopts
EGs and
Empl.
Recs

Competitiveness
Council endorses
IM Strategy

Other Councils follow up

inclusion (Commission 2003). These objectives largely incorporated the previous four pillars (employability, entrepreneurship, adaptability and equal opportunities) and were undertaken in order to rationalize the EES with the Lisbon Strategy and the BEPG (Ardy et al. 2006: 125). Beginning with the 2003 Employment Guidelines, a three-year cycle was introduced in addition to the annual reports, thereby synchronizing the EES and BEPG timetables (Ardy et al. 2006: 134). The purpose of the three-year cycle is to provide the opportunity for a revision of the guidelines, whereas the annual cycle assesses their implementation.

The ten Member States that joined in 2004 were quickly incorporated into the EES that same year with the submission of their first NAPs for employment. The process of integrating the new states had begun in 1999 with the creation of Joint Assessment Papers (JAP) which identified major issues in employment policy. The Commission along with the European Training Foundation evaluated the initial conditions that the candidate countries found themselves in, and the candidate countries themselves worked in close cooperation with the Commission on the JAP drafts. By the beginning of 2002 JAPs had been established for the Czech Republic, Slovenia, Poland and Estonia. Malta, Hungary, Slovakia, Cyprus and Lithuania quickly followed suit the following year, and by the fall of 2002 Romania, Bulgaria and Latvia signed their JAP.

By 2004 the Commission acknowledged that the European Union would clearly not be able to fulfil its stated goals, and thus the reform process of Lisbon I began. The Commission proposed the prioritization of the project focusing on economic growth and employment. A High-Level Group was set up to contribute an independent analysis to the mid-term review, the result of which is known as the Kok Report (2003). This report also criticized the lack of progress made during the preceding years, noting the 'disappointing delivery' which resulted from 'an overloaded agenda, poor co-ordination and conflicting priorities'. Ultimately, however, the Member States had failed to rise to the task. Like the Commission report, the Kok Report emphasized the lack of ownership, stating 'Lisbon is about everything and thus about nothing. Everybody is responsible and thus no one.' The following priorities were set: increasing the adaptability of workers and enterprises; bringing more people into the labour market; investing more in human capital, both quantitatively and qualitatively; and devising better governance procedures for the implementation of reforms. Finally, 'the High Level Group advises the EU and Member States to focus on growth and employment in order to underpin social cohesion and sustainable development'.

In February 2005 the Commission proposed a new Lisbon Strategy that prioritized jobs and growth (COM (2005) 24 of 2.2.2005). The revised Lisbon strategy was dubbed the Partnership for Growth and Jobs, which would have an action plan at the EU level and be implemented by the Member States' NAPs. Moreover, the Lisbon Agenda 'must become part of national political debate' in order to create more 'ownership' of the reform process. In March the European Council officially reformed the Lisbon Strategy and its ambitions were scaled back substantially, calling for a focus on growth, innovation and employment. The social and environmental elements of the original agenda would still be encouraged, but it signalled an even greater shift in the European Union's priorities towards market-oriented policies. At the Member State level, the Integrated Guidelines for Growth and Jobs (2005–2008) constituted the basis for the National Reform Programmes (thus replacing NAPs), integrating the BEPG and the Employment Guidelines. The development of a common energy policy was also added to the Lisbon Strategy. At the same time, the Commission would create a Community Lisbon programme for activities that would be done at the EU level. No separate procedures currently exist for the Eurozone, the coordination of structural policies applies to the entire European Union. However, the spring 2006 European Council noted:

> the special importance of enhanced structural reforms in Member States of the euro area and stresses the necessity of effective policy coordination within this area, i.e. as a requirement to more effectively deal with asymmetric developments within the monetary union.

BEPG and later the Integrated Guidelines have increasingly mentioned the need for structural reform in the euro area, and offered specific recommendations to Eurozone members which emphasize reforms that would aid in adjusting to the loss of the exchange rate and to a single monetary policy (van den Noord et al. 2008: 26–8).

The Commission presented its Community Lisbon programme in July 2005, which outlined steps for the European Union to take in order to refocus the agenda on jobs and growth. No new initiatives were proposed, and the policy measures fell under three categories: knowledge and innovation for growth, making Europe a more attractive place to invest and work, and creating more and better jobs. Some of the concrete measures included the completion of the Internal Market for services, developing a common strategy towards economic migration, and completing the Doha round. At the EU level, the Commission would 'complement the efforts of Member States ... offer[ing] a clear value added because of action being taken or coordinated at the Community level' (COM (2005) 330 of 20.7.2005).

The main tools of the revised EES are:

- Integrated employment guidelines: the Commission prepares an annual proposal that establishes common priorities for employment policies in Member States, which is approved by the Council.
- National reform programmes (NRPs): each Member State submits a programme detailing how the guidelines will be implemented on a national basis.
- Joint employment reports: the Council adopts the Employment chapter of the annual progress report, thus creating the Joint Employment Report.
- Recommendations: the Commission makes a recommendation for a specific country, which must then be approved by a qualified majority vote of the Council.
- EU annual progress report: an annual assessment in which the Commission monitors and evaluates progress at the level of the Community and the Member States in implementing the Community Lisbon Programme. This report can form the basis of proposals to further amend the programme.

The OMC no longer seems to be the future of European governance. In a speech at the European Policy Centre in Brussels in November 2005, Commission president Barosso admitted that the 'naming and shaming' element of the OMC was ineffective and that the new approach would stress the NRPs.

In October 2006 the Commission published a strategy paper which added a trade dimension to the Lisbon Agenda. According to the report, 'the renewed Lisbon Strategy set out the steps we must take in Europe to deliver growth and jobs .... This internal agenda must be complemented with an external agenda for creating opportunity in a globalized economy, encompassing our trade and other external policies' (Commission 2006b). The major policy proposals included the creation of new free trade areas with emerging economies, with ASEAN, Korea and Mercosur as priority regions; ensuring a level playing field for European companies conducting business abroad by improving the regulatory environment; obtaining reciprocal agreements from trading partners that would open up public procurement markets to EU exporters, and implementing intellectual property rights.

While trade policy rose in significance with the revised Lisbon Strategy, other policies faltered. Lisbon 2's social policy orientation is considerably weaker. The emphasis on jobs and growth has pushed social exclusion further down the list of the European Union's objectives. In addition, combining the economic and employment processes of Lisbon 1 served to further marginalize social policy.

A 2007 IMF statement commented that Lisbon 2 'still has some way to go in fostering ownership, harnessing the national and area-wide synergies among reforms, and becoming more transparent'. However, the country-specific policy recommendations and the national reform programmes were praised as having the ability to promote greater cooperation. Indeed, studies show that Member States have shown signs of policy learning through the sharing of best practices. The Luxembourg process has also increased the visibility of employment policy, further encouraging coherence within Member States. Nevertheless critical structural reforms such as labour market reform not covered by the EES still need to be undertaken (Ardy et al. 2006: 131–2).

In light of the economic upswing from 2006–08, the European Council returned to social concerns. At the launching of the 2008–10 cycle, the Slovenian presidency issued a press release announcing:

> Economic growth and high-quality jobs are a guarantee of social progress and social cohesion. The new cycle of the Lisbon Strategy ensures a better balance between concern for citizens and the environment on the one hand and efforts for a competitive, knowledge-based market economy on the other.

Theoretical considerations

Ideas

The academic community immediately embraced the Lisbon Agenda and in particular the OMC for its innovative approach to integration.

Abbott and Snidal (2000) delineated conditions where the use of soft law would be appropriate, namely in areas requiring the reduction of negotiating costs as well as sovereignty costs, where uncertainty over outcomes exist, and when compromise is required so as to alleviate bargaining tensions. Enthusiasts noted that this new form of governance could lead to enhanced cooperation and improve the legitimacy problems of the European Union by involving more social actors in the policy process (Hodson and Maher 2001, Eberlein and Kerwer 2004), although it has been more effective in some areas (Luxembourg process) than others (Cologne process) (Ardy et al. 2006). Through the benchmarking and peer review processes, a dialogue is created that can transform preferences (Kerstin 2004) as well as aggregate diverse preferences at multiple levels, thus creating an instance of 'democratic experimentalism' (Eberlein and Kerwer 2004). The OMC encourages a more gradual approach to integration through policy learning and incremental change (Ferrera et al. 2001, Hodson and Maher 2001, Trubek and Mosher 2003).

Achieving procedural legitimacy via public argument and deliberation (Habermas 1996, 2002; Cohen and Sabel 2003) contrasts with legitimacy through policy output, such as achieving specific economic goals like an inflation target or growth rate (Scharpf 1999). The former type of legitimacy envisages the forging of a common will and possibly a common identity in the process. Indeed, as Jacobsson (2005) notes, in order for the OMC to work, participating actors must believe in it and strive towards common goals. For example, a recent study of the EES and German labour markets notes how the former intensified the effects of pre-existing policies and at times even steered policy towards certain directions (Zohlnhöfer and Ostheim 2005). Such deliberation contributes to the viability of the democratic process, thus boosting claims for the legitimacy of the OMC and by extension the European Union (Cohen and Sabel 2003).

However, the Lisbon Agenda and the OMC also faced detractors regarding their effectiveness, legitimacy and policy outcomes. In terms of the effectiveness of the OMC, it is unclear whether or not soft law promotes further cooperation. Its voluntary nature makes it difficult to ascertain whether reforms were undertaken as a result of policy learning or whether they would have been adopted anyway. It is uncertain whether policy learning via the OMC is even realistic; while peer review and benchmarking have played a constructive role in the business world, their application at the international level is difficult and unlikely to promote innovation (Lodge 2005) given the more limited resource of national governments (James et al. 2004). States are still reluctant to sacrifice their sovereignty in this policy dimension, thus change must come from a variety of actors at the national level who are involved in complicated political processes (Trubek and Mosher 2003). Jacobsson (2005) found that committee members act as national representatives with political mandates, perhaps indicating less openness to policy learning and dialogue than proponents indicate. One study concluded that the 'EES did not possess the capacity to Europeanise German labour market policy to any significant extent ... reflect[ing] the insignificance of the EES so far' (Fleckenstein 2006). Others have pointed to the ambiguous governance structure, which makes it difficult to assign responsibility for job creation, thus weakening the coherence and legitimacy of the EES (Ardy et al. 2006). Finally, 'benchmarking fatigue' (Zängle 2004) could have deleterious effects on integration itself if the European Union sets ambitious policies that it is unable to achieve. Even Ireland, despite its many economic successes in the last decade, fell short of its Lisbon objectives by not 'increase[ing] social cohesion while at the same time promoting growth and employment' (Zängle 2004: 7).

The Lisbon Agenda's ultimate policy objectives have also been questioned. Rather than true policy innovation, the sound money paradigm upon which monetary union was founded continued to form the basis of all subsequent economic policy initiatives (Dyson 2000). It was developed in the context of an overtly political process involving Council members, which was 'risky in terms of consistency of diagnosis and solutions', as it continued to prioritize controlling inflation and budget deficits over policies that would promote economic development (Pochet 1999). According to Trubek and Mosher, 'For the pessimists, the move to soft law is at best a waste of time, and at worst a smokescreen behind which the welfare state might be dismantled' (2003: 2). Furthermore, the scientific basis on which the Lisbon Agenda rests can also be questioned. Although social protection can coexist with reduced unemployment rates (Blanchard 2004), research has not shown a decisive link between improving employability and reducing unemployment (Calmfors 1994, OECD 1997, Pochet 1999).

Interests

Integration via the OMC was seen as less threatening to those that were averse to further integration, as the states retained their ability to direct and implement the economic and social policies associated with it (Mosher 2000, Ferrera et al. 2001). Instead of the black holes of nondecision (Scharpf 1999) that beset the European Union and left it prone to deadlock, cooperation could proceed on a more informal basis, thus creating a complementary form of governance (Trubek and Mosher 2003). Indeed, the OMC is generally introduced after traditional methods of cooperation fail (Eberlein and Kerwer 2004), thus demonstrating its utility in keeping integration in motion. For example, Member States are loath to harmonize their different welfare models, but the OMC allowed for a dialogue that encourages convergence, if not harmonization (de la Porte 2002). In addition, the line between hard law and soft law is not as rigid as it may initially appear (and as seen by the non-application of rules in the SGP), and the European Union may simply be evolving in terms of governance, rather than retreating, as some critics have argued (Daly 2006).

However, empirical studies have shown mixed results regarding the extent to which Member States have been impacted by these European-level processes and accompanying deliberation at the national level. Meyer and Kunstein (2007) found differences between Member States and between policies in the extent to which public debate has been Europeanized. While Europeanization appears strong in Germany, it is only moderate in France. In addition, the European measures did not appear to make a difference in employment policy debates, as covered by major media outlets. This lack of relevance contributes to the ownership problems discussed previously, as well as the poor implementation of measures by some Member States. Some states did seem more prone to policy adaptation as a result of peer pressure, further suggesting that national-level explanations are an important explanatory variable. Regarding employment policy, for example, some countries appeared strongly influenced as a result of the EES whereas in other countries change was more sluggish when it did not dovetail with national policy agendas. National priorities still dominated the policy process, and institutional innovation was not particularly pronounced. Jacobsson and Schmid (2002: 87) write that the EES:

is administered by international offices which work much like diplomatic missions: they represent national policies and interests in a European process, but have little direct influence on what actually happens in their domestic labour markets.

Hartwig (2007) characterized the process as Member States 'paying only lip-service to the programmes'.

Studies on the impact of the BEPG have similarly concluded a negligible impact on national policies. One study of the changes made by Member States as a result of country-specific recommendations indicated that 34 per cent of the recommendations were modified, 26 per cent of them substantially so. Linsenmann (2007) describes the BEPG as a statement of intent rather than a credible contract on the part of the Member States, although the BEPG are useful insofar as they promote policy coherence at the EU and Member State level.

Institutions

In contrast to the 'hard law' of the original SGP that referred to the use of sanctions, the 'soft law' of the BEPG aimed at improving economic coordination through jointly agreed targets, peer pressure, benchmarking, and naming and shaming recalcitrant Member States in order to promote policy learning (Meyer 2004). Thus the European Union expanded its modes of governance from its use of the traditional Community method that relied on directives and the harmonization of policy, to incorporate methods that took into account the increasing diversity of its Member States and their reluctance to cede sovereignty over politically sensitive policy areas (Gerstenberg and Sabel 2000).

However, soft law mechanisms have also been questioned over their efficacy in promoting policy learning. Multilateral surveillance had already been used in other organizations like the OECD and IMF with questionable results. Scant evidence exists demonstrating that such measures lead to better policy coordination or encourage policy changes. Schäfer (2006: 70) concluded that 'governments select voluntarist procedures mainly to secure their own competencies rather than to realize common goals. Effective problem-solving is therefore not necessarily the dominant objective of soft law.' Nevertheless, policy initiatives based on soft law proliferated through the 1990s, beginning with the creation of an EU-level employment policy.

Although it was originally touted as making the policy process more democratic via the social dialogue, the OMC can be criticized for exacerbating the legitimacy problem because of the lack of transparency in the process, the limited role that civil society plays in practice, and the muted role for the more democratic institutions of the European Union (like the European Parliament) and of national governments (national parliaments) (Borras and Jacobsson 2004, Szyszczak 2006). Indeed, accountability is quite difficult in a system that easily conflates decision making with implementing policy (Radaelli 2003). Rather than a more participatory system, the OMC encourages the development of an expertocracy (Eberlein and Kerwer 2004). In assessing the democratic quality of the OMC in the employment sector, de la Porte and Nanz regard it as 'mixed' (2004: 283), finding it of only medium quality regarding transparency, learning and participation, and of low quality in terms of public debate (2004: 276).

Gros et al. (2005) have referred to the '*immobilisme* of economic policies' as a result of the contradictory objectives in the short run versus the long run, adding that 'European policymakers tried to achieve too many things at the same time, and ended up with weak growth, a weak fiscal position and a minimalist reform effort' (2005: iv–v).

Conclusion

The implementation of a project is rarely as exciting as its launch. The policies devised to support monetary integration (the Stability and Growth Pact, the Broad Economic Policy Guidelines, the Lisbon Agenda) did not attract the same kind of attention as the decision to proceed with monetary union. Thus the results of these policies (at best ambiguous, at worst disappointing) did not generate a strong reaction from either the general public or market actors. The creation of the Eurozone seems to have been the biggest hurdle faced by the European Union, and markets have been relatively sanguine about differences that in the past might have triggered a crisis. That in itself may be a testament to the utility and success of monetary union, the creation of more stable expectations and the elimination of large amounts of risk.

However, the long-term health of monetary union does require a certain amount of policy coordination. While reform fatigue and blame-shifting characterized the early years of the SGP, it did not seriously harm the euro. Nevertheless, economists agree that structural reforms must be undertaken in order to avert a crisis as populations age and strain state coffers. The reformed Lisbon Strategy can help Member States adjust at the national level in a way that does not negatively impact their European partners and can potentially help offset the costs of adjustment through more job creation and stronger economic growth.

In order to do this, however, the political will must be found at the national level. A convergence of ideas on how to best handle the coordination of economic policy has not emerged the way that it did in the case of monetary policy. This is why the European Union resorted to soft law methods like the flexible version of the SGP and the OMC. But the effectiveness of soft law is still being debated. The discussion in the context of the reforms of both the SGP and the Lisbon Strategy in 2005 regarding the importance of 'national ownership' indicates that domestic politics remain a key element in the ultimate success of either. Larger states can lead the way in terms of policy setting (as seen in the SGP reform), but even smaller states (as seen with Ireland) cannot be forced to adjust their policies, particularly in the face of a recalcitrant electorate. While the SGP and the Lisbon Strategy (and OMC) have expanded the European Union's involvement into new issue areas, the implementation of both indicates the limits of what can be done at the supranational level.

Chapter 7

The European Union without EMU: the United Kingdom, Denmark, Sweden and the accession countries

European Monetary Union has the distinction of being among the few EU policies not to require the participation of all EU Member States. This indicates the politically divisive nature of monetary union, as without the possibility of derogation it is unlikely that the Treaty would have been ratified. While in other contentious EU policy areas (such as the Common Agricultural Policy) states were expected to adopt the entire *acquis* despite reservations about any specific issue areas, monetary union was treated differently in order to ensure that monetary integration would not be derailed due to a small number of recalcitrant Member States. Thus neither Denmark nor the United Kingdom is obliged to adopt the euro in the future.

Of course, Eurozone membership is not simply a matter of the desire/consent of applicant countries. Though all non-Eurozone countries without derogations are eventually expected to become members, they must first comply with the Maastricht Treaty convergence criteria. Slovenia succeeded in becoming the first among the newest members to satisfactorily comply with the criteria and officially became the 13th member on 1 January 2007. Cyprus and Malta acceded to the Eurozone in 2008, joined by Slovakia in 2009.

This chapter begins with the mechanics for a country to become a member of the euro area, followed by a discussion of the economic and political rationale for the three states of the EU15 to remain outside of the Eurozone in the 1990s and what have been the effects (economic and political) of not joining EMU. This is followed by an analysis of the accession countries, what kind of impact monetary integration has had on them already, how euro area membership will influence these countries, and how these countries are likely to impact the functioning of the Eurozone. The next section highlights significant economic and political theories that have played into the debate over EMU enlargement, using the framework established earlier of looking at the interplay between ideas, interests and institutions. The chapter will conclude with a reflection on the impact a multi-speed EMU has had on European integration more generally.

How to become a member of the euro area

EMU was launched on 1 January 1999 with 11 participants (Austria, Belgium, Finland, France, Germany, Ireland, Italy, Luxembourg, Netherlands, Spain, Portugal). In 2001 the Eurozone was joined by Greece, and in 2007 Slovenia became the first of the CEECs to qualify for EMU, followed by Cyprus and Malta in 2008 and Slovakia in 2009. All of these countries were required to meet the Maastricht Treaty's convergence criteria, in accordance with Article 109j of the Treaty on European Union (see Box 7.1).

Upon becoming a member of the European Union, a country's exchange rate policy becomes a matter of 'common interest', though this has not been defined in practice. Economic and fiscal policies are coordinated in Ecofin, and countries are obliged to remove restrictions on capital controls. The next step towards membership is joining the ERM II for at least two years. When the Maastricht Treaty was signed in 1992, the ERM I was in operation, which had a 2.25 per cent fluctuation margin. Though the ERM II specifies a fluctuation band of plus or minus 15 per cent, states have been evaluated against the old 2.25 margins of the ERM I.

All members of the European Union are committed to meeting the Stability and Growth Pact's targets. Though non-EMU members are not subject to the excessive deficit procedure, failing to achieve the SGP goals can still have serious consequences, as Council Regulations 1164/1994 and 1264/1999 stipulate that the failure to correct an excessive deficit can lead to the denial of financial support for new projects and even prevent the disbursement of funds to complete new stages of existing projects. Member States not participating in the euro area are also subject to 'convergence reports' that are generated either every two years or upon request of the Member State in question. These reports analyse the compatibility of legislation within the Member State with its future treaty obligations and the European System of Central Banks'

Box 7.1 The Maastricht Treaty convergence criteria

Price stability: a Member State has a price performance that is sustainable and an average rate of inflation, observed over a period of one year before the examination, that does not exceed by more than 1 percentage points that of, at most, the three best performing Member States in terms of price stability. Inflation shall be measured by means of the consumer price index on a comparable basis, taking into account differences in national definitions.

Budgets: The criterion on the government budgetary position referred to in the second indent of Article 109j(1) of this Treaty shall mean that at the time of the examination the Member State is not the subject of a Council decision under Article 104c(6) of this Treaty that an excessive deficit exists.

Exchange rate stability: A Member State has respected the normal fluctuation margins provided for by the exchange rate mechanism on the European Monetary System without severe tensions for at least the last two years before the examination. In

⟶

---

statutes. In addition, the report assesses the progress of the state's ability to fulfil the obligations required by EMU membership, including meeting the Maastricht criteria. In accordance with the Treaty, the Commission submits a proposal on which states fulfil the convergence criteria and sets a date for Eurozone accession. The Council then takes a decision. Once the euro has been adopted, the national currency ceases to exist and the ECB officially assumes control of monetary policy.

Opting out – the United Kingdom and Denmark

The United Kingdom

The United Kingdom has a difficult history with European integration more generally. It was not one of the founding members of the European Economic Community in the 1950s, declining membership due to the infringements on sovereignty that it implied and

⟶

particular, the Member State shall not have devalued its currency's bilateral central rate against any other Member State's currency on its own initiative for the same period.

Interest rates: Observed over a period of one year before the examination, a Member State has had an average nominal long term interest rate that does not exceed by more than 2 percentage points that of, at most, the three best performing Member States in terms of price stability. Interest rates shall be measured on the basis of long-term government bonds or comparable securities, taking into account differences in national definitions.

The Council shall, acting unanimously on a proposal from the Commission and after consulting the European Parliament, the EMI or the ECB as the case may be, and the Committee referred to in Article 109c, adopt appropriate provisions to lay down the details of the convergence criteria referred to in Article 109j of this Treaty, which shall then replace this Protocol.

Source: Protocol (No 6) On the convergence criteria referred to in Article 109j of the Treaty establishing the European Community, http://europa.eu/abc/treaties/archives/en/entr8g.htm

because of its aspirations for a more international role. These concerns still colour the United Kingdom's relationship with the European Union, as the country has tried to balance its economic interest in integration with the political demands placed on it by other members. Shortly after joining the EC in 1973, the government called a referendum for 6 June 1975. The question posed to the British public was 'Do you think the United Kingdom should stay in the European Community (Common Market)?' 67 per cent of voters responded affirmatively, seemingly paving the way for greater involvement and a more constructive role for the United Kingdom within the European Community.

However, three years later during the negotiations for the European Monetary System, the Callaghan government kept the pound outside of the Exchange Rate Mechanism. The Conservative government, then in opposition, argued in favour of full membership (George 1994). Therefore when the ERM went into effect in

March 1979 it was without British participation. But when Margaret Thatcher took office a couple of months later, she also declined to link the British currency to it, as the economic conditions were deemed inappropriate (George 1990).

When the pound was brought into the ERM in October 1990, it was done so reluctantly, with the economic benefits still under debate. By this time negotiations were under way for the Maastricht Treaty, placing Britain under greater pressure to join the ERM as the other Member States pushed for a single currency. The British government tried to slow the tide in terms of its own membership and EMU while not stoking concerns of its partners regarding traditional British Euroscepticism. A 1989 Treasury report stated that the:

> UK Government reaffirms that it will join the ERM when the level of UK inflation is significantly lower, there is capital liberalization in the Community and real progress has been made towards completion of the single market, freedom of financial services and strengthened competition policy.

However, monetary union would place severe constraints on Member States' budgetary policy, which ran counter to the Community's principal of subsidiarity and provided another reason for urging caution and adopting 'an evolutionary approach' to EMU, as opposed to 'the Delors Report [that] envisages moving by administrative fiat and institutional change.' Moreover, an independent central bank with no means of accountability to the national parliament was regarded as an anathema (HM Treasury 1989).

European monetary integration proved to be a divisive subject within Britain and even within Thatcher's own cabinet, with notables like Geoffrey Howe (Chancellor of the Exchequer 1979–1983, Foreign Secretary 1983–89), Nigel Lawson (Chancellor of the Exchequer 1983–89) and John Major (Chancellor of the Exchequer 1989–90) all voicing their support of monetary integration despite Thatcher's objections. Bank of England Governor Robin Leigh-Pemberton also expressed his positive proclivities towards monetary integration with Europe. The 1980s had been a turbulent decade for the British economy, with the pound's volatility contributing to the economy's poor performance. Indeed, Chancellor of the Exchequer Nigel Lawson hoped that by tying the hands of the government, the economy would become more competitive and would control costs when exchange rate devaluations were no longer an option (Lawson 1993: 1058, Buller 2006).

Despite rising support among Conservative elites, Britain remained sceptical towards monetary union. In June 1990 chancellor of the Exchequer Major responded to the Delors plan with the idea of a parallel currency instead of a single currency. The 'hard ECU' would allow the national currencies to remain and compete against it. Unlike her chancellor of the exchequer, prime minister Thatcher was not concerned about Britain becoming isolated on the issue, expecting the Germans (pressured by the Bundesbank) to back up Britain's refusal. She unwillingly relented to internal pressure to join the ERM in October 1990, much of it emanating from Major (Thatcher 1993). Joining the ERM was not enough to placate her party, however. Major shortly succeeded Thatcher as prime minister when her Europe policy (and domestic issues like the poll tax) led to her downfall within the party.

As prime minister, Major negotiated an opt-out from monetary union during the Maastricht Treaty negotiations in 1991. Despite his support for ERM membership, he still harboured doubts about monetary union. His hard ECU idea went nowhere, so he committed to a wait-and-see approach to monetary integration as Britain adjusted to the ERM, locked in at an exchange rate that many noted was too high, at 2.90 marks to the pound.

Its participation was short-lived, as the pound was ejected from the ERM after massive currency speculation on 16 September 1992, 'Black Wednesday'. In the failed attempt to save the pound, interest rates had been raised to 15 per cent, and the Bank of England spent £3 billion. Major declared that the ERM contained 'fault lines' and refused to consider re-entering. Britain eyed EMU even more cynically, and in 1995 the government vowed not to take Britain in without a referendum, a move quickly followed by a similar pledge from the Labour party (Gamble and Kelly 2002: 103).

The question of British membership in EMU (which would require parliamentary approval) was postponed until Stage 3 commenced (set for 1999). When the Conservatives were voted out of power in 1997, the new Labour government under Tony Blair quickly dismissed British participation in the first wave of EMU. The new government did grant the Bank of England independence, thus bringing Britain into line with the institutional demands of EMU (though this was not the official intent). A series of economic tests were developed to ensure that Britain would not join monetary union before its economy converged with those in the Eurozone in a way that would enable the British economy to benefit; Chancellor of the Exchequer Gordon Brown stated the benefits to the British economy must be 'clear and unambiguous'. These tests concerned convergence, flexibility, investment, financial services and growth, stability and jobs (see Box 7.2). Not surprisingly, the United Kingdom's tests are more flexible than the Maastricht convergence criteria, both in terms of their definition and in how they can be assessed (Ardy et al. 2006). Indeed, when introducing the tests, the chancellor offered no concrete timetable and admitted that 'to demonstrate sustainable convergence will take a period of years'. Nevertheless, Brown attempted to differentiate this policy announcement from previous examples of British Euroscepticism, declaring, 'We are the first British government to declare for the principle of monetary union' (Brown 1997). In 2003 the British government concluded that the tests had not been fulfilled because of continued problems with the convergence and flexibility criteria.

The issue of British membership is a curious one given how well its current economic policies mesh with those of the euro

---

Box 7.2 The five economic tests

1. Are business cycles and economic structures compatible so that we and others could live comfortably with euro interest rates on a permanent basis?
2. If problems emerge is there sufficient flexibility to deal with them?
3. Would joining EMU create better conditions for firms making long-term decisions to invest in Britain?
4. What impact would entry into EMU have on the competitive position of the UK's financial services industry, particularly the City's wholesale markets?
5. In summary, will joining EMU promote higher growth, stability and a lasting increase in jobs?

Source: http://www.hm-treasury.gov.uk/documents/international_issues/the_euro/assessment/report/euro_assess03_repintro.cfm area. It is already committed to the sound money paradigm, the Bank of England has been independent since 1997, and it was one of the earliest countries to remove its capital controls. Nevertheless the political discourse of British membership in EMU portrays monetary integration as an assault on British sovereignty that threatens to make the United Kingdom a regional player as opposed to a global one (Gamble and Kelly 2002). Indeed, the differences between monetary policies followed by the United Kingdom versus the ECB are rather small, with only slight differences in long-term economic outcomes (Rollo 2002).

Popular sentiment against monetary integration seems more consistent than in Denmark or Sweden. Moreover, unlike in these countries, the idea does not strongly resonate among the political elite, either. The latter remain divided, though the divisions have changed over time (with the Tories being pro-monetary cooperation in the 1970s and 1980s and Labour being against before their positions flipped during the 1990s) (Gamble and Kelly 2002). Interest groups also differ in their preferences: manufacturing interests may prefer the stability offered by the euro (Gamble and Kelly 2002) but the City of London has favoured delaying entry (or even staying out) (Talani 2000). For the general population, their support for monetary union or lack thereof is not tied to party identification but rather issues of national identity and apprehension regarding the accountability and legitimacy of EU governance more generally (Gabel and Hix 2005).

In January 2006 the excessive deficit procedure was launched against the British government. As a non-member of the Eurozone, however, this did not have any serious policy consequences for Britain. The Labour government remains committed to the fulfilment of the five economic tests before membership. No doubt a referendum would also be put to the British people, given its rocky history with monetary integration and the disaster of Black Wednesday still invoked when the issue arises. The success of the British economy after leaving the ERM emboldened critics of EMU, pointing out the superior performance of the British economy to the large countries within the Eurozone. No indications have been given that the British will seek membership in the near future, as it has not even rejoined the ERM since leaving in 1992 (participation in the ERM II for two years is part of the Maastricht criteria).

Denmark

The other country that secured a derogation from EMU during the Maastricht Treaty negotiations (through the subsequent Edinburgh Agreement that added a protocol) was Denmark. Both economically and politically, Denmark has been doing well outside of the euro area, much like Britain (Marcussen 2005). Denmark's history with Europe does not contain the same rhetoric regarding the need for peace or a shared destiny as with the original EU Member States. Indeed, even among its supporters participation in European integration is treated pragmatically, though opponents address possible threats to Danish culture and democracy. Economically speaking, participation in EMU should not cause great adjustment problems for Denmark. For many years a 'sound policy consensus' has existed that advocates low inflation, stable exchange rates, and low levels of debt and deficit (Marcussen and Zolner 2001: 382–4).

Denmark has an ambivalent relationship with European integration. The country has held six referenda on the subject of European integration, the most pertinent ones for monetary union occurring in 1992 (Maastricht Treaty), 1993 (Maastricht Treaty with Edinburgh Protocol) and 2000 (EMU). The two 'no' results in 1992 and 2000 contributed to Denmark's reputation for Euroscepticism, though the majority of referenda on Europe have passed (Qvortrup 2001). The reasons for Denmark's frequent resort to referenda are legal and political. According to Article 20 of the Danish constitution, any law that would cede sovereignty and is not approved by a five-sixths parliamentary majority is subject to a referendum. However, the application of this statue was not always straightforward.

For example, in 1971 all of the major parties were in accord regarding Danish participation in the European Community, yet it was still put to a referendum. The same thing happened in the case of the Treaty of Amsterdam, but the Treaty of Nice was not put to a referendum. The use of referenda in Denmark stems from the politically divisive nature of European integration, as referenda have been used to separate domestic political issues from the Europe question. When a European issue threatens to derail domestic policymaking, parties prefer to put the issue to a referendum and thus remove European integration from the equation (Buch and Hansen 2002: 8). The results of the referenda on European monetary integration illustrate why political parties have sought confirmation of their policies to move forward, as the referenda generate a high voter turnout and the outcomes are often close (see Table 7.1).

The ambivalence towards monetary integration shown by the Danish public contrasts with the commitment of the government and elites involved in the monetary policy making process in Denmark to the sound money principles. Ever since the government announced in 1982 that it would no longer consider devaluation as a policy option, Danish elites have been among the most steadfast supporters of the sound money paradigm and capital liberalization. Banking and industry both supported monetary union from the start (Marcussen and Zolner 2001: 386). The official report on monetary union enumerated numerous advantages to the Danish economy (liberalizing capital flows, giving Denmark more influence on monetary and exchange rate policy) and noted instances where EMU policy corresponded well to existing Danish policy (non-monetization of budget deficits) (Danish Ministry of Economic Affairs 1989). Nevertheless concern over the threat that monetary integration might pose to the welfare state continues to fuel tensions over EMU membership despite the attempt of the Social Democratic Party to recast monetary union as a project that has evolved in the wake of the Lisbon Agenda and now is tightly linked to the creation of jobs (Marcussen 2002).

This is in contrast to the allegedly more neoliberal Maastricht Treaty that the Danes voted on in June 1992. The no vote came as a surprise to both participants and observers, as there was no alternative plan to the Maastricht Treaty; everyone had assumed that the referenda that were called (in Denmark, Ireland and France) would be formalities. The Danish rejection of the treaty threw

TABLE 7.1   *Danish referendum results on EMU issues*

Year / issue	Percentage in favour	Turnout
1992 / Maastricht Treaty	49	83
1993 / Maastricht Treaty supplemented by		
Edinburgh Agreement	57	87
2000 / euro	47	88

Source: Buch and Hansen (2002: 14–15).

Europe into a tailspin as monetary union no longer appeared certain, and speculation began against the weaker currencies (see Chapter 2). The Danish government was persuaded to put the question to the people again after the Edinburgh Summit in December 1992 added protocols to the Treaty that gave Denmark opt-outs on the issues of European citizenship, cooperation in internal (police) and external (defence) security, and monetary union. The results of the May 1993 referendum (not required by Danish law) yielded a favourable outcome but provoked rioting in Copenhagen (de Vreese and Semetko 2004: 706).

In August 1993 the fluctuation bands of the ERM had widened to plus or minus 15 per cent. This change was institutionalized at the Amsterdam European Council in June 1997, and the ERM II went into force on 1 January 1999 as it officially succeeded the European Monetary System. In January 2001 Denmark had the distinction of being the only ERM II participant after Greece joined EMU (Marcussen 2005: 50).

Polling data show similar reasons across the referenda for voting against further monetary integration, the most important and consistent ones being the loss of sovereignty and the threat it would pose to national identity. In the case of the 2000 referendum on joining the euro area, the euro's decline against the dollar was also cited (Buch and Hansen 2002: 14-15). That year's Eurobarometer survey had already noted one of the lowest levels of support for the euro in the European Union (behind the United Kingdom) (Eurobarometer 2002), though in the weeks prior to the vote many remained undecided (de Vreese and Semetko 2004: 712). However, after the euro's introduction in 1999, polls indicated growing popularity for the new currency, a major factor in Prime Minister Rasmussen's decision to call for a referendum on 2 March 2000 that would be held on 28 September 2000. (Marcussen and Zolner 2001: 385–6). This referendum was not required for constitutional reasons but for reasons of custom on European issues. The Danish opt-outs from the Edinburgh Agreement following the Maastricht Treaty made a referendum essential for political reasons (Qvortrup 2001: 190–1).

In anticipation of the referendum, a slew of reports were issued on the costs and benefits of euro area membership. On 7 April 2000, the government report 'Denmark and the EMU' was released. It was based on the European Commission study, 'One market, one money' that presented a strong microeconomic case for EMU. Opponents labelled the report propaganda that relied on biased evidence. On 8 May 2000 the Danish Foreign Policy Institute issued a report that presented the political case for participation, arguing that remaining outside the Eurozone threatened Denmark's influence in the European Union. On 17 May 2000 the Danish Economic Council released its report, arguing that economic benefits of Danish membership were likely to be small, describing EMU as a political project. After the release of this final report, public sentiment once again shifted against EMU (Marcussen and Zolner 2001: 388–90).

The negative result of the Danish referendum shelved the issue of monetary union for the time being. The Danish currency remains a part of the ERM II, so membership would be a quick and straightforward affair if and when the government makes this decision. Its economy is among the strongest in the European Union, and remaining outside of the Eurozone has not had tangible repercussions in other issue areas.

States without opt-outs

Sweden

Sweden shares a sceptical attitude towards European integration with Britain and Denmark, and this has surely influenced public opinion towards monetary integration. As in Denmark, a divide exists between the political elites and the public; while the latter's enthusiasm for integration remains among the lowest in Europe, a consensus has emerged between the major parties of government (save certain members of the Green Party and the Left Party) that Sweden should be at the heart of Europe's integration. Miles (2005) characterizes the Swedish strategy, like that of Britain, as a 'hitchhiker'. As with Britain, Sweden is comfortable remaining on the outside of the euro area (Lindahl and Naurin 2005). Thus Sweden has pursued a policy of 'conscious outsidership' towards the euro while trying to be an 'insider' in regards to the European Union more generally (Lindahl and Naurin 2005: 65–7).

Sweden's participation in European exchange rate cooperation predates EU membership. It was part of the Snake from 1973–77, after which it pegged its exchange rate against a currency basket. In 1991 the government unilaterally tied the Swedish krona to the ECU. Sweden willingly undertook the initial steps towards monetary union, as it abolished capital controls (Stage One) and granted independence to its central bank, the Riksbank. But Sweden fell victim to exchange rate speculation during the 1992 ERM crisis, though not officially participating in the ERM (Sweden was not a member of the EC at the time). The Swedish government raised interest rates to 500 per cent before abandoning its exchange rate peg, and the economy fell into a recession. GDP fell and unemployment rose rapidly; unemployment averaged from 1986–90 had been 2.0 per cent, but in the 1990s it hovered around 8 per cent (Commission 2006c). In order to stem the crisis, the government guaranteed bank obligations, costing taxpayers about 2 per cent of GDP (Englund 1999). The krona has been floating ever since, with the central bank (Riksbank) targeting inflation.

When the government negotiated Sweden's EU membership, it did not formally opt-out from monetary union but rather declared that EMU participation would be decided upon by the parliament. The 1994 referendum on Swedish membership did not deal with monetary union per se, but after the referendum it became a hot topic as it became linked to the possibility of Sweden seceding from the European Union (Lindahl and Naurin 2005: 68). As Swedish participation in EMU continued to garner support from politicians as well as business, the public remained sceptical. The well-respected Riksbank also supported membership. A group of scholars was commissioned to study the benefits of EMU for Sweden, and the Calmfors Commission argued for remaining outside EMU while preparing for membership at a later date so as to minimize potential costs of remaining on the periphery. Economically, EMU was seen as potentially aggravating the country's unemployment problem. In addition, the weak state of government finances made the Maastricht Treaty criterion on budget deficits too restrictive. Politically, there was not an overwhelming amount of public support in favour of joining, and the first round of EMU would likely comprise just a small group of countries anyway, so Sweden would likely be in the majority as a euro-outsider (Calmfors Commission 1997).

Thus in 1997 the Swedish parliament passed an Act, Sweden and Economic and Monetary Union, which requires a popular referendum before the government can commit to monetary union. Only then can the government proceed with an application for Eurozone membership. From the perspective of the European Union, because Sweden does not have a formal opt-out it is theoretically required to join the euro area upon fulfilling the Maastricht criteria. It is for this reason that Sweden has not joined the ERM II, participation in which is required for two years prior to membership.

On 14 September 2003 the government held a referendum on EMU. This vote was not necessary from a constitutional point of view, though all of the major parties promised to respect the results. The real reason for calling the vote was to avoid splitting the Social Democratic government on the issue, as division in this area could have spilled over into other issue areas as well (Aylott 2005: 543). The 'no' votes carried the day with 55.9 per cent and a scant 42 per cent voting in favour, with voter participation at 82.6 per cent. This stands in stark contrast to the 'strong and stable majority in favour of entering the EMU Third Stage' in the parliament (Lindahl and Naurin 2005: 72). Whereas the proponents of Swedish membership highlighted the economic advantages, its opponents pointed out the weakness of the euro, the independence of the ECB, and the failure of euro area members to respect rules like the Stability and Growth Pact. Both groups also made more general arguments regarding its importance to European integration/peace (by proponents) and fear of the unknown/legitimacy of an unelected body creating interest rate policy (by opponents) (Lindahl and Naurin 2005: 74).

An important differentiation that can be made between Swedish voters and their counterparts in Denmark is their perceptions of the benefits of EU membership are generally lower. Polls show that 27 per cent consider membership 'a bad thing', the highest percentage from any of the EU15 states (Aylott 2005: 546). However, there is also a growing tendency within Sweden to differentiate between policies (for example, EMU versus CAP). Thus it seems possible for Sweden to be an important participant in European integration in some fields while taking a backseat in others (Lindahl and Naurin 2005: 78). A common reason given for the reluctance of Sweden and Denmark to join the euro area is their commitment to a strong welfare state and the constraints that EMU membership would place on spending. However, Finland also subscribes to similar social welfare principals, yet monetary union enjoyed strong support among the Finnish population in both the run-up to the euro and during its first years of implementation. Nevertheless, the Finnish experience has not obviously influenced the debate in the other Nordic countries (Tiilikainen 2005).

Sweden has also performed well economically, mitigating internal pressure to quickly join the euro area. Moreover, if Sweden were to strictly adhere to the Maastricht convergence criteria, it would need to join the ERM II for two years prior to membership. Thus Swedish membership in EMU in the near future is unlikely.

The 2004/2007 accession countries

After the fall of the Berlin Wall signalled the end of communism, attention soon turned to the fate of the former members and satellites of the Soviet bloc. The bulk of these countries sought rapid economic and political integration with the West, including the European Union and, by extension, EMU. Upon becoming members of the European Union, all of the states participated in the economic and budgetary cooperation mechanisms as well as economic surveillance. The differences between these states quickly became apparent. In 2004 six of the ten new Member States (Cyprus, the Czech Republic, Hungary, Malta, Poland and Slovakia) recorded a deficit above the 3 per cent of GDP reference value outlined in the SGP. Cyprus and Malta also overshot their government debt targets of 60 per cent of GDP. The Commission subsequently produced a report with recommendations to reduce the deficits under the excessive deficit procedure, though non-Eurozone members are not subject to either enhanced budgetary surveillance or sanctions. Moreover, these recommendations were not done mechanistically but took into account the differences between the Member States, which were given different timetables to rectify their economic difficulties.

Dyson (2007) elaborates on the different strategies assumed by the new Member States, arguing they are shaped by an interaction of:

- Different geostrategic concerns that link euro entry to state security.
- Different economic and trade structures.
- Differences in debt and deficit levels that have their origins in their communist histories in their institutional capacity to impose or negotiate compliance with EU fiscal norms.
- Social and regional disparities between states that make it necessary for governments to have a different balance between the observance of EMU fiscal rules and protecting social services.
- Ideology and how this is manifested in the objectives of political

parties and the way issues are portrayed in electoral politics (2007: 431–2).

While EMU conveniently has divided the European Union into two groups (participants versus non-participants), such a characterization underestimates the differences within the latter. Even among the newer Member States that await EMU membership, both their strategies towards EMU and the effect that EMU has had on their political economic development differ greatly. Domestic political considerations such as electoral factors, national institutions, party competition and existing economic structures have yielded different outcomes across the new members (Dyson 2006: 9–10). This applies to both monetary policy and fiscal policy strategy, with domestic institutional structures and party politics impacting fiscal institutions and thus the viability of a country's candidacy for monetary union, as they have a significant effect on debt and deficit levels (Hallerberg 2004, Dimitrov 2006). Thus the newer Member States have approached monetary integration with different strategies and timetables. For example, two years in the ERM II are needed to join the euro area, and Table 7.2 shows how some states have joined earlier in order to fast track their application.

The Member States that acceded to the European Union in 2004 comprise a diverse set of economies that Schadler et al (2005) have argued can be divided into two groups: Hungary, Poland, and the Czech Republic will likely have more difficulties adjusting to EMU, while the rest of the accession countries should have an easier time of it (this analysis did not originally include Bulgaria and Romania). The first group's problems concern their ability to meet the debt and deficit criteria, which will require painful structural

TABLE 7.2   *The Exchange Rate Mechanism II*

Member State (national currency)	Central rate (EUR 1)	Fluctuation band	Date joined
Denmark (krone)	7.46038	+/- 2.25%	1 January 1999
Estonia (kroon)	15.6466	+/- 15%	28 June 2004
Lithuania (litas)	3.45280	+/- 15%	28 June 2004
Latvia (lats)	0.802804	+/- 15%	2 May 2005

Source: http://www.europa.eu/scadplus/leg/en/lvb/l25082.htm

reforms to achieve. Economically, membership could pose a problem given the potential impact of monetary shocks on these countries. Politically, monetary integration has not provided the political impetus to enact the reforms that would enable rapid accession.

Hungary's economic difficulties make rapid EMU membership impossible, and its political elites have been unable to institute the reforms needed to reach the criteria in the near future. First of all, its economy is not sufficiently integrated with countries in the euro area, making EMU less attractive. For example, Jones and Kutan (2004) find that monetary shocks emanating from the Eurozone could be destabilizing for Hungary's industrial production. In addition, Hungary suffers from a high budget and has been subject to the excessive deficit procedure since 2004. Its deficit hit 9.2 per cent of GDP in 2006, the highest in the European Union, which provoked the threat of a freezing of EU funds until the government got its house in order. The Hungarian government undertook an austerity programme in the form of tax hikes and announced public sector reforms. By 2007 the deficit was estimated to be safely below the target of 6.8 per cent passed by the Hungarian parliament on 21 December 2006. In June 2007 the Commission deemed the country on track to meeting its 2009 deadline for correcting its deficit.

Nevertheless the country's road to EMU is likely to be rocky, as political battles between the two main electoral blocks have seized on monetary integration as a mechanism to further aggravate the economic divide, resulting in 'Euro-populism' and the lack of an effective economic strategy to steer the country into monetary union (Greskovits 2006). In addition, the promise of monetary union could exacerbate the deficit bias in Hungary (as well as in the other the new Member States) by creating a moral hazard problem, suggesting the need to implement national-level reforms to remove the deficit bias and not be too reliant on EMU rules to tie the hands of governments (Gyrffy 2007). Hungary is not part of the ERM II and its target goal for membership is 2012.

In **Poland**, everyday monetary policy has primarily been directed towards internal objectives rather than monetary integration per se (Kokoszczynski 2002). Electoral politics have prevented the country from achieving fiscal rectitude despite the central bank's efforts to fast track the country to EMU membership (Zubeck 2006). Though in the long run Poland stands to gain significantly from

EMU membership, with the estimated costs of foregoing monetary sovereignty rather modest (Borowski 2004), it suffers from a public expenditure problem and high debt. Poland is at a higher risk in terms of social conditions, making EMU less of a priority for the government (Rhodes and Keune 2006). Poland is not a member of the ERM II and does not have a date for EMU membership.

The **Czech Republic** has a marked lack of enthusiasm for monetary integration despite the presence of an independent central bank modelled after Germany's. Indeed, the bank's relationship with the government has been tense since the late 1990s, as the former has pressed the government on the need for structural reforms that would be required to achieve the convergence criteria, in particular the deficit criterion (Bonker 2006). The ruling government has declined to set a date for EMU membership, having renounced its previous target of 2010 with little impact on Czech politics, given the government's ambivalence towards the project (*Financial Times*, 3 April 2007). It is not a member of the ERM II.

Bulgaria has taken great strides towards becoming a member of the Eurozone, tying its hands in order to force fiscal discipline as a result of its fiscal crisis in the 1990s that led it to adopt a currency board (Dimitrov 2006). Indeed, countries with small open economies that have already strong ties to the euro through the presence of a currency board or euroized economies may find the move to monetary union less difficult, as they have already foregone monetary sovereignty. The benefits of euro area participation are clearer in euroized economies (Vujcic 2004). Nevertheless it is not a member of the ERM II and EMU membership will likely not occur before 2012 due to the structural reforms needed to make membership viable from a long-term perspective.

One thing that these cases share is varying degrees of acceptance of the 'sound money' paradigm among relevant domestic actors. Indeed, commitment to these principles appears to be lower in the group above than in the countries discussed below. Whereas central banks tend to accept the tenets, politicians have been willing to be more flexible in their interpretation. In **Romania**, another country likely to encounter problems on the road to EMU, the central bank was described as 'a lonely island of technical excellence in a sea of low institutional capacity (Papadimitriou 2006: 215). Another similarity is that these countries tend to have more westernised welfare systems, with more structured labour markets, stronger product market regulation and a stronger welfare state. These Member States benefit from a macroeconomic policy that already supports the 'sound money paradigm', flexible labour markets, and support among both political elites and the general public (Feldmann 2006).

In contrast with larger new Member States, the **Baltic states** had smaller governments and fewer social benefits (Rhodes and Keune 2006). The size of such countries and their economic openness towards the European Union makes monetary integration less problematic, as these states could arguably form an optimum currency area with the Eurozone (Ross and Lättemäe 2004). In addition, central bank independence seems firmly rooted, as attempts to circumvent its authority were quickly rebuffed (Greskovits 2006, Zubeck 2006). Estonia and Lithuania had originally wanted to enter the Eurozone early, but their inflation rates prevented them from achieving the Maastricht criteria, causing the Estonian government to withdraw its application. The decision on Lithuania in 2006 sparked some controversy regarding its fulfilment of the criteria. The Maastricht Treaty states that applicants must have an average annual inflation rate below the average of the three lowest rates in the European Union, plus 1.5 per cent. However, the lowest rates belonged to Sweden and Poland, two states not in the Eurozone. Had Lithuania been evaluated against the three lowest inflation rates of Eurozone countries, it would have been admitted. Moreover the criterion was created for advanced industrial economies and does not take into account the different needs of post-Communist countries (see the 'Ideas' section below on the Balassa–Samuelson effect). The European Union refused to re-evaluate the convergence criteria, leaving Slovenia as the only country to join in 2007.

Given their Treaty obligation to eventually join EMU via the Maastricht Treaty, states have little room for manoeuvre. The European Union provides technical assistance to Member States to help them prepare for Eurozone accession, with the ECB, Eurostat and the Commission being the bodies that are most intensively involved in this (Dyson 2006: 15). Nonetheless, the need to fulfil the criteria in advance gives states some breathing room in terms of being able to manipulate the timing of monetary union, the sequencing and pacing. This allows them more domestic monetary autonomy in the short-run (Dyson 2006: 29–30).

The new Member States appear well on their way to EMU

accession. Financial markets appear increasingly integrated as long-term sovereign bond yields have converged towards those of the European Union (both local currency bonds as well as euro denominated bonds), euro-denominated corporate bond yields are similar to those of the more established EU countries, and convergence also seems apparent in the banking sectors and the stock markets (Dvorak 2007). The home bias in portfolio investments in the new EU countries has decreased, institutional consolidation has already commenced, and the financing of large projects no longer depends on personal relationships but is more arm's-length (Bottazzi and Giavazzi 2005). Nevertheless, banks still dominate the financial sectors while equity markets remain small (Cerps 2005), making the newer states still a work-in-progress with some way to go before catching up to their Eurozone counterparts.

Theoretical considerations

Ideas

An influential economic idea is optimum currency areas (Mundell 1961, Krugman 1990). According to optimum currency area theory, giving up the currency as a policy instrument requires labour mobility, wage flexibility, a common fiscal policy, or some combination thereof in order to compensate for the loss of the exchange rate. Without such measures, an asymmetric shock could destabilize the area by making a single monetary policy inappropriate for the region. How does such a theory judge EMU enlargement? While labour mobility in the new Member States is rather low, labour flexibility is not (Backé et al. 2004, Ederveen and Thissen 2004), as the wage bargaining systems tend to be decentralized and the unions generally do not enjoy the same strength as their counterparts in Western Europe (Boeri 2005). Though this allows some of the non-EMU members like Britain, Denmark, Sweden and the Baltic countries an important means of adjustment, it could be problematic for them in terms of sharing a currency with states that have substantially more labour rigidity. Dellas and Tavlas (2005) concluded that countries with rigid labour markets in wages do well when joining up with other rigid markets; however, countries whose wage markets are more flexible are worse off, making membership expensive.

Some economists argue that the new Member States do not fit the optimum currency area criteria and that important differences in adjusting to shocks remain (Frenkel and Nickel 2005), though it is possible that they will be as trade flows increase (von Hagen and Traistaru 2005: 166). Regarding the synchronization of business cycles, another important determinant of whether or not an optimum currency area exists, the new states exhibit different characteristics. Slovenia as well as the Visegrad states' manufacturing cycle correlates strongly with the euro area (Menasce and Gianella 2006), but not that of the Baltic states (Dyson 2007).

Artis (2006) reviews British membership in the context of optimum currency area theory, noting that three of the five economic tests address OCA concerns. However, he also raises concern about the continued relevance of OCA theory. Prior to the creation of the euro area, some feared that convergence would occur more rapidly among its members, and it is no longer clear that is the case. In fact, 'globalization may be proceeding faster than Europeanization' (Artis 2006: 12, see also Bovi 2003). And though some trade creation did occur after 1999, it is difficult to separate the causal forces as the states also participate in the Single Market, etc. (Artis 2006: 18).

The lack of an optimum currency area at the start of single currency may not pose a problem if its development is endogenous. As Frankel and Rose (1997) argue, an optimum currency area could develop among members over time by virtue of a single currency's effect on business cycles and trade patterns. Exogenous factors like the Lisbon agenda have also allowed countries to move closer towards forming an optimum currency area, indicating that an 'OCA theory in reverse' may be plausible (Mongelli 2008).

Opting out of monetary union does not mean that a state cannot still follow the sound money paradigm. Indeed, the Europeanization element of the sound money idea is only one part of the globalization process that more generally inculcates monetary elites into following a doctrine that privileges price stability and capital mobility (Dyson 2006, 2007). For instance, in Denmark the monetary elites worked in a relatively permissive atmosphere in which the central bank was a prestigious and influential institution and a consensus existed on the need to follow sound money principles. The Danish elites remained in close contact with their European homologues despite their exclusion from the Eurogroup, as numerous other forums (Ecofin, Economic and Financial Committee, etc.) also exist and allow them to participate in debates (Marcussen 2002).

For the newer Member States, much of the debate concerns the appropriateness of EMU. As transition economies, the 'Balassa–Samuelson effect' notes the higher natural rate of inflation that these economies have compared to their counterparts in developed economies due to the transmission of prices in tradable goods to nontradable goods. While economic indicators like the inflation rate (de Grauwe and Schnabl 2005) and real exchange rate (Khan and Choudhri 2004) seem to confirm the validity of the effect, some economists take a more cautious view and attribute this to other factors such as the relatively high share of food items in inflation indices combined with price regulation (Egert et al. 2003). In addition, the price effects are unlikely to be so large as to be unmanageable within the Maastricht criterion (Deroose and Baras 2005).

Regarding the exchange rate stability requirement, much has changed since the EMS was originally created and tying one's hands in a fixed but flexible exchange rate system was seen as beneficial. This has been replaced by the 'corners' view that states should choose between the extremes of an exchange rate float and a fixed exchange rate. Von Hagen and Traistaru (2005) have argued that applicant countries should spend only the minimum required time in the ERM II, as evidence does not show ERM membership itself to have beneficial effects on macroeconomic policy and it can, in fact, put currencies at risk of speculation. Furthermore, if the economy is still in transition, the risk of the currency being pegged at an inappropriate rate increases (Begg 2006b), thus making it vulnerable to speculation (Begg 2002, Buiter 2004). Angeloni et al. (2007) argue that some of the new Member States should retain their exchange rate flexibility in order to absorb shocks. Joining the ERM II too soon could make a currency vulnerable to market pressure, thus jeopardizing its fulfilment of exchange rate stability prior to joining EMU (Van Poeck et al. 2007). Indeed, low-income countries seem to find flexible exchange rate systems particularly beneficial (Eichengreen and Leblang 2003: 800). One suggestion is that countries retain floating exchange rates and target inflation levels, rather than have a hard peg. The argument is that lower per capita income levels in the newer Member States mean that they will have a larger price level gap to close while also being at risk for credit booms and overheating, so some real convergence is necessary prior to EMU membership (Darvas and Szapáry 2008; see also Begg 2008).

Thus it appears that the applicant countries would assume more risks in joining EMU than the current Eurozone countries did, as measures needed to prepare for membership could be costly, and the membership of the CEECs would have little impact on the current Eurozone (Neck et al. 2004).

Finally, the expansion of the Eurozone, like the European Union's enlargement more generally, brings increased diversity that risks watering down European integration so as to accommodate so many different interests. The ability to find a consensus and to enhance cooperation through persuasion diminishes as the number of participants increases. This also has repercussions for the legitimacy of monetary integration, as the informal dialogue that takes place between Member States in venues such as the Eurogroup and in technical committees includes the possibility of contestation. This contestation potentially assuages the legitimacy problems of monetary integration by enhancing its 'input legitimacy' (Scharpf 1999). However, enlargement of the Eurozone puts this at risk as a larger number of participants could preclude the ability of all governments to voice their opinions regularly (Puetter 2007).

Interests

In recent history the performance of the euro area has not been so impressive as to make membership become a priority for any of the states. Economically the larger states have dragged down the overall growth and employment levels posted by the Eurozone. Politically the uneven application of the SGP rules indicated favouritism towards larger states (Chang 2006) and weakened the credibility of the euro area by making decision making less transparent due to the flexibility allowed in complying with and applying the rules (Dyson 2007). The EU-15 countries do not seem to have suffered economically from being outside the Eurozone. Indeed, their economies ranked among the strongest in Europe since the introduction of the euro, with growth and unemployment rates comparing favourably with that of the Eurozone (see Figures 7.1 and 7.2). Studies also show that non-Eurozone countries benefited from lower costs of capital due to financial market integration despite being outside the euro area (Askari and Chatterjee 2005).

The newer Member States are also registering healthy growth rates higher than the Eurozone average, as seen in Figure 7.3.

Nevertheless, there are reasons to believe that at least some of them could have thrived within the Eurozone as well. One of the reasons for the creation of the euro was the currency instability of the 1980s, a concern that was resurrected in the early 1990s and in 2008. EMU membership protects participants from large currency fluctuations during unstable economic times, leading states like Denmark (*Financial Times*, 5 November 2008) and Poland (*Financial Times*, 29 October 2008) to reconsider more rapid Eurozone membership.

A fixed exchange rate is particularly advantageous for a small open economy, which most of the non-Eurozone countries are. Given that the bulk of their trade is with the Eurozone, joining the single currency would remove exchange rate risk from a large percentage of their economy. Rose (2000, 2001) argues that EMU membership possibly could have tripled both the United Kingdom's and Sweden's trade with the Eurozone, making non-membership quite costly from an economic perspective. This would seem to corroborate existing evidence that trade flows within the Eurozone increased after EMU, and that the trade-enhancing effect may even be generalisable to non-Eurozone countries (Micco et al. 2003). Moreover, monetary integration may have a dynamic effect in promoting further trade between countries sharing the same currency and thus encouraging a convergence of business cycles.

Other economists have sharply criticized such optimistic analyses. In fact, their exports to the euro area increased about 7 per cent, very close to the 9 per cent increase in trade creation that occurred among the Eurozone members. EMU seems to have positive external trade effects for all countries due to trade liberalization by the EMU participants. Baldwin (2006a, 2006b) argues the trade effects would be much smaller than Rose's view, estimating that the United Kingdom would see export increases in the order of $3 billion, with Denmark and Sweden facing similar albeit smaller gains because of their smaller size. Sweden could expect a 1 per cent increase in exports and Denmark between 1–6 per cent. Similarly, Bun and Klaasen (2007) estimate the trade effects as closer to 5–10 per cent. Thus the trade benefits may, in fact, be quite modest and not exclusive to Eurozone members (trade was created as a result of EMU but apparently not diverted).

Furthermore, EMU membership purportedly brings with it greater foreign investment. The rise in capital inflows, in fact, points to the need for applicant states to institute measures beyond those required to meet the Maastricht criteria so as to keep demand for capital in check. This, along with the relatively large proportion of government size, poses the biggest threat to applicant countries on the fiscal front (von Hagen 2005).

Perhaps the most dangerous risk of staying outside of the Eurozone is political, namely the potential loss of influence. This factor seems to weigh heavily in the decisions of the newer EU Member States. However, analysts have argued that this has not been the case in either Sweden or Denmark, as they have been able to harness networks and other means of influence to ensure that their outsider status does not harm their political influence in Europe (Lindahl and Naurin 2005, Marcussen 2005). Indeed, Sweden's Presidency of the EU Council in 2001 was well regarded, as was Denmark's in 2002 (Lindahl and Naurin 2005: 81). Moreover, the United Kingdom was a key player in the October 2008 European response to the global financial crisis despite not being a member of the Eurozone.

Arguments for delaying entry into the Eurozone include the loss of the exchange rate as a policy tool, and the relatively small role that the conditions in most of the states (except Britain) will factor into any ECB interest rate decisions. Indeed, using the Irish case for comparison, its business cycle (like Britain's) was not closely aligned to that of the Eurozone, making the single interest rate inappropriate for both economies (Hay et al. 2006). Additional problems could arise due to rising capital flows (Rollo 2006: 68) and the lack of EU-level policies to help applicant states cope with adjustment (Begg 2006b: 77). Historically the entry rate has important consequences for economic growth, as the impact of exchange rate regimes on

FIGURE 7.1   Annual growth rates, 1999–2006

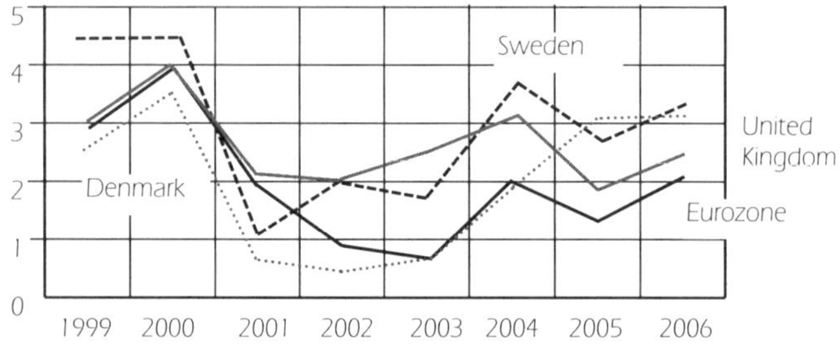

Source: data from European Commission.

FIGURE 7.2   Annual unemployment rates, 1999–2006

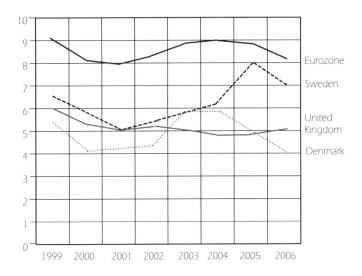

Source: data from European Commission.

FIGURE 7.3   Annual GDP rates, 2000–09

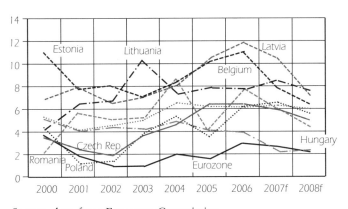

Source: data from European Commission.

growth depend on such contexts (Eichengreen and Leblang 2003). Such effects can have long-lasting repercussions for the standard of living and take years to correct; thus the accession countries should take pains to enter at the correct rate so as to avoid wiping out their competitive advantage of lower costs with a stronger real exchange rate (Pain and Van Welsum 2003: 838–9).

Sceptics argue that the higher growth of the transition economies could also result in higher volatility, which means economic levels between the euro area and the accession countries are less likely to be synchronized (Thimann 2005). However, given their different economic profile in comparison to most Eurozone countries, asymmetric shocks will likely be larger and more discretion should be used in deciding when to admit an applicant. Instead of rigidly following the Maastricht criteria, other factors like real convergence should also be taken into account (Ahearne and Pisani-Ferry 2006).

Related to monetary integration is the Lisbon Agenda's system of economic policy coordination, with the goal of improving innovation so as to promote competitiveness and growth. Most of the new states are not well positioned to participate intensively in this exercise, as they lack the resources to invest substantially in research and development activities (one of the primary calls for action in the Lisbon Agenda). This magnifies the importance of cohesion funds for these states, the receipt of which is in part dependent on their ability to comply with the Stability and Growth Pact budget limits (Dyson 2007: 424). This is further complicated by the fact that the co-financing rules of EU cohesion policy may demand that governments invest more resources in public investment, which would have the effect of creating fiscal problems in the short run (Begg 2006b). The Visegrad states, for example, lure foreign direct investment through generous subsidies. Though this has the effect of improving intra-regional trade with the Eurozone and promotes foreign direct investment (FDI) by large firms investing in cutting edge technology, it also harms their ability to fulfil the Maastricht criteria (Dyson 2007: 433).

From a political economy perspective, a j-curve effect could arrive upon entry into the euro area, referring to the temporary downturn in economic performance once a change is initiated followed by an upward trend as performance improves. Depending on how deep the downward dip is and how protracted a process it is for the trend to reverse itself, in the short- to medium-term euro area membership could be quite costly for a government, as it could undermine its own public support (Begg 2006b).

Another way to group the states is according to size, which could also lead them to different economic and policy preferences. According to Duval and Elmeskov (2006), large countries are likely to be more reticent to commit to monetary union because they have more to lose in regards to their macroeconomic flexibility. Reforms would thus become even more difficult after a larger country joined EMU because it would not have as much macroeconomic flexibility to offset the effects. The up-front costs involved in qualifying for monetary union could actually delay needed reforms and exacerbate the poor fit between existing members and applicants (Hallett et al. 2005).

From a political perspective, putting off entry allows the newer states more time to deal with conflicting domestic interests associated with the single currency (Dyson 2007: 418). If one were to extrapolate from the experience of the current euro area countries, most of the newer states can take heart, as the smaller states seemed to have an easier time in implementing needed structural reforms (Duval and Elmeskov 2006).

Institutions

In regard to the newer Member States, entering the Eurozone sooner rather than later can enhance their credibility in monetary and fiscal policy, sending an important signal to wage setters. Moreover these countries would also benefit from the low interest rates that have been enjoyed by the euro area, thus encouraging more domestic and foreign investment (Rollo 2006). Indeed, financial market integration with Eurozone countries would likely pick up speed along with trade flows (Begg 2006b). And while the symmetry of shocks in applicant countries versus current EMU countries may be large right now, this effect will likely change after EMU membership (Schadler 2005). States also stand to benefit from seignorage gains upon entering the Eurozone, though some states will benefit more than others (in particular Bulgaria and Romania) (Gros 2004).

There is also the issue of assessment. According to the Maastricht Treaty, Member States must achieve nominal convergence in regard to their inflation rate, interest rates, exchange rates, and compliance with specified debt and deficit limits. Real convergence, however, looks at matters such as the convergence of business cycles (Frankel and Rose 1997, Alesina et al. 2002). Though business cycle patterns are not part of the optimal currency area literature and it 'treats [them] as exogenous to the monetary regime, there are good reasons to believe that they are not. Cyclical correlation patterns are shaped by structural characteristics ... which are likely to change due to increasing economic and monetary integration' (von Hagen and Traistaru 2005: 159). Indeed, 'the Maastricht criteria ... have proven to be ill-designed to assess whether structural convergence is sufficient to make participation in EMU sustainable' (Ahearne and Pisani-Ferry 2006: 1).

Another institutional factor is the importance of price stability and the efficacy of an independent central bank in pursuing this task. In the long term governments could not influence economic output through either monetary or fiscal policy, the best that it could do was offer a stable macroeconomic environment. Despite the history of a dependent central bank in the United Kingdom, this has not played a large role in the economic debate within the United Kingdom. Regarding the newer Member States, the sound money paradigm was part and parcel of the international economic governance system that had become dominant just as they became participants in the international economy. Thus adherence to the sound money paradigm comprised a part of its relationship not only to the European Union but also the IMF, World Bank, and ERBD that promoted trade in goods and services, privatization, capital mobility and foreign direct investment (though the emphases differed across institutions) (Rollo 2006: 48–9). However, the commitment to the sound money paradigm may not be uniform across societal actors. Johnson (2006) argues that after EU accession became certain in Hungary and the Czech Republic, only the central bankers remained committed to early adoption of the euro and the constraints that it would place on the management of the economy. Indeed, public support in Poland for EMU membership, for example, has also been described as 'rather shallow' (Johnson 2005: 111). Such findings are congruent with other research that has argued for stronger amounts of Euro-scepticism in these countries (Beichelt 2004).

A related issue is the plan for a rotation system of the ECB's Executive Board, discussed in Chapter 5. This could be problematic from a political economy perspective as the larger countries have what amounts to 'reserved' seats, which could pose problems and undermine the democratic credentials of the ECB (Begg 2008).

In addition to structural explanations of monetary integration, one must also consider how domestic politics play in to the decision-making process, in particular why countries choose to remain outside of the euro area (in the case of Britain and Denmark) or take a slower pace in adopting the euro. Elections are a big factor, as the three EU15 countries have made monetary integration an issue to be decided ultimately by a referendum. The preceding section outlined how in some of the newer Member States monetary integration (and the reforms it entails) has been politically divisive, making rapid membership politically impossible.

In addition to achieving the convergence criteria one must also consider the longer-term viability of a country's participation in EMU and its ability to respect the Stability and Growth Pact. Prominent theories on budget formation suggest that political institutions can help predict how well a government will be able to do so. The CEEC countries are largely comprised of multi-party coalition governments in which a 'contract model' would be optimal. In such a model total there would be binding budgetary targets for overall spending levels with a strong finance minister who would be capable of executing the budget (Hallerberg and von Hagen 1999). Weak institutions, on the other hand, could result in a 'deficit bias' (Gryffy 2007). Other institutional factors that authors have argued to be of relevance include the strength of the prime minister and finance minister (Brusis and Dimitrov 2001, Gleich 2003), and focusing on controlling expenditures rather than revenue (Afonso et al. 2006). Considering the different economic structures of the newly acceding countries to the European Union, EMU also provides them with an incentive to stabilize their financial markets, which is arguably more relevant than have them achieve price stability and low budget deficits (Schelkle 2004).

An important institutional consideration is the connection between monetary integration and European integration more generally. Dyson (2006: 8) has emphasized the role that monetary union has played as 'a new historic project' within the European Union that 'has a better claim than any other policy sector to represent an embryonic "core" Europe'. Such a relationship has no clear legal basis in any EU Treaty, but concerns over an informal core and periphery developing in the European Union between EMU versus non-EMU participants is present. While officially those outside of the euro area have tried to treat monetary integration as a separate issue from European integration more generally, there is nevertheless a tension between those inside the euro area to further enhance cooperation (such as through the Eurogroup) and those outside to try to stop such potential losses in influence. On the other hand, the multi-speed nature of EMU can also be viewed as part of a larger trend in European cooperation that is more flexible in order to account for an European Union that is more diverse and can be considered part of an 'enhanced cooperation framework' (Allemand 2005).

Conclusion

Monetary integration is both one of the most important symbols of European unity and one of its most controversial policies. The desire for some to proceed with monetary integration met with such resistance that the 'opt-out' was invented, though subsequently revoked for future members. Nevertheless this precedent for staying on the fringes of EMU was set, and the initial three non-members did very well. Although governments had cited various economic reasons, the decision clearly rested on political considerations. Monetary union impinged too much on state sovereignty in countries already known for being less than enthusiastic about the supranational elements of European integration. Thus monetary union is akin to issues considerably thought of as 'high politics' such as matters of security and defence, immigration, foreign policy, and internal security in the institutional safeguards taken by certain members to avoid a slippery slope in terms of giving up policymaking responsibility. Though the three EU15 members chose not to be in the Eurozone (and in the case of Britain and Denmark, negotiated additional opt-outs) this has harmed neither the countries involved nor the Eurozone from an economic standpoint. One can argue that these countries (and/or the euro area) could have done better with the inclusion of these three nations, but their absence has been accepted and there is not a strong push for their inclusion. The use and promised use of referenda to a certain extent ties the hands of governments in that they are loath to call a referendum until they are sure that it will pass. It is in the interest of neither the government nor the European Union to have a failed referendum on the subject.

From a political standpoint having these countries on the outside is a bit more problematic. The three states from the EU15 have been able to exert influence in other issue areas and do not appear to be ostracized for not participating. On the other hand, monetary union is one of the most important ventures ever undertaken by the European Union, and their reticence has an impact on the underlying level of solidarity within the European Union as well as perceptions from the outside. The Europe à la carte model allowed the European Union to continue to integrate without the threat of the veto in the 1990s, but that situation now stands as an exception. The new Member States must adopt all of the *acquis*, including the euro.

For some of these states euro area membership presents similar domestic political problems in terms of varying levels of public support for further integration. This is compounded in some states by the integration fatigue similar to those countries that had worked to join EMU in 1999. After enacting numerous reforms to qualify for EU membership in 2004 and 2007, the 12 states then had an additional set of criteria to become 'full' members of the European Union. For some countries like Slovenia this was a political priority enjoying widespread support, enabling rapid membership. For countries like Poland it interferes with domestic political objectives and takes a back seat to other projects. In any case, the European Union has not pressured the states for rapid accession. Before joining the European Union some countries raised the idea of simultaneous EU/EMU accession. This was rejected in favour of adhering to the Maastricht timetable and discouraging accession before an adequate level of economic convergence had taken place. EMU membership would not be a panacea to a country's economic ills and could easily become a political scapegoat if the economy faltered upon accession. Thus all of the newer states must join eventually, though they are not pressured to do so according to a specific schedule.

The presence of euro area ins and outs does, however, raise questions of the European Union's *raison d'etre* and how much integration is tolerable versus desirable. European integration has always been an elite-driven affair, but in an age of higher flows of information along with European policies that affect more aspects of daily life than ever before, it may no longer be possible for elites to lead the way. This could serve as a harbinger for the slowing of integration to more pragmatic issues rather than politically charged ones that are fraught with symbolism. The EU inside-outside dichotomy is a constant reminder of the different priorities held by Member States and the at times conflicting goals they hold for integration.

Chapter 8

The international role of the euro

Since French president Charles de Gaulle decried the United States' 'exorbitant privilege' and its misuse of this power in the 1960s, the potential benefits and prospects of Europe taking over such a role have figured among the most important implications of European monetary cooperation. While it would entail both economic and political costs, the gains could be substantial. This chapter evaluates the international role of the euro. It first reviews the progress that the Eurozone has made in achieving the status of an international currency and its ability to represent itself in international fora. It continues with an evaluation of economic and political theories associated with these topics. The conclusion considers future prospects for the euro as an international currency and dollar alternative in light of the inertia that favours the dollar and the governance structure that impedes the Eurozone.

Challenging the dollar?

The dollar has served as the anchor currency of the international monetary system since the days of Bretton Woods, and the introduction of the euro has not yet altered this configuration. The use of a currency as an international currency can be classified according to its use as a medium of exchange, a unit of account and its store of value (see Table 8.1).

A currency as a medium of exchange refers to its use by public and private actors in commercial and financial transactions. Central banks could use a currency for exchange market interventions, for example. As a medium of exchange, the euro has made some progress, though it is rather limited. The stock of euro notes in circulation outside of the Eurozone is estimated to be about 10 per cent of the total euro notes in circulation, equal to €55 billion in June 2005, whereas the currencies it had succeeded had a distribution

TABLE 8.1 *The US dollar versus the euro as an international currency*

Function	Private use	Public use	Dollar versus euro
Medium of exchange	Settle international financial transactions. Vehicle currency in foreign exchange markets. Parallel currency.	Intervention currency in foreign exchange markets. Balance of payments financing.	Private: dollar, though euro use on the rise, albeit largely within Eurozone. Public: dollar, esp. in central bank intervention.
Unit of account	Invoicing foreign trade, quotation, and denomination of international commodities and financial instruments. Parallel currency.	Anchor or reference currency for exchange rate regimes.	Private: dollar, euro primarily used within region. Public: dollar, with euro increasingly attractive.
Store of value	Denomination of deposits, loans and bonds. Portfolio allocation.	Official reserves and assets held by monetary authorities.	Private: euro as serious rival, in some cases surpasses dollar. Public: dollar, with euro increasingly attractive.

Sources: Commission (2008: 118), Kenen (1983), Hosli (2005: 80), Pouvelle (2006).

equivalent to €39 billion in 1998 (Pouvelle 2006: 41). In financial markets, the euro is also used more than the previous national monies; in mid-2005 the euro comprised 31.5 per cent of international financial obligations, compared with the 20 per cent share of the previous national currencies in 1999. Meanwhile the dollar's share went from 40 per cent to 44 per cent (ECB 2005). The additional liquidity from the increase in notes in circulation makes it easier for the euro to assume an important role in this regard. However, while foreign exchange transactions saw an increase in the share of the euro, it was at the expense of the Japanese yen and the British pound, not the dollar. In foreign exchange transactions, the euro comprised 39 per cent of daily settlements from mid-2005 to the end of 2006, whereas the dollar's share was 93 per cent (ECB 2007: 32–3).

Nevertheless, the use of the euro clearly has risen, both publicly and privately (Becker 2007). As indicated in Table 8.2, the number of banknotes denominated in euros has increased steadily since its introduction, whereas the number of dollars in circulation has actually decreased a bit from a high in 2005. However, most of the euro notes are used within the Eurozone (10 to 20 per cent), whereas the bulk of dollar banknotes (50–70 per cent) are used extraterritorially. The most commonly traded pair of currencies was the dollar and the euro, which comprised 28 per cent of global exchange transactions. In contrast, dollar–yen transactions comprised 17 per cent, and the dollar–pound 14 per cent (BIS 2007). Publicly, however, the euro's gains have been more modest, and the dollar has maintained its dominant position. The euro's use as an intervention currency by foreign banks has been rather limited, with Asian banks often intervening in support of the dollar. The dollar continues to enjoy certain advantages such as the

TABLE 8.2   *Banknotes in circulation*

Date	Euro	Dollar
December 2003	354.5	584.3
December 2004	501.3	564.2
December 2005	565.2	668.0
December 2006	628.2	618.9
March 2007	608.5	571

Source: Becker (2007: 3).

greater liquidity of government securities as well as repo markets (Galati and Woodridge 2006).

As a unit of account, goods or services are denominated in a specific currency. For example, private actors use an international currency for the invoicing of commodities like oil, or governments select a currency or currencies to act as an exchange rate anchor. In regards to its use as a unit of account, the dollar is still king. Nearly half of world trade remains invoiced in dollars, with oil and other commodities generally using the dollar for invoicing purchases (although Iran invoices in euros). The Eurozone has been invoicing its trade in euros, as well as EU countries outside the Eurozone, but the overall impact is limited. EU Member States and candidate countries are the most likely to invoice their trade in euros, reaffirming previous reports that the euro's use as a settlement currency is particularly pronounced within its region (ECB 2007).

In addition, even trade between Europe and the United States tends to be billed in dollars rather than euros; almost five years after the euro's introduction, over 90 per cent of US exports to Europe and 80 per cent of European exports to the United States were denominated in dollars (Bernanke 2005). In this respect, the euro shows signs of hysteresis in that it has been characterized more by inertia, rather than a strong aggregation effect in which case the euro would have surpassed the sum of its constituent national currencies (de Boisseu 2005).

Publicly, the euro serves as the anchor currency for some 40 countries in Europe and 50 countries and territories worldwide, compared with 75 for the dollar. Countries with special ties or institutional arrangements with the European Union include the non-Eurozone EU countries, the Balkans, Russia and numerous countries in the Mediterranean and North Africa. This is slightly less than the 56 countries that used the old national monies before 1999, which can be explained, at least in part, by the rising preference for floating exchange rates in emerging market economies (Pouvelle 2006: 41).

The euro has also benefited from the diversification of several countries that have gone from using the dollar as an anchor currency to a basket of currencies. Russia has steadily increased its euro holdings since February 2005, rising from 10 per cent to 45 per cent a mere two years later (Pouvelle 2006: 42, ECB 2007). A 2004 International Monetary Fund (IMF) study listed 150 pegged currencies, of which 40 used the euro as the anchor. This does not include countries that do not publish their target values, such as China and Singapore (ECB 2005). The increasing attraction of the euro is apparent, and its movements have had a rising impact on other currencies both formally and informally aligned. The Swiss franc, Danish krone, Norwegian krone and Swedish krona have all been matching the movements of the euro closely, and the movements of the newer Member State' currencies unsurprisingly have also mirrored those of the euro more than the dollar. It is unclear whether or not this change is long-term/structural as opposed to cyclical (Galati and Woodridge 2006).

Regions such as Montenegro and Kosovo have 'euroized' their currency through unilateral adoption of the euro, similar to the dollarization that occurred in Ecuador and Panama (Becker 2007). However these neighbouring countries of the European Union are not as strong economically as the Asian and Latin American countries that use the dollar; the EU neighbouring countries comprise 2 per cent of world GDP, compared with 17 per cent for Asia and Latin America, explaining further the gap between the use of the euro versus that of the dollar internationally (Pouvelle 2006: 43). Overall the dollar enjoys pre-eminence over the euro as a unit of account, although it is not as dominant as previously (Galati and Woodridge 2006).

Finally, a currency is used as a store of value in that it is assumed to be a stable asset. For example, private agents might hold a currency to diversify their investments, and central banks retain specific currencies in their official reserves as an investment (Cohen 2003, Pouvelle 2006). Privately, the euro has made much progress when it comes to its liquidity and the types of instruments offered. The euro securities market is the second largest in the world (to the dollar). In some markets such as those for derivatives, the dominance of the dollar is vanishing. The liquidity for euro securities rivals those for dollar securities, and the turnover of euro-denominated interest rate swaps dwarfs those of the dollar (Galati and Woodridge 2006). In 2006, initial international bond offerings were issued primarily in euros (46 per cent, followed by the dollar at 39 per cent). Meanwhile, the dollar's proportion of international bonds in circulation dropped from 50 per cent to 43 per cent (Becker 2007: 4). By 2007 the euro's position as the international bond market's top currency solidified, with $4,836 billion worth of debt denominated in euro, compared with $3,892 billion in dollars, according to the International Capital Market Association.

TABLE 8.3 *Countries with exchange rate regimes linked to the euro*

Region	Exchange rate regime	Countries
EU (non-euro area)	ERM II	Cyprus, Denmark, Estonia, Latvia, Lithuania
	Euro-based currency boards	Bulgaria
	Peg arrangements with fluctuation band based on the euro	Hungary
	Managed floating with euro as reference currency	Czech Republic, Romania
	Pro memoria: independent floating	Sweden, United Kingdom, Poland
Candidate and potential candidate countries	Unilateral euroization	Montenegro
	Euro-based currency boards	Bosnia and Herzegovina
	Peg arrangements or managed floating with the euro as reference currency	Croatia, FYR Macedonia, Serbia
	Pro memoria: Independent floating	Albania, Turkey
Others	Euroization	Kosovo, European microstates, French territorial communities
	Peg arrangements based on the euro	CFA franc zone, French overseas territories, Cape Verde, Comoros
	Peg arrangements and managed floats based on the SDR and other currency baskets involving the euro (share of the euro)	Seychelles (37.7%), Russian Federation (40%), Libya, Botswana, Morocco, Tunisia, Vanuatu

Source: ECB (2007: 41).

Thus debt denominated in dollars stood at 37 per cent, compared with 45 per cent for the euro. The primary forces behind the issuance of euro-denominated debt were companies and financial institutions, thus attesting to the growing liquidity of European capital markets (*Financial Times*, 14 January 2007). Indeed, this is the one area in which a dramatic aggregation effect took place since the introduction of the euro (de Boisseu 2005). Such figures of the euro's share of international debt markets can vary substantially, however, depending on how it is measured. Table 8.4 shows that the euro's share can vary anywhere from almost 28 per cent to 47 per cent. The figures for the dollar, however, are more stable.

The euro as a store of value has been used more extensively than the previous national currencies, although it also falls short of the usage of the dollar. Nevertheless countries have increasingly chosen to incorporate more euros into their reserves. When the euro was launched in 1999, it comprised 18 per cent of global foreign exchange reserves. It rose to 25 per cent by the end of 2003, where it has roughly remained ever since (see Table 8.5). The dollar's share reached a high of a little over 70 per cent in 2001 before falling to 66 per cent of reserves and 59 per cent of deposits by 2006 (BIS 2007). Some have estimated by the end of 2010 that it would approach 30 to 40 per cent (Becker 2007). In 2005 several

TABLE 8.4 *Alternative measures of debt securities supply and major currencies' shares (fourth quarter of 2006, values at current exchange rates)*

	Amounts outstanding (US$ billion)	Euro shares (%)	US$ shares (%)	Japanese yen shares (%)
Narrow measure, excluding home currency issuance	7,857	31.4	44.1	5.3
Broad measure, including home currency	18,435	47.0	36.3	2.7
Global measure, including domestic issuance	68,720	27.8	42.2	13.0

Source: ECB (2007: 14).

central banks of emerging economies (such as the banks of Japan, South Korea and China) announced their intention to increase their stock of euros and reduce that of the dollar. This development corroborates a study done by Central Banking Publications (2005, cited in Pouvelle 2006) in which 65 central banks which held 45 per cent of official reserves worldwide were polled, and over two-thirds of those surveyed intended to raise their proportion of euro holdings in the coming years, largely at the expense of the dollar (Pouvelle 2006: 42–3).

However, several qualifications are in order when considering such figures. The IMF calculates the share of the euro in official reserves, but only two-thirds are covered in its survey because several Asian countries with large holdings do not fully take part in it, as they prefer not to specify the composition of their reserve stocks. Moreover, the data are also influenced by exchange rate fluctuations. When the currency value is held constant, the euro's increase is not as marked (Papademos 2006).

In summary, the euro has been increasingly used as a means of finance and as an official reserve. However its growth has been weaker as an invoicing instrument and as a currency in foreign exchange transactions. In addition, its international role remains largely a regional one (Pouvelle 2006). The continued dominance of the dollar does not pose any problems for official policy, as the European Central Bank (ECB) has not pursued greater international use of the euro. Its main priority is the pursuit of price stability, which may have contributed indirectly to its use as an international currency though this was not a stated objective (Becker 2007: 6). Such decisions regarding the use of a currency are arguably best left to market forces rather than overt state pressure (Henning and Padoan 2000).

TABLE 8.5   *Use of currencies as percentage of foreign exchange reserves*

	1999	2001	2003	2005	2006
US$	71	71.4	65.9	66.5	64.7
EUR	17.9	19.3	25.3	24.4	25.8
JPY	6.4	5.1	3.9	3.6	3.2
GB£	2.9	2.7	2.8	3.7	4.4

Source: BIS *Quarterly Review*, September 2007.

External representation

As the euro rises in importance, the ability of the Eurozone to conduct itself effectively and coherently within international fora becomes ever more critical. Shortly after the launch of the euro, one observer optimistically extrapolated from the Eurozone's favourable economic conditions, positing:

> Euroland will equal or exceed the US on every key measure of economic strength and will speak increasingly with a single voice on a wide range of economic issues .... Economic relations between the US and the EU will rest increasingly on a foundation of virtual equality.
>
> (Bergsten 1999)

The relationship between economic conditions and political leadership in international financial institutions is not so direct, however, and the complicated governance structure of the European Union and how it impedes its effectiveness as an international actor have increasingly come under scrutiny.

The legal basis of the European Union's external representation under EMU is found in Article 111 of the Maastricht Treaty. The Council acts as the external representative, with the ECB and the Commission also becoming involved in certain cases. However, the Commission is subordinate to the Council when it comes to the euro's exchange rates, with the Council free to take up proposals submitted by the ECB (Coeuré and Pisani-Ferry 2007).

The European Union is well represented in international institutions like the IMF, the G7 and the G10 (see Table 8.6). This is largely due to the economic conditions prevailing at the time of the creation of these organizations, and these institutions have not been substantially updated since in order to reflect new political and economic realities. In 1944 the European states comprised a disproportionate share of international trade and financial transactions, hence their leading role in Bretton Woods institutions like the IMF. In the 1960s European countries held significant amounts of reserves in dollars, thus leading to their presence in the G10, which originally concerned itself with the dollar exchange system. Similarly, when the G7 was instituted in the 1970s, European countries naturally took a leading role in managing this nascent institution that would govern international monetary and financial relations.

TABLE 8.6   *Selected international fora and member countries*

IMF Executive Board	G7	G10
Germany	France	Belgium
France	Germany	France
United Kingdom	Italy	Germany
Belgium	United Kingdom	Italy
Netherlands	Canada	Netherlands
Italy	Japan	Sweden
Finland	United States	Switzerland
Switzerland		United Kingdom
United States		Canada
Japan		Japan
Venezuela		United States
Australia		
China		
Canada		
Egypt		
Saudi Arabia		
Malaysia		
Kenya		
Russian Federation		
Iran		
Brazil		
India		
Peru		
Rwanda		

Source: Ahearne and Eichengreen (2007: 129).

While European countries are well represented, their effectiveness within some of these organizations is another story. The governance structure of the European Union and the Eurozone complicates its ability to function effectively as a unit in international fora such as the G7 and the International Monetary Fund (Cohen 2006). In contrast with the World Trade Organization in which the European Union has sole competence and delegates power to the Commission to broker negotiations on its behalf, authority in the financial sector is divided between the Member States, the European Central Bank, and, to a lesser extent, the Commission. This contrasts with other industrialized countries like Japan, in which the Treasury assumes full responsibility.

In addition, levels of integration across EU countries differ substantially. The most glaring example is, of course, Eurozone membership. Coordinating EU versus Eurozone membership could become complicated as some share a currency and monetary policy while others retain these policies as national prerogatives. This is complicated further by the fact that cooperation in fiscal and economic policy remains under control of the Member States and is only loosely coordinated across the European Union. Financial policy coordination is even more complicated given the diffusion of competencies across Member State governments, the Commission, and numerous Lamfalussy committees (Smaghi 2007).

IMF

When considering the external representation of the Eurozone, the IMF is a good place to start. As one of the core institutions created by the Bretton Woods Agreement of 1944 (along with the World Bank and the General Agreement on Tariffs and Trade, GATT, now the World Trade Organization, WTO), it is a foundation of the postwar global economic governance order. The IMF's Executive Board comprises 24 directors, five representing countries and the rest acting on behalf of groups of countries, or constituencies (see Table 8.7). Reformed in September 2006, the IMF's 184 members agreed to a deal that granted greater weight to China, South Korea, Turkey and Mexico. Despite this being a step in the right direction, most considered this agreement woefully inadequate in addressing existing biases favouring European countries, and it did not advance Eurozone representation as a bloc.

The IMF operates much like a company with shareholders, with voting weights distributed according to the size of the country and its role as a debtor or creditor. Some states enjoy a greater level of representation than others. G7 countries hold the bulk of votes, and they meet prior to IMF meetings in order to hammer out a common position. Thus the European G7 countries of France, the United Kingdom and Germany have their own seat, while the remaining euro area countries are spread across six different constituencies and the remaining EU countries across seven. Some of the states are permanent chairs of their respective constituencies (Belgium, Italy and the Netherlands), whereas others serve as chair as part of a rotation system (the Scandinavian countries and Baltic states), others hold the position of alternate, or deputy, executive director, and some do not hold any directorship at all. Such elements influence the agenda of the respective Member States as well as what kind of alliances they can construct (European Network on Debt and Development (Eurodad) 2006). Each constituency can only support one perspective, making it necessary for members to compromise or abstain from casting a vote.

This system of subsidiarity presents three problems for external coordination in the IMF, as well as in other venues:

- In addition to Member States retaining authority over actual policy, the processes governing cooperation differ from soft coordination (such as that which dominated the Lisbon Agenda) to more communautarized examples (like the internal market programme).
- It is the European Union rather than the Eurozone that coordinates policy, making a separate representative for the Eurozone more complicated given the implications for non-euro area countries.
- The Commission and the Council share power (we can also add the ECB to this list in the case of exchange rate cooperation) (Eurodad 2006, Smaghi 2006).

The birth of the euro added to the European Union's representation on the IMF. First is the chair of the presidency of the Eurogroup, who speaks on behalf of the Eurozone when issues regarding the euro are under consideration. The statement is prepared in advance with the consultation of the ECB (a representative of which also goes to IMF Board meetings as an observer when the euro is on the agenda). In addition, the ECB received observer status on the IMF Board in December 1998, and subsequently established a permanent representative in Washington, DC in February 1999 in order to participate in its duties of surveillance and the conduct of the euro's policy (although it can neither vote nor table proposals and amendments) (Horng 2004: 331).

The prospect of a single currency heightened awareness of the importance of the external representation of the Eurozone and the European Union, leading to the efforts to improve cooperation in the IMF among EU countries via the creation of two committees, one in

TABLE 8.7 *IMF executive directors and voting power (Eurozone countries in bold)*

Country	Non-EU countries in constituency	Director *Alternate*	Total votes[1]	Percentage of fund total[2]
United States		Meg Lundsager *Vacant*	371,743	16.79
Japan		Daisuke Kotegawa *Hiromi Yamaoka*	133,378	6.02
United Kingdom		Alex Gibbs *Jens Larsen*	107,635	4.86
Germany		Klaus D. Stein *Stephan von Stenglin*	130,332	5.88
France		Ambroise Fayolle *Benoit Claveranne*	107,635	4.86
Austria	Belarus Kazakhstan	Willy Kiekens (Belgium)	18,973	0.86
Belgium	Turkey	*Johann Prader (Austria)*	46,302	2.10
Czech Republic			8,443	0.38
Hungary			10,634	0.48
Luxembourg			3,041	0.14
Slovak Republic			3,825	0.17
Slovenia			2,567	0.12
Bulgaria	Armenia	Age F.P. Bakker (Netherlands)	6,652	0.30
Cyprus	Bosnia and Herzegovina	*Yuriy G. Yakusha (Ukraine)*	1,646	0.07
Netherlands	Croatia		51,874	2.34
Romania	Georgia, Israel, Macedonia, former Yugoslav Republic of Moldova, Ukraine		10,552	0.48

Spain	Costa Rica El Salvador Guatemala Honduras Mexico Nicaragua Venezuela, República Bolivariana de	Roberto Guarnieri (Venezuela) Ramón Guzmán (Spain)	30,739	1.39
Greece	Albania	Arrigo Sadun (Italy)	8,480	0.03
Italy	San Marino	Miranda Xafa (Greece)	70,805	3.20
Malta	Timor-Leste		1,270	0.06
Portugal			8,924	0.40
Ireland	Antigua and Barbuda Barbados Bahamas Belize Canada Dominica Grenada Jamaica St Kitts and Nevis St Lucia St Vincent and the Grenadines	Jonathan Fried (Canada) Peter Charleton (Ireland)	8,634	0.39
Denmark	Iceland	Tuomas Saarenheimo (Finland)	16,678	0.75
Estonia	Norway	Jon Thorvardur Sigurgeirsson (Iceland)	902	0.04
Finland			12,888	0.58
Latvia			1,518	0.07
Lithuania			1,692	0.08
Sweden			24,205	1.09
Poland	Azerbaijan Kyrgyz Republic Switzerland Republic of Serbia Switzerland Tajikistan Turkmenistan Uzbekistan	Thomas Moser (Switzerland) Andrzej Raczko (Poland)	13,940	0.63
Total Eurozone			504,110	22.78
Total EU			616,039	27.83
Total IMF			**2,213,434**	

Notes: 1 Voting power varies on certain matters pertaining to the General Department with use of the Fund's resources in that Department. 2 Percentages of total votes 2,214,651 in the General Department and the Special Drawing Rights Department. *Source:* IMF.

Brussels (SCIMF) and the other in Washington (EURIMF) (Eurodad 2006). The SCIMF (EU Sub-Committee on IMF matters) is a subset of the Economic and Financial Committee. It was created in 2001 and works on the IMF and other related subjects. Two representatives per country from finance ministries and national central banks in addition to two members of the Commission and two representatives from the ECB comprise what was originally a working group and is now a permanent sub-committee. The role of the Commission in the SCIMF is different than in normal comitology in that the EFC's status precludes it from playing an active role through voting, agenda setting or coordination (Eurodad 2006). In addition, someone from the EU presidency on the IMF Board also sits in on SCIMF meetings in order to maintain consistency with representatives working at IMF headquarters in Washington, DC.

The SCIMF prepares common understandings on a range of issues from crisis prevention to inter-institutional cooperation with the World Bank, which are endorsed by the Economic and Financial Committee (EFC) and Ecofin. It was made a permanent sub-committee of the EFC in 2003. The group convenes in Brussels approximately eight times a year, with the Commission serving as its secretariat (but not voting) and the European executive director of EURIMF (the EU Member States' IMF representatives, a group created in 1998) also attending the meetings (Ahearne and Eichengreen 2007). This committee considers long-term priorities and principles, and prefers to operate according to consensus, although legally votes are taken by a simple majority. However it has not been able to translate its consensus into specific agreements or legislation (Eurodad 2006).

The other coordinating body for the European Union is Washington-based EURIMF, which is comprised of the European executive directors of the IMF and other Member State representatives for those countries without directorships, as well as a representative from the Commission delegation in Washington and one from the European Central Bank. In addition to the EURIMF, a mini-EURIMF also meets on an ad hoc basis so that a limited number of participants (one per chair) can convene as necessary to discuss issues of common interest in a smaller, more informal forum reminiscent of pre-enlargement EU meetings. This body provides European states with a venue in which to exchange viewpoints, although they do not enter these meetings with a prior obligation to reach a joint position. They primarily consider the IMF's

economic surveillance functions under Article 4. The country holding the presidency of the European Union prepares a European
position paper (also known as a 'grey') to present to the IMF's
Board as well as coordinates between the EURIMF and SCIMF
(Eurodad 2006).

One of the most common suggestions for the reform of the IMF
is the reduction of European representation through the creation of
a single seat for the Eurozone or European Union. This would pose
an institutional challenge for the IMF in that its statutes accord
power to nation states rather than groups/institutions like the
European Union, so this would require legal changes on its part.
However this does not present the biggest obstacle for IMF reform,
as many developing and developed nations (including the United
States) already have argued for the need for a reduction in the
number of seats occupied by European countries. Indeed, the European Union is overrepresented in this forum, largely at the expense
of emerging economies.

Paradoxically, this overrepresentation has not translated these
votes into greater influence. A single seat could make the European
bloc more effective within this organization, which has largely been
dominated by the United States. Indeed, the European Union has
almost twice the percentage of votes of the United States but has not
been able to make its voice heard. Despite the potential for greater
EU influence, individual countries within the EU/Eurozone have
resisted such a move, as it would reduce the prestige of the Member
States that stand to lose a seat in favour of single EU representation
(Smaghi 2004, 2006). Both larger states and smaller states have been
reluctant to give up their seats, as individual Member States within
the IMF and as states holding executive director positions (McNamara and Meunier 2002: 858). Additional reasons outlined by
Ahearne and Eichengreen (2007) in favour of greater centralization
in the external representation of the European Union include the
reduction of negotiating costs; EU states share similar preferences;
and economies of scale would accrue.

Besides, according to Smaghi (2004: 241–3) the current system
of coordination actually limits the effectiveness of the European
Union in the following ways:

• The constituency system can place some EU countries in the
  minority within their constituency and thus prevents them from
  promoting a European view.

- EU positions may not be cohesive in issues regarding Member States' roles as creditor versus debtor nations. The divided representation of the European Union in the IMF Executive Board encourages differentiation rather than consensus (as consensus pre-empts the participation of all EURIMF countries in discussions).
- The changing representation of the European Union, in particular its rotating presidency, makes the European Union a difficult and uneven negotiation partner.

Another positive impact would be an increase in the legitimacy of the IMF, which is sometimes viewed as a postwar relic that does not adequately account for the interests of emerging economies such as China and India. Indeed, the IMF in recent years has faced an identity crisis in which it struggles to find its *raison d'être* in the face of competition from private market actors in providing funding for developing economies. A rebalancing of institutional power in favour of emerging economies would go a long way in restoring its legitimacy and sense of purpose, something that the reduction of European representatives could make possible (Smaghi 2006). The advantages that these authors point out make a compelling case for a rationalization of EU representation, for the sake of both the European Union and the IMF as an organization.

Nevertheless various arguments have been raised against changing the current governance system of the IMF, as such a reform could have a negative impact by altering the mixed constituency system in a way that would render it weaker and thus less cooperative in nature (Mahieu et al. 2005). Similarly, the Executive Board could become prone to greater polarization and find itself under regular conflict with the United States, leading to a shared veto and worsened relations with developing economies which would then be under pressure to intensify their coordination (Smaghi 2004: 237). Furthermore, given the quota system that determines the voting weights of states, pooling their quotas together would lead to a loss of voting weight once intra-EU trade and financial flows were excluded from calculations (McNamara and Meunier 2002: 858).

Despite these reservations, most agree that a rationalization of EU representation in the IMF would be a good thing for both the European Union as a whole and the IMF as an organization. But a common seat at the IMF demands a shared viewpoint, which the European Union currently does not possess. The ability of the

European Union to streamline its representation must take into account multiple interests (at the national, EU and international levels) which can be contradictory (Eurodad 2006). At the national level, Member States have different interests in organizations like the IMF which will vary according to how much that country has invested in it. Organizational considerations will also come into play, as a Member State considers how any reform would affect its constituency (especially if it holds the directorship). At the EU level, treaty obligations will limit the extent to which the European Union can take on a higher profile role in international institutions in regard to how the European Union's mandate is defined and its interests specified. Finally international considerations will also factor into the equation of any changes in EU representation, particularly as emerging economies exert greater pressure for the reform of international organizations and are often backed by the United States. According to Truman (2005), forging a common external representation for the EU/Eurozone in international fora can only be done incrementally, because of the limited political will of the Member States

Smaghi (2004) notes the major differences among the EU Member States, which include the role of the IMF in the international financial system, crisis prevention and resolution, and the role of the IMF in poor countries. While the EU countries may broadly agree and share similar interests, in specific policy matters their geopolitical interests may diverge, or the Member States may decide that individual rather than concerted action would be more efficient. In areas where the EU states share a common position, such as in multilateral surveillance, the role of the IMF has become less significant. Indeed, despite efforts of the Commission and the European Parliament to promote a more unified external representation for the European Union during negotiations for the Constitution, the Member States were reluctant to push forward. Instead of delegating greater power to the Eurogroup, for example, at the 2002 Ecofin meeting in Oviedo they agreed that informal coordination would be pursued rather than the rationalization of the Eurozone's representation (Ahearne and Eichengreen 2007). Smaghi (2004: 236) summarizes, 'the current situation can be characterized as one of increasing co-operation on an ad hoc, informal basis. There is no *ex ante* commitment to achieve and defend common positions.' Thus despite the myriad of benefits that could accrue to the Eurozone or European Union as a group and the IMF as an institution, continued differences between Member States regarding policy as well as the benefits of a single IMF seat will hinder substantial progress toward the rationalization of EU representation for some time to come.

World Bank

Coordination among EU states at the World Bank is less developed yet in some ways more successful than in the IMF. While the IMF has committees in both Brussels and Washington, the only structure in place for the World Bank's European representatives is in Washington; no analogue to the SCIMF exists. The European Union's coordination efforts are further impeded by the fact that the representatives are from a variety of ministries: approximately half from finance ministries, a third from development ministries and the remainder from foreign ministries. This combined with a weak bureaucratic structure (such as the lack of committee in Brussels in order to provide background support, and the impermanent leadership of the EU presidency, which does little to contribute to the profile of the European Union's efforts) poses serious challenges for EU coordination. However, despite these constraints and the more limited opportunities for coordination, the European Union has been able to establish joint positions in the World Bank, something it has not been able to do in the IMF. This is in part because politically sensitive issues are still handled in national capitals (Eurodad 2006).

G7

Unlike in the IMF, within the G7 Member States attempt to construct a consensus on general policy issues as well as specific policy points (Smaghi 2004: 236). Like in the IMF, speaking with a single voice has proved to generate similar challenges to those described above. Discipline and consistency among euro area members has been difficult to achieve, as numerous actors play their respective roles in representing various EU interests at the supranational and national levels. Article 111 lays out the competences of the various institutions. The Chairman of Ecofin and/or the Eurogroup represents the Eurozone externally, and the president of the ECB may also participate in G7 meetings if the subject entails matters dealing with the exchange rate or other macroeconomic issues (otherwise the national central banks participate)

(Pisani-Ferry et al. 2008). However, the Eurozone states are not obliged to coordinate their national fiscal policies, nor does the Eurogroup president hold authority over these states in negotiations (Henning and Meunier 2005: 87).

The addition of the ECB president, Eurozone president and Commission upon the birth of the euro caused consternation within a group that prized its small size and the informal discussions that this allowed. Thus beginning in June 1999 the structure of the meetings were altered so as to allow the relevant actors to participate in a way that would still minimize the number of players involved via splitting the meetings into two parts (Everts 1999: 22–3). The first part concerns the surveillance of economic policy and conditions. The ECB president takes over for the national central bank governors of the Eurozone G7 members (France, Germany and Italy), accompanied by their respective finance ministers. The president of the Eurogroup and the ECB president effectively represent the Eurozone during the surveillance discussions (Smaghi 2004). For the second portion of G7 meetings concerning the international financial architecture and economic development, all of the G7 Finance Ministers attend, in addition to their national central bank governors. The creation of the Eurozone added two European members to this meeting, the ECB president and the Eurozone president.

Far less research has been devoted to the effectiveness of the European Union's representation in the G7. This group is already small, so further reducing the number of representatives would have less of an impact than it would on an organization the size of the IMF. In addition, there are similar disagreements between EU Member States and institutions to those described for the IMF, making a single seat a remote possibility in the near future within this institution as well. In addition to actors like the Commission, ECB, Ecofin and the Eurozone, other potential players in an international agreement include the General Affairs Council and the Development Council, particularly when dealing with issues of aid (Everts 1999: 46–7).

Exchange rate policy

The question of the European Union's external representation also refers to its exchange rate policy. According to Article 111, the Ecofin must approve by a qualified majority vote a proposal from the

Commission or ECB on any exchange rate orientation for the euro. In the absence of a formal orientation (like a fixed exchange rate), the ECB has a considerable amount of discretion in regards to foreign exchange market interventions (Henning and Meunier 2005: 85). Other actors who could become involved include the chairs of the Eurogroup (speaking on behalf of the finance ministers), the EFC and the ECB (Henning and Meunier 2005: 87). Henning (2007) writes of the development of Eurozone foreign exchange intervention. While the euro is a free-floating currency, the Ecofin has the option of setting 'general orientations' for the euro, so long as it does not prejudice the ECB's pursuit of price stability. While such an orientation has not been fixed, in 2000 Eurozone members clashed with each other as well as the ECB when determining what action, if any, should be taken to prop up the value of the currency that was weakening against the dollar. The resulting agreement gave a substantial (though incomplete) amount of latitude to the ECB, though this responsibility was not fully delegated and could be altered in the future. ECB board member Lorenzo Bini-Smaghi (2007) praised the system that was set in place, claiming it ensured that Eurozone policy fulfilled the following desiderata:

- 'First, to be supported by consistent domestic policy action;
- Second, to be taken in concert with the euro area's two major partners, i.e. the US and Japan; and
- Third, to be well explained to financial markets.'

In addition to the external representation of the Eurozone as a whole, we can consider the external relations of specific institutions. The European Central Bank is of particular interest given that it is the only new institution with the legal status to come out of EMU (the Eurogroup is still, as of this writing, an informal group despite its participation in various international fora as described above). Thus its presence necessitated some alteration to the respective duties of the Commission and Council (Henning and Meunier 2005: 86). According to Horng (2004: 327), the external relations of the ECB comprise:

- the recognition of the ECB
- the international representation of the ECB
- compatibility of the ECB's status in international organizations and conferences

- participation of the ECB in international agreements and other legal instruments
- the application of international law to the ECB.

In addition to its participation in the IMF and G7/G10, the ECB also participates in the OECD and the Basel Committee on Banking Supervision (the latter as an observer) (Horng 2004: 331–2).

The role of the ECB is complex. In its relations with the euro area Member States, the ECB has exclusive competence on monetary policy. In regard to non-Eurozone Member States, the ECB coordinates monetary and exchange rate policies via the ESCB, the ECB General Council, and Ecofin. As to the Commission and other EU institutions, the ECB coordinates monetary and exchange rate policies with them through its General Council, although it only has the right of consultation when it comes to forming exchange rate policy, negotiating and concluding agreements dealing with monetary or foreign exchange regime matters, and in decisions and common positions that deal with the Eurozone at the international level. As far as relations with third countries and international organizations are concerned, the ECB's role is more mixed. When it comes to open market and credit operation and the collection of statistical data, the ECB has exclusive competence. However is only an observer in institutions like the IMF, G10 and the BCBS (Horng 2004).

Future prospects

Given US policy, in particular its large trade deficit, the continued strength of the dollar has been seemingly unsustainable for many years. Yet its resilience has provoked economists to devise explanations of why its strength persists, which Krugman summarized as:

- too much savings globally
- better rates of return on the part of American investors
- Bretton Woods II
- statistical manipulation that downplays the overseas assets of US investors by leaving out the export of American multinationals' 'hidden assets such as expertise and reputation' (2007: 450).

While not all economists agree on the validity of such arguments, rumours of the death of the dollar over the years have tended to be exaggerated, despite the inability to agree on the reasons for its long life.

In late 2007 several events occurred that made the prospect of the euro overtaking the dollar seem more plausible than ever before. First was the subprime mortgage crisis in the United States, which contributed to the downgrading of its future economic prospects. The United Arab Emirates and Qatar in November openly contemplated dropping their exchange rate peg to the dollar. The greenback continually weakened, reaching record lows with the euro. Historically the Eurozone has been more passive about such developments, but by November its top representatives became more active in their approach to international exchange rate management, sending ECB president Jean-Claude Trichet, Eurogoup president Jean-Claude Juncker and economics commissioner Joaquin Almunia on a mission to China. This marked the first time that the Eurozone embarked on such a high-level mission devoted to macroeconomic policy.

Despite the long-term significance that these developments could portend, the relatively large contingent being sent to China once again illustrates one of the primary impediments to the Eurozone exerting strong leadership, its complicated governance structure. In particular, the nature of financial crises makes rapid decision making critical in order to minimize their damage. Events such as the Asian financial crisis in the 1990s or concerted efforts among major financial powers like the Plaza and Louvre accords of the 1980s all require greater coherence if the European Union is to take a leading role (most likely at the expense of the United States). The need for so many actors to approve any agreement means that in the near future, the United States will continue to dominate such events despite the rising use of the euro in international financial markets. Political leadership and political will are critical characteristics for the holder of the leading international currency.

If the Eurozone were to pursue a stronger international role, how would it go about it? According to Smaghi (2007) the major area for improvement in this area is in its communication strategy. The Eurogroup prepares its common position in conjunction with the ECB in advance of meetings at international forums such as the G7 and the IMF. Although the technical details are well specified in advance, 'the publicity surrounding them often leads to conflicting signals ... often in an attempt to influence the meeting ... [but which] tends to weaken the negotiating position of the euro area'.

Another way in which the Eurozone could enhance its effectiveness externally is greater financial market integration (de Boisseu 2004, Papademos 2006, Portes and Rey 1998, Bibow and Terzi 2007). In particular, Europe has no public debt security that can compete with the US Treasury bill. The Eurozone's debt market remains segmented, with national differences in legal and administrative systems imposing substantial costs on business (Bibow and Terzi 2007). In a similar vein, the entrance of the British pound would also improve the euro's international standing, considering the size of the British economy and in particular the highly developed British capital markets (de Boisseu 2005, Portes and Rey 1998). Henning (1997) notes that historically the reserve currency was backed up by the most developed capital markets, further making the case for the need for greater Eurozone financial integration.

The prospect of the euro overtaking the dollar and establishing itself as the international anchor currency is limited by several factors. Its reduced potential for economic growth along with demographic trends make the euro less attractive as an asset (Becker 2007, Cohen 2006). Inertia of international financial actors also favours the continued use of the dollar. The concept of hysteresis highlights how the effects of something persist, even after the initial cause no longer exists, making it difficult to dislodge an anchor currency unless the alternative can not only match the advantages of the anchor but also apply additional benefits (Cohen 2004). Some of the advantages of inertia arise from the reduced transaction costs in the economies of scale in using an existing international currency (Bénassy Quéré et al. 1998) as well as accompanying network effects (Portes and Rey 1998). Such inertia is a factor for central banks as well. Papademos (2006) notes that emerging market central banks look not only to potential yields when determining the composition of reserves but also to considerations like a currency's suitability to serve as a reference for monetary policy and how a country's external trade and debt are invoiced, making decisions on reserve composition of a long-term nature.

Finally, one of the biggest impediments to the Eurozone moving beyond its status as an 'accidental player' (Ahearne et al. 2006) in global economic governance is the improvement of its institutional representation (Bergsten 2005). Indeed, the international arrangements within the European Union and its complex system of governance leave it open to a variety of participants, opening up the number of possible veto gates and making rapid decision making difficult at best. Monetary and financial crises require a speedy resolution in order to prevent contagion and overshooting by financial markets. The restoration of confidence is critical, and the lack of a leadership role that the European Union can assume given its current institutional structure is a significant impediment to its ascension as the leading monetary actor in the international system. Some have argued that the locus of power should thus be the Eurogroup, albeit working in close consultation with the Commission and ECB (McNamara and Meunier 2002). But a larger issue is the role that politics plays in the euro's trajectory to become the international currency. While some have noted the complex governance structure that hinders its effectiveness (Cohen 2006, Sapir 2006), other analysts have gone even further to argue the need for political unification (de Grauwe 2006).

On the positive side, numerous factors bode well for the euro as a leading international currency. Its economic fundamentals are largely healthy in that the Eurozone has not contributed significantly to the global imbalances problem. Indeed, several central banks in emerging economies (such as Russia, China, South Korea and India) have announced in recent years their intention to diversify their reserves in favour of the euro (Pouvelle 2006). Enlargement of the Eurozone is inevitable and will by definition increase its use. In addition, as progress continues on the integration of European financial markets, the euro will become a more attractive currency as transaction costs diminish (Pouvelle 2006).

However the issue of global imbalances (referring largely to the US current account deficit and the current account surpluses in Asia and the Middle East – see Gros et al. 2006) directly impacts the Eurozone, even if 'Europe is not part of the problem of global imbalances' (Ahearne and von Hagen 2006: 4). Lane and Milesi-Feretti (2007) explain how the current situation differs from the global imbalances prevalent during the 1980s in three ways:

- The Asian and oil-producing economies run surpluses relative to the large industrialized economies, thus the major players in the debate have expanded to include non-G7 nations.
- The European economy is more open (and therefore vulnerable) than it had been previously, in particular its asset and liabilities with the United States have tripled in the last 20 years.

• The euro has changed the situation in that the dollar's fluctuations no longer have the same effect on intra-European exchange rate movements.

The euro's vulnerability to dollar movements is important but perhaps not as important as for the Asian markets.

The unwillingness of the United States to change its policies and the concomitant reluctance of Asian countries to allow their currencies to depreciate against the dollar have placed upward pressure on the euro. This poses a serious problem for the Eurozone, as it would depress economic growth and worsen existing economic divergences among the Eurozone economies. Eurozone product and labour markets lack the requisite flexibility to adjust to a steep rise in the euro, and the governance structure of the European Union would delay a response even further. Indeed, analysts have warned the European Union of the need to prepare for such a development through structural adjustment (especially labour market flexibility) and fiscal consolidation so that it will be in a better position to respond (Ahearne and von Hagen 2006).

Financial linkages between the United States and Europe have risen sharply, so shocks from one would have strong repercussions on the other. A rising dollar would make European exports less competitive, and slowed growth in the United States would further reduce demand for European goods. Increasing European demand internally (via structural reforms in goods and labour markets) as well as weakening currencies in Asia are critical to dealing with such an eventuality (Lane and Milesi-Ferretti 2007).

The different interests of Europe and the United States would be better served if the Eurozone could act as a unit. For example, during the Mexican financial crisis in the mid-1990s, the United States took the lead in the IMF-sponsored bailout, aided by disagreement among European states. Again during the Asian financial crisis a few years later the United States dominated discussions in the IMF's rescue of several nations affected by the crisis. The role of the IMF has changed several times since its inception and it is currently struggling to reinvent itself once again as emerging economies turn to private finance for help rather than the IMF and the structural adjustment programmes that loans often demand. Indeed, the legitimacy and efficacy of the IMF are under question, and the European Union has a major stake in its continuation. It will be difficult for Europe to stand on the sidelines despite the myriad obstacles it may face on the way to exhibiting greater leadership.

Theoretical considerations

Ideas

Broadly speaking, what makes a currency the international reserve currency? We can view this in terms of a set of political and economic preconditions combined with the political will of the country involved. Although there is a broad consensus regarding the elements that go into making a reserve currency, there are different ideas regarding the likelihood of the euro achieving this role. In order to make such a transition, the currency generally exhibits several traits:

- International economic preeminence, measured by such factors as a country's share in world output and trade, contributes to its use as an anchor currency and in invoicing trade. It also makes it likely that it would be an important component of official reserves. Additionally, the balance of payments of the issuing country should be sustainable.
- The economic stability of a country, both internal and external. In particular price stability is necessary for the emergence and continuation of a reserve currency.
- A well-developed financial market increases the likelihood that the currency will be used for intervention. It may also be necessary as a counterweight to export interests seeking a weak currency in order to increase trade.
- Network externalities play an important role in the emergence of a reserve currency. Others must want to use the currency, thus factors such as positive economic growth/investment yields could be important in influencing such decisions. Nevertheless international currency status tends to be path dependent and resistant to change (Galati and Woodbridge 2006, Pouvelle 2006).

In addition to these economic considerations, the stability of a currency is linked to the political stability of the issuing country (Tavlas 1998), making stable and predictable policy developments key to obtaining and keeping market confidence. Politics affect market estimations of a country's future economic conditions, such as what sort of policy decisions a government will make and the type of economic conditions that will emerge in the future. Political factors such as cabinet duration, length of a government's time in office, a government's partisanship and the timing of elections, can all impact how markets perceive the long-run trajectory of the economy and thus impact more immediate economic indicators such as the exchange rate (Bernhard and Leblang 2002a, Chang 2004). Therefore political stability and the expectation that the issuing country is willing and able to fulfil its financial obligations are also critical to market confidence and the ability of a currency to become the anchor currency.

How does the Eurozone score on all these factors? As reviewed in the first part of this chapter, the euro has become an increasingly important currency internationally, and in a few respects its use has even outstripped that of the dollar. However the Eurozone cannot lay claim to 'dominance' in the global economy. It is questionable that even the United States could claim 'dominance' given the increasing interdependence of economic actors and the open nature of the international trading and financial system. No consensus has emerged on the issue, with some prominent economists arguing that the euro will not displace the dollar as the reserve currency (Cohen 2003, Feldstein 1997, Frankel 1995, Portes and Rey 1998) and others predicting that the importance of the euro will match or even exceed that of the dollar, albeit with varying time horizons (Bergsten 1997, Chinn and Frankel 2007, Kenen 1995, Masson and Turtleboom 1997). While the United States continues to enjoy a situation of preeminence, in part because of the inertia of financial markets (Cohen 2003, 2006), it is also reasonable to see the future as no longer revolving around a single currency but for multiple currencies to compete against one another as the criteria above become harder and harder to fulfil. Indeed, the evolving 'geography of money' increasingly calls into question the relationship between a currency and state sovereignty (Cohen 1998).

Interests

Should the Eurozone want the euro to displace the dollar? What advantages accrue the international anchor currency? Cohen (2006) notes that the United States has enjoyed numerous benefits, such as seignorage gains, more leeway in conducting macroeconomic policy (as it can use the dollar to finance its deficits), international prestige, as well as the option of using the currency as a form of hard power via the exploitation of other countries' dependence on the dollar. These elements specify the 'exorbitant privilege' that de Gaulle referred to years ago in that the United States can run economic and monetary policies that are simply not an option for other countries due to the preeminent status of the dollar. The willingness of foreigners to hold dollars as assets means that the United States was able to run deficits that would lead to a currency run and higher interest rates in other countries, thus giving the country issuing the reserve currency a liquidity discount (Portes and Rey 1998: 309, Bibow and Terzi 2007).

Everts (1999) describes how for decades the United States has used the dollar as a weapon in order to pressure European governments to enact economic policies in accordance with US preferences, such as in 1978 when the United States pressured the German government to act as a locomotive of world growth and loosen its fiscal policy. The subsequent fall in the dollar hurt German exports as well as wreaked havoc on the other trade-dependent European economies. This manifest dependence on the dollar is what helped prompt the relaunching of monetary integration the following year with the European Monetary System.

Kirshner (1995) has gone further in explaining how a currency can be a tool of statecraft and how it can be used to promote a state's non-economic interests, including its security interests. This can be done in three ways: currency manipulation, monetary dependence (done by the leading state, exploiting a vulnerable state's monetary/financial situation) and systemic disruption (most often practised by medium-sized states threatening the dominant state and/or smaller states in the system). The line between hard power and soft power is more blurred than perhaps is expected when it comes to the politics of monetary relations.

Institutions

Given the economic and political advantages that accrue to the issuer of the international reserve currency, it is no surprise that the international role of the euro is such an important preoccupation. But it is not clear that the Eurozone would necessarily benefit from all of these advantages. In particular, its aforementioned inability to speak with one voice is in part the result of different economic and political interests of its member states. This makes it difficult not only for the Eurozone to consolidate its representation in the first place, but it logically follows that even if this hurdle were overcome there would be substantial disagreement among actors as to how to best wield the enhanced influence, particularly when it comes to non-economic issues.

This is perhaps why the Eurozone does not have an explicit policy on the issue of becoming the leading currency, preferring to leave such decisions up to financial markets. It could also be in order to maintain a greater margin for manoeuvre in dealing with internal developments, as opposed to being concerned with monetary and financial developments outside its borders. For the ECB in particular such a policy would be in line with that of its predecessor, the Bundesbank, which never overtly sought or accepted monetary leadership of the European Monetary System and concentrated on German price stability and economic conditions, even when its policy had clear implications for other countries. The EMS only became a relevant policy factor occasionally and under duress (Everts 1999: 14). Indeed, a greater international role for the euro could bring with it an increased possibility of currency speculation as more euros are circulated outside the Eurozone (and thus outside the control of the ECB). Eventually the ECB could be expected to perform the role of lender of the last resort when financial crises arise (de Boisseu 2004).

Becoming the key international reserve currency could have serious implications for the ECB's policy, in particular its evaluation of monetary aggregates and exchange rate fluctuations (Hartmann and Issing 2002). Others have argued that this would not necessarily be the case: ECB board member Lorenzo Bini-Smaghi (2007) remarked, 'The fact that the dollar is the major world currency does not seem to affect the conduct of the US monetary, fiscal or exchange rate policies …. Why should then the euro area be different?' The decision to pursue monetary hegemony thus rests on a calculation of the benefits that would accrue versus the constraints a state would face once achieving such a status. Nevertheless the Commission (2008) has criticized the Eurozone for not having a clear international strategy, arguing that the euro could better shield the Member States from the turbulence resulting from global imbalances and growing demand for energy and other primary products.

Conclusion

One of the most pressing issues facing the future of the Eurozone is the status of the euro internationally. Comparisons between the euro and the dollar are inevitable given their similar status economically. Furthermore, the status of international reserve currency would do much to enhance the political prestige of the euro and perhaps grant the Eurozone great policy autonomy, such as has been enjoyed by the United States for decades. But the greatest impediment to such a development is the internal politics of the Eurozone itself. In particular the complex governance structure and unwillingness of Member States to give up national prerogatives in favour of a streamlined European representation mean that the Eurozone will be unable to exercise strong leadership in the foreseeable future. The euro therefore does not provide a credible alternative to the dollar when considered from a holistic sense and including political variables, not just economic ones. The political will of the issuing currency and its economic preponderance in international financial markets must both be present in order for a country to assume international financial and monetary leadership.

Chapter 9

The Eurozone: an initial balance sheet

A central theme in this book is the political ramifications of the adoption of the single currency in Europe. The reasons for its creation were largely political, as discussed previously, though much of the rhetoric surrounding it rests on technocratic arguments related to how it would improve the functioning of the Eurozone economy. This chapter considers both the economic and political consequences of the euro thus far. Has the euro measured up to economic and political expectations? Why or why not?

Economic consequences of the euro

Ultimately monetary union was supposed to make the European economy more competitive and thus improve economic growth. Economic and Monetary Union (EMU) would promote market efficiency, price stability, public finances, and give the European Union the advantages of issuing an international currency (reduced risk, seignorage). Further, it could assist in the development and convergence of poorer Member States via synergies from national development programmes, the single market programme and EMU. These benefits were laid out in the Commission's 'One market, one money' (1990) report and were backed up by academic research. Later research added trade enhancement as another expected benefit of monetary integration.

The Commission's 1990 report predicted that a single currency would first of all render the European economy more efficient by reducing transaction costs and exchange rate uncertainty, thus saving 0.5 per cent and at least 0.4 per cent of the EC's GDP, respectively (1990: 63). The enhanced efficiency of the European economy would presumably encourage greater investment (a reduced risk premium of 0.5 per cent could translate into a 5–10 per cent increase in income for the EC (1990: 63) and hence foster

economic growth. The variability of exchange rates among countries participating in the Exchange Rate Mechanism was estimated
to be 0.7 per cent a month, and removing this risk would offset the
expected seignorage loss of up to 1 per cent of GDP that could be
expected from the creation of a single currency. Indeed, the introduction of a single currency has eliminated exchange rate fluctuations and the threat of currency speculation between Eurozone
members.

Although exchange rate variability between Eurozone members
has obviously been erased, the high level of the euro in recent years
has caused some concern. The Commission (2007a: 5) published a
report that estimated the appreciation of the euro since 2000
caused growth to recede 0.6 per cent, though the report took pains
to note that this is a relatively small percentage of the 5 per cent
annual export growth. It should be balanced against the 0.5 per
cent gains in the late 1990s when the euro was relatively weak.

The second major predicted benefit of EMU was what later
would become known as the 'sound money' paradigm in which
governments pursued low inflation and fiscal solvency. Already in
practice in Germany, its institutionalization as part of EMU meant
that it would become even more widespread in Europe and create
a virtuous circle in which stable prices and public finances would
allow for lower interest rates, encourage investment and lead to
stronger growth. The Commission report envisaged an independent Eurofed (later named European Central Bank) which prioritized price stability. Following the Delors Report, benefits were
expected to begin to accrue as early as Stage 1 of EMU and would
increase over time. The 1970s and 1980s were turbulent decades in
European currency markets, and the preparation for the euro and
the institutionalized commitment to price stability coincided with
a long-term decline in and convergence of interest rates in the
European Union, and stable inflation expectations. In the early
1990s the average inflation rate in the Eurozone was double that
of the 2 per cent enjoyed by the area in recent years (see Figure
9.1). Consequently long-term interest rates have also declined
significantly over the last few decades (see Figure 9.2). In addition,
the variability of the prices of goods traded within the Eurozone
from 1990–2001 was reduced in half to a level similar to that of
goods traded within the US (Rogers 2007). However, most of the
convergence occurred during the consolidation of the Single
Market rather than in the run-up to the euro.

A few caveats are in order. First, Eurozone countries exhibit varying degrees of interest rate sensitivity due to differences in housing markets. In countries such as the Netherlands and Ireland, for example, most mortgages are linked to variable interest rates, making the effect of interest rate changes more acute. On the other hand, in

FIGURE 9.1   Average annual inflation rates, 1981–2006

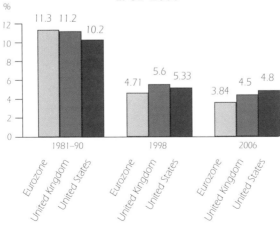

Source: data from European Commission.

FIGURE 9.2   Average nominal long-term interest rates, 1981–2006

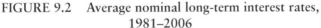

Source: data from European Commission.

countries such as Germany and Italy most mortgages are fixed to long-term interest rates. In addition the consumer credit markets in these countries are also tighter, further insulating them from interest rate changes relative to other countries (Tilford 2006).

Second, it is not clear that the inflation and interest rate benefits are necessarily attributable to the euro (Lane 2006). A recent paper (Angeloni et al. 2007) asked the question, 'Price setting and inflation persistence: Did EMU matter?' and responded negatively. Looking at consumer prices and inflation levels in six Eurozone countries both before and after the introduction of the euro, Angeloni et al. (2007) find that 1999 did not mark a change in the behaviour of market actors or inflation levels. Although there was evidence that inflation had permanently declined after the mid-1990s, non-EMU countries (such as the United Kingdom) and non-EU countries (such as the United States) experienced similar declines, casting doubt on the idea that preparation for EMU was the cause (see Figure 9.2). While prices in the Eurozone have been stable, it is possible that EMU is not directly responsible, or only indirectly.

Prices in Europe were quite stable over the last two decades, but the perception of the citizenry is that EMU contributed to higher prices as a result of shopkeepers rounding up prices during the 2002 changeover from national monies into the euro as a physical currency. The actual economic impact of this was relatively minor, but the perceptions surrounding the euro's introduction as inflationary persist. The main point of contention was the increase in prices in certain items purchased relatively frequently, such as milk, coffee and haircuts, with countries like Italy being more affected by this than others. However the overall levels of inflation did not increase substantially as a result, with the Commission reporting a one-off 0.1–0.3 per cent increase in prices in 2002 due to the euro. A Commission study (2002b) done after the euro became a physical currency nevertheless indicated widespread concern about price hikes, with interviewees from Italy, Spain, Greece, Ireland, France, Belgium Luxembourg, Germany and the Netherlands all expressing anxiety on this issue, as well as citizens of Portugal, Austria and Finland, albeit to a lesser degree.

The 2007 accession of Slovenia showed similar patterns, with higher prices as a result of the switch from the tolar to the euro cited as the biggest concern (Commission 2007b). Such fears continue even though many favour Eurozone membership: a 2007 Eurobarometer poll showed 53 per cent of those interviewed in the new Member States believe the euro will be beneficial, varying from 34 per cent in Latvia to 67 per cent in Romania (2007: 16). Despite this overall positive score, three quarters of those interviewed still expressed their belief that the introduction of the euro will be accompanied by higher prices (2007: 20).

The effect of EMU on public finances was supposed to include greater budgetary discipline, lower interest rates and a more efficient public sector, according to the Delors Report and reiterated in 'One market, one money' (Commission 1990). The latter noted that the seignorage losses of up to 1 per cent that the more inflationary countries enjoyed would be more than compensated for by lower interest rates. While EMU did provide states with strong incentives to reduce budget deficits in the 1990s, its effect on fiscal conditions has weakened since then (see Figure 9.3). The Maastricht Treaty threatened exclusion from EMU should a country fail to meet its debt and deficit targets, and the Stability and Growth Pact (SGP) carried the threat of sanctions if the debt targets were breached post-EMU membership. Therefore in order to fulfil the Maastricht Treaty convergence criteria, states made strong efforts to consolidate public finances. But after the euro's introduction in 1999, many states' finances slid back into deficit.

Hughes-Hallet and Lewis (2007) found that although fiscal consolidation seemed to occur prior to EMU, by 2004 the disciplinary effect had disappeared. Rather than engaging in reforms that would streamline government costs, governments counted on economic growth in order to achieve fiscal targets. In fact, economists even detected the return of political business cycles in which governments implemented expansionary policies prior to elections (Buti and van den Noord 2004). The poor implementation of the SGP and the high number of countries that have fallen foul of its rules attest to the more limited effects that monetary union and the 'stick' of the SGP have had, as opposed to the 'carrot' of qualifying for monetary union. While in 1996 almost all of the countries ran some sort of deficit, with most exceeding the 3 per cent Maastricht Treaty limit, by 2000 almost all of them had achieved the SGP's target level. By 2006, however, many fell once more into deficit. The economic upswing in Europe in 2007–8 did lead to better results.

The trade benefits of the euro were not among the primary considerations in the establishment of EMU, as macroeconomic benefits were the real focus. However academic literature provided additional rationale for monetary union, with a single currency arguably having a positive effect on trade. An oft-cited paper by Andrew Rose (2000) reported that historically speaking, a significant increase in trade occurred between countries participating in a currency union. Ensuing research on Europe predicted that the euro could also be expected to contribute to deepening Eurozone trade, albeit with more modest estimates (Baldwin 2006a).

Intra-Eurozone trade has increased from 5 per cent to 10 per cent since the introduction of the euro according to empirical reports, and this was not accompanied by a significant amount of trade diversion (Baldwin 2006b). However, some of this rise can be attributed to cyclical conditions as well as the weakness of the currency during its first years of operation. In addition the euro's trade effects have differed from country to country. For example, Belgium/Luxembourg, Finland, Germany, Ireland, the Netherlands, Portugal and Spain benefited from a rise in trade thanks to the Eurozone membership, whereas Greece, Austria and France did not (Aristotelous 2006, Baldwin 2006a). Ireland and Portugal have seen their real exchange rates strengthen, but with a different impact on exports. In Germany and France the real exchange rate has weakened, but Germany's exports have increased whereas France's have not (Ahearne and Pisani-Ferry 2006). Thus far the

FIGURE 9.3   Government deficit as percentage of GDP, 1996–2006

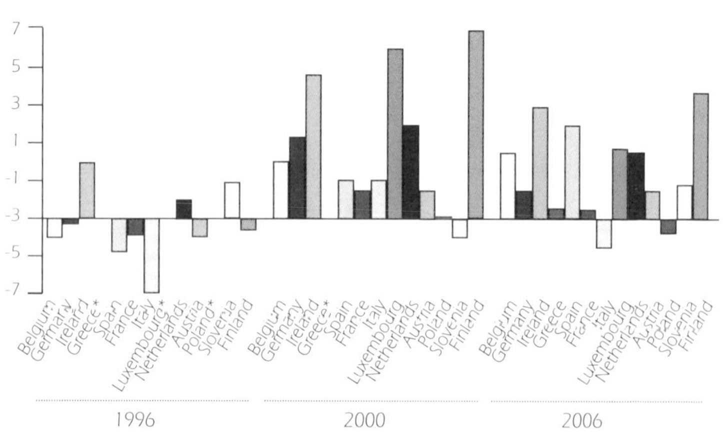

Source: data from European Commission (* = no data available).

role of trade in monetary integration has not gone entirely according to expectations. A rise in trade did occur, but the extent to which it can be attributed to the euro is questionable. In addition, the increased trade flows did not contribute to price convergence, nor play a role in lowering transaction costs (Baldwin 2006a).

Furthermore, Eurozone trade generally has increased with the rest of the world, leading Lane (2006) to conclude that intra-EMU trade has not increased substantially in proportion. Indeed, the exports of Britain, Sweden and Denmark to the Eurozone increased by 7 per cent. Baldwin (2006a) observes that countries in the Eurozone liberalized trade broadly, thereby lessening the impact of Eurozone membership. This has implications for the trade benefits of Eurozone membership, as Baldwin predicts that would-be Eurozone members should expect to see a stronger rise in imports rather than exports. For example, if the United Kingdom joined the Eurozone, its exports would increase by $3 billion, whereas its import levels would increase by $18 billion. The ramifications of the small rise in trade between Eurozone countries therefore include a weakened case for Eurozone membership.

'One market one money' noted that monetary integration also could assist in economic convergence through spillover effects. While over half of the EC countries at that time (Germany, France, Belgium, the Netherlands, Luxembourg, Denmark and Ireland) were relatively similar in terms of inflation and costs, other countries (Ireland, Spain and the United Kingdom) would likely converge within a few years' time. Greece and Portugal had even greater challenges to overcome, but they could still become members of the Eurozone by the start of EMU if enough political will could be mustered. International Monetary Fund (IMF) studies (1996) predicted that EMU could spark further reform and benefits once the Member States achieved the Maastricht criteria.

However in order for these countries to catch up, monetary union would need to build on national reforms as well as the completion of the internal market. Sadly the political will to implement necessary reforms has been lacking in critical areas. Ironically, the Eurozone's implementation of internal market directives ranks among the worst, lower than Denmark, Sweden and the United Kingdom. Across the Eurozone, productivity has generally been disappointing due to the continued protection of the services sector (IMF 2007). The Eurozone's largest economies (France, Germany and Italy) are among the worst offenders as they have diluted initiatives like the directives on services and takeovers in order to protect vested interests (Tilford 2006).

Reforms within the Eurozone have not exceeded the pace of reform outside, and the introduction of the euro did not spur further reform. There is even some evidence that reforms slowed down (Duval and Elmeskov 2006). The Eurozone's reform record is particularly bleak in the services sector, as national regulators continue to impede convergence (Commission 2006c, ECB 2003). Mongelli and Varga (2006) write that although the intensity of structural reforms undertaken from 1994 to 2004 was greater than in the OECD, this was an EU phenomenon rather than one limited to EMU. Moreover, reforms slowed down in EMU countries from 1999 to 2004, but not in the non-Eurozone EU countries. Given the continued disparity within the Eurozone, a single monetary policy is inappropriately loose for some and tight for others, making renewed efforts towards structural reforms essential to promote convergence (OECD 2007).

The report also envisaged the extension of cohesion policies normally undertaken at the national level to the European level, so as to further promote convergence, or at least not exacerbate existing disparities between countries. The regional policies already used (such as the 1975 European Regional Development Fund, the Guidance Section of the European Agricultural Guidance and Guarantee Fund, and the European Social Fund) were mentioned as precedents and rationalizations for the need to increase the European Commission's structural policies, as national policy would become more constrained as a result of EMU. The economies of the peripheral countries would likely weaken before strengthening, thus requiring additional assistance from the European Commission in order to maintain social cohesion. Greece, Ireland and Portugal, the recipients of structural interventions, were targeted as the countries that would be most affected by the loss of the exchange rate. (Spain's poorer regions and the Italian Mezzogiorno were mentioned but already lacked exchange rate sovereignty because of their participation in a national currency area.) The academic literature on the subject concurred that the hard core of the Eurozone (like Germany and France) would be the primary beneficiaries of EMU, and that the southern countries like Spain and Italy would likely face some challenges (Ardy et al. 2006: 141).

The economic disparities between Member States narrowed

during the 1990s as states implemented reforms to qualify for monetary union. Although substantial differences remained, this did not prevent the initial wave of the Eurozone being much larger than the expected mark zone, including almost all of the countries that sought membership despite not fulfilling all of the convergence criteria. The periphery states did benefit from the creation of cohesion funds, and in the cases of Ireland and Spain enjoyed some of the strongest growth in the European Union. The mark zone, however, generally experienced weaker growth and more problems during the first decade of EMU, in particular problems with the SGP.

Overall, EMU did not lead to as much economic integration/convergence as some might have expected. Altavilla (2004) notes that significant differences in the size and timing of business cycles remain in Europe, with Ardy et al. (2006) obtaining similar results and also finding that inflation and the structure of fiscal policy and debt across the Eurozone (and the European Union) still vary significantly. For example, the Eurozone economies came out of the economic slowdown in the early part of the decade in different positions: while Ireland, Greece and Spain emerged with their economies not only intact but growing, other countries like Germany, the Netherlands, Luxembourg and Portugal experienced much weaker economic growth. In regard to fiscal policy, Denmark, Finland, Luxembourg, Ireland and the United Kingdom have had a relatively easy time meeting their targets (although British deficits have been moving upwards in recent years), while France and Germany had well-documented problems meeting their targets. In addition, Belgium, Italy and Greece all suffered from relatively high debt levels. The start of EMU also failed to herald greater price convergence; Engel and Rogers (2004) find that although price dispersion decreased throughout the 1990s, after January 1999 they found no such tendency when examining an extensive range of consumer prices. According to Pisani-Ferry et al. (2006) these differences in growth, wages and prices are rooted in domestic shocks and policies, as they largely originate in the non-traded sector.

But perhaps the biggest divergence concerns unemployment (see Figure 9.4). Indeed, prior to EMU versus afterwards this is particularly marked, with Germany exhibiting weakness over the entire period and France and Italy initially showing strength but later suffering from high unemployment. Denmark, Sweden and the Netherlands enjoyed relatively lower rates of long-term unemployment in comparison with Italy, Greece and Germany. Thus a single macroeconomic policy poses a difficult challenge given the different needs of these economies, as they continue to demonstrate different policy preferences, varying predispositions to economic shocks, and they also respond differently to both the shocks and the policy levers that would be used to manage them (Pisani-Ferry et al. 2006: 36).

Greater economic convergence was both encouraged and expected because of the longer-term spillover effects of the changes that had been occurring in Europe over the past two decades. The creation of the single currency can be viewed in part as the completion of the internal market, the functional logic suggesting that it would be needed in order to fully realize all of the potential benefits of the world's largest single market and eventually a more dynamic economy. More integration would follow, such as what happened in the Eurozone financial sector. Financial market integration is expected to yield 'growth dividends' for Eurozone economies as companies have greater access to capital (Guiso et al. 2004). An ECB study (Cappiello et al. 2004) analysing financial market integration indicated greater co-movements of stock and government bond markets after 1999. Larger countries with bigger stock markets have made greater strides in financial integration than smaller countries. Guiso et al. (2004) document the integration of Eurozone bonds, both private and sovereign bonds in

FIGURE 9.4   2006 unemployment rates

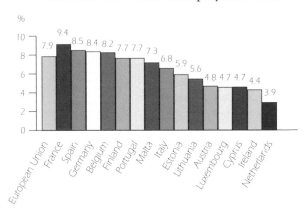

Source: data from European Commission.

primary and secondary markets. As a result of EMU greater liquidity exists in secondary markets. Nevertheless small yield differentials for sovereign debt remain because of corresponding differentials in fundamental risks. In equity and bond markets, financial integration has seen important increases; although most mergers in the banking sector have been domestic, cross-border banking mergers have also become more common recently. According to Pisani-Ferry et al. (2008), money markets have become fully integrated, and the share of bonds and equities of fellow Eurozone countries in national portfolios has risen substantially. Yields on euro-denominated bonds and other same-category assets have converged (ECB 2007). Cross-border holdings of financial assets have expanded within the Eurozone (Lane 2006). Again, the aforementioned differentials between Eurozone countries are significant in these sectors as well: financial integration has been more significant in bigger countries with correspondingly larger stock markets (Mongelli and Varga 2006).

Despite these strides, substantial room for improvement remains. Credit markets continue to be fragmented as different regulations and tax systems in the Member States limit cross-border competition (Pisani-Ferry et al. 2008). Other challenges include: the need to address the disparity between German-denominated futures and the underlying cash market, reducing the manipulation of cash markets by large financial institutions, completing the integration of clearing and settlement systems in the Eurozone bond market, and creating joint bond issuances by Eurozone countries (Pagano 2004).

In addition, oversight of the banking system is done at the national level, making it difficult for the Eurozone to adequately handle any systemic crises (Pisani-Ferry et al. 2008: 62). Given the continued importance of bank loans (as opposed to securities) in financing debt, this presents a major hurdle in the full integration of financial markets. Issing (2006) estimates that 90 per cent of debt financing in the Eurozone is composed of bank loans, compared with 75 per cent in the United Kingdom and less than 60 per cent in the United States.

The rising volume of cross-border banking has made problematic the traditional system of entrusting responsibility for banking supervision to the legal jurisdiction of the bank. The 2007 crisis involving Northern Rock of the United Kingdom and Industriekreditbank of Germany demonstrated the difficulty of coordinating between national authorities (Pisani-Ferry et al. 2008: 63). Ecofin recently arrived at an agreement for a set of common principles regarding the European Union's financial stability so as to protect the stability of the financial system in all of the Member States in a manner that minimizes any harmful economic effects at the lowest collective cost (Ecofin 2007). Other areas that could benefit from further integration include the commercial paper market, stock market harmonization, and cross-border equity investments (Bernanke 2005).

The record of the Eurozone countries is not without positive elements. In addition to the reforms linked specifically to the Maastricht Treaty, governments also have undertaken some reforms to improve competitiveness and foster growth. In Germany, for example, companies took strong measures to reduce unit labour costs (Dyson and Padgett 2006). In France the government has made some strides in the reform of the public sector: the Raffarin government passed a law raising the amount of time public sector employees need to work in order to qualify for a pension from 37.5 years to 40. Over the last decade the Eurozone countries have taken on more structural reforms than other countries in the OECD, with smaller countries taking the lead (Duval and Elmeskov 2006). However this appears to be an EU-wide phenomenon which is not limited to the Eurozone. Besides, Eurozone reform took place at a faster pace during the years prior to the euro's introduction (1994–98) than during the early years of the euro. Non-Eurozone countries did not see such a difference between the periods. Thus much like trade integration, the impact of the run-up to the euro seems to have had a stronger effect than its actual introduction, again indicating the reform fatigue that many Eurozone countries battle. The ability of countries like Greece and Portugal to undertake further reforms in view of their already high fiscal deficits and growing debt is questionable, however. Although the Spanish economy has experienced strong growth, its productivity has not improved significantly and its competitiveness has declined (Dyson 2007). If this is not something the Member States are able to overcome, the affect of the euro will continue to be seen as limited. As Wyplosz (2006: 222) argues, save for Greece, 'the relative average country performance has not changed significantly'.

A study published by the Commission (2006d) points out the adjustment problem faced by the Eurozone and its continued internal economic divergence, highlighting Germany, Italy, the Netherlands, Portugal, Spain and Ireland as deviating the most from the area average in terms of growth, inflation, and competitiveness. The report focuses on five main causes for these continued divergences:

- Countries are still adapting to the decreasing interest rate levels and ease of credit, a process that began shortly before the euro's introduction. Germany presents a special situation because of the long-lasting effects of its unification.
- Although lower interest rates gave governments the chance to consolidate public finances, not all countries took advantage of this opportunity, so they feel the loss of the exchange rate as an instrument of adjustment more acutely.
- Wages and prices have been relatively sticky and unresponsive to changes in competitiveness and national cyclical conditions.
- Some countries have seen spillover effects from economic conditions such as domestic housing booms, which affected demand for traded goods and the interest rate levels in other Member States.
- Countries have different policy approaches, which are thus reflected in their growth and competitiveness.

Portugal and Italy have faced particularly difficult challenges in adopting the euro, as they are no longer able to rely on exchange rate devaluations to increase their competitiveness. The Commission report notes that Portugal would benefit from structural reforms to bolster its competitiveness. Similarly Italy has encountered a 'dramatic slowdown' in productivity and requires serious structural reforms to regain competitiveness. Tilford (2006) elaborates that the complacency and reform fatigue that have plagued Italy since 1999 are also doing it a disservice: 'There is no real sense of national crisis, despite the fact that its economy is heading for serious trouble.' Gros et al. (2005) have gone so far as to argue that the divergence between Italy and Germany in particular threatens the long-term cohesiveness of the Eurozone.

Although the stable currency and low interest rates have been helpful, more needs to be done to ensure the long-term economic health of the euro area. This includes better governance and budgetary coordination so that Member States can implement economic reforms that would be mutually reinforcing, and to give the euro area a stronger voice in international monetary affairs (Commission 2006c, 2008). Following the publication of the 2006 Commission report, European commissioner for economic and monetary affairs Joaquín Almunia admitted, 'The adjustment in the euro area has been slower than we would like and we cannot ignore this fact. We need to promote structural reforms' (*Financial Times*, 22 November 2006). However, such statements fail to take into account the reforms already undertaken by Member States and the reform fatigue that has taken root in many countries. Even more serious is the possibility that despite all the sacrifices made by the Eurozone states to meet the convergence criteria, 'There is little doubt that it has been costly and no evidence that it has been helpful, even in the limited sense of providing an incentive to "clean the house"' (Wyplosz 2006: 224).

The ultimate potential economic benefit of monetary union is economic growth, towards which policies on enhancing competitiveness are designed. In this regard the salutary effects of the euro also proved to be less dramatic than optimists had hoped. After the French U-turn in the 1980s, its policy of competitive disinflation did not yield the expected improvements in unemployment and growth (Blanchard and Muet 1993), and the extension of this policy to the Eurozone has had similarly disappointing results. Critics have repeatedly pointed out the weakness of the Eurozone's growth compared with the United States, a situation which began to be reversed only in 2007 (see Figure 9.5). While most have focused on the sluggishness of the Eurozone economy as a whole, when disaggregating the Eurozone the situation looks different. Some economies have thrived under monetary union while others have faltered (see Figures 9.6 and 9.7). According to Aghion et al. (2006), the level of a country's technological and financial development affects which exchange rate regime contributes to optimal growth.

Productivity gains have been weak under EMU, contrasting with the expectation that greater price transparency would promote competition and competitiveness. The Eurozone compares unfavourably with other countries of similar economic development. Moreover, productivity increases seem to involve a trade-off with employment increases, as the Eurozone sees rising employment in areas with slow productivity gains, as well as the reverse (Pisani-Ferry et al. 2008: 19).

What of the costs of the creation of a single currency? The 'One

FIGURE 9.5   Annual growth rates for Eurozone and United States, 1999–2008

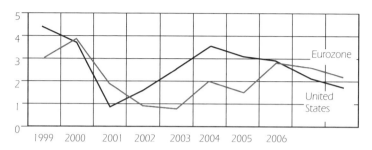

Source: data from European Commission. Data from 2007 and 2008 are estimates.

FIGURE 9.6   Average growth rates in Eurozone countries, 2001–07

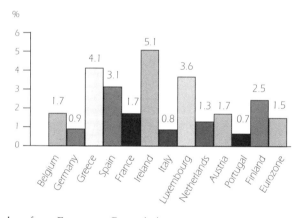

Source: data from European Commission.

market, one money' report (Commission 1990) noted that the main cost likely would be the loss of the exchange rate as an adjustment tool. However this option was already restricted given the confines of the Exchange Rate Mechanism of the EMS, in that states had delegated monetary policy to the Bundesbank in order to maintain their fixed exchange rate relative to the mark. The convergence of economic conditions that would follow monetary union would further obviate the need to resort to the exchange

FIGURE 9.7   Average unemployment rates in Eurozone
countries, 2001–07

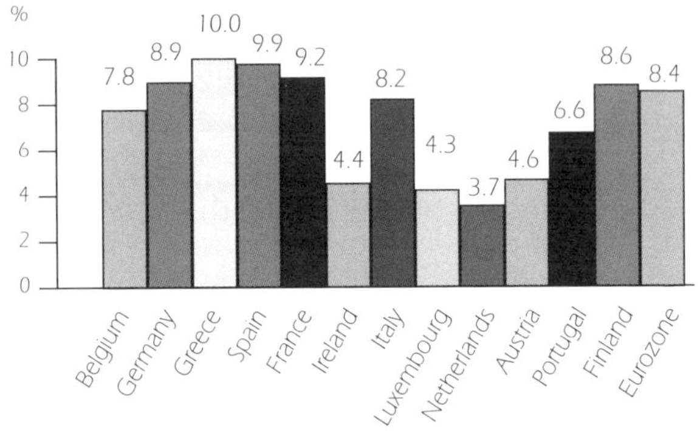

Source: data from European Commission.

rate, as it would lower the incidence of country-specific shocks. Thus labour costs would be the primary mechanism of adjustment, in addition to national and Community budgets, presuming that monetary union would be accompanied by 'an effective economic policy coordination function' (1990: 13).

Labour can compensate for the loss of an exchange rate in numerous ways. First it can increase government credibility and promote wage restraint. Economic research has yielded ambiguous results on the effect of monetary union in this regard. While some argue that monetary union has had a positive impact on wage restraint (Posen and Gould 2006), both the United Kingdom and Sweden also enjoyed greater wage restraint after employing inflation-targeting strategies post-ERM crisis, indicating that monetary union is unnecessary. Indeed, Schelkle (2006) found that EMU did not confer greater credibility in labour markets. Greater credibility in financial markets and the ensuing lower interest rates could have had the effect of boosting demand, easing borrowing constraints and thus removing pressure for labour market adjustment. The experience of labour markets under EMU indicates that credibility must be earned, and that new institutions cannot serve as a quick fix.

Another way to ease adjustment is greater labour market flexibility. Eurozone countries have again been rather slow to undertake measures that would promote greater flexibility. Eurozone's employment protection is slow to change and offers a higher degree of job protection than any country save Japan (Pisani-Ferry et al. 2008). This is consistent with a recent study that finds that membership in a fixed exchange rate regime, or monetary union does not contribute to structural reform in labour markets, particularly in larger countries (Duval and Elmeskov 2006). However other research (Enderlein 2006) indicates that monetary integration has contributed to reform and caused Eurozone countries to adjust their domestic fiscal and wage-setting institutions. Such reform has not led to the convergence of national practices but rather increased divergence, with some wage bargaining systems becoming more coordinated and others decentralized. Although EMU may exert similar pressures for change, it may have different policy results (Herrmann 2005).

From an economic perspective, it seems that the introduction of the euro contributed to the key objective of ensuring stable prices throughout the Eurozone. This allowed interest rates to be lowered substantially, and some countries have enjoyed strong economic growth. However there are questions regarding the extent to which the introduction of the euro should be given credit; global trends indicate similar developments elsewhere in terms of reduced inflation and interest rate levels. While many of the predicted benefits of monetary union came to fruition, overall there has been a palpable sense of disappointment. Sluggish growth in the larger economies and stubbornly high unemployment levels have dampened enthusiasm for EMU. Trade benefits proved to be relatively modest and not limited to EMU members. Public finances in many states have worsened since EMU, with the SGP proving to be an insufficient mechanism to keep down deficits. Finally questions remain about the euro's contribution to economic growth as well as the continued divergence between Eurozone economies. The latter could have important political repercussions, which will be considered in the next section.

Political consequences of the euro

Monetary integration was planned at the highest levels of government, and the political roots and implications of such a project were apparent at every stage of its history. Despite the temptation to dismiss monetary policy as a matter left for technocrats who are better positioned to construct policy that will improve social welfare, EMU has created winners and losers. It is one of the most ambitious experiments ever attempted by the European Union, and thus much prestige and momentum for further integration ride on its success. The euro is the most visible symbol of European unity, and the policies associated with monetary integration have significant implications for state sovereignty.

Although the economic case for monetary union is not as strong as it could be, the economic and political success of the euro is important to the success and momentum of European integration more generally. The *raison d'être* of monetary union was political rather than economic. Despite the importance of central bankers in the design of EMU, prominent central bankers publicly acknowledged that EMU's success rests on political union and not simply on following economic theories (Padoa-Schioppa 1987).

So how has the euro done in political terms? Prior to its introduction both academics and practitioners warned of the political challenges of monetary union. The 1990 Commission study emphasized the need for effective policy coordination to ensure the ultimate success of EMU, writing primarily about fiscal policy although other economic policies could also be subsumed under this rubric. The report noted, 'An excessive emphasis on monetary coordination at the expense of fiscal coordination might be suboptimal, if not counterproductive' (1990: 190). Indeed, fiscal policy would need to bear part of the adjustment as short-term stabilization and medium-term adjustment policies such as monetary policy would be constrained. Monetary stability could be threatened if one or more Member States' budgetary situation led to its default or the monetization of its debt. The ECB would then be under pressure to ease monetary policy and even bail out the debtor country, despite the explicit inclusion of a no-bailout clause in the Maastricht Treaty. Thus the Commission predicted that fiscal policy should be coordinated in order to avoid spillovers that could negatively impact fellow Eurozone members, while recognizing the need to balance Member State autonomy with fiscal policy coordination. Finally economic policy coordination in a broader sense would also be required, as it had long been recognized that the European economies would have to undertake structural reforms to make them more competitive. Both the internal market programme and EMU would presumably encourage such reforms at the national level.

The complex governance mechanism of monetary and economic policy in the European Union that emerged has been routinely criticized as hampering the effectiveness of the single currency. The troubles that Member States have had with abiding by the terms of the SGP were outlined in a separate chapter. The fact that the bulk of economic and structural reforms rest with national governments and are only subject to very loose coordination mechanisms without sanctions for failure to comply with recommendations has meant that progress in institutionalizing structural reforms has been piecemeal, particularly in larger economies like France. European labour markets remain segmented, for example, and the long-awaited Services Directive was substantially weakened after it evoked much controversy. In the absence of substantial economic convergence, policy coordination has proven difficult, something that Feldstein predicted would engender strife both internally and externally:

> For many Europeans, reaching back to Jean Monnet and his contemporaries immediately after World War II, a political union of European nations is conceived of as a way of reducing the risk of another intra-European war among the individual nation-states. But the attempt to manage a monetary union and the subsequent development of a political union are more likely to have the opposite effect. Instead of increasing intra-European harmony and global peace, the shift to EMU and the political integration that would follow it would be more likely to lead to increased conflicts within Europe and between Europe and the United States.
>
> (Feldstein 1997: 60)

Feldstein's most polemical assertion was the prediction that Europe's rising political ambitions combined with its economic affluence would encourage greater militarism and contribute to international disagreements. In this respect the actual fallout has been far more limited than predicted by Feldstein. Disagreements in fora such as the WTO have occurred, but even the possibility of this extending to military action has not arisen. The Eurozone has become more vocal in the issue of global imbalances; in November 2007 the Eurozone sent its three most senior members (ECB president Jean-Claude Trichet, Eurogroup president Jean-Claude Juncker and European economics commissioner Joaquín Alumunia) to China to discuss the strength of the Chinese currency, the prospect of encouraging domestic demand and the banking system's large level of savings (*Financial Times*, 27 November

2007). This marked the first time that the European Union had engaged with China on macroeconomic issues (previously the relationship focused on trade). After meeting with Chinese Central Bank president Zhou Xiaochuan, the two parties agreed to 'take comprehensive measures to enhance structural economic adjustments, avoid big swings in currency movements and make respective contributions to an orderly adjustment of global imbalances' (*Financial Times*, 28 November 2007). While no concrete measures emerged, it was another stage in European activism in this issue area which could bring it into conflict with the United States; however, the extension to military action still appears remote.

Feldstein's other prediction was that internal disagreement would arise from conflict over monetary policy, assuming (correctly) that business cycles would continue to diverge after EMU and make the single monetary policy sub-optimal for some. The demands of the SGP would exacerbate tensions and eventually require a European Union capable of redistribution and not just regulation, implying the ability to tax. The concomitant process of political integration, especially the accession of the Central and Eastern European states, would increase strain and further divide members over matters involving power sharing and resource distribution. While the uneven application of the SGP did provoke criticism and disagreement among Member States, its reform did not result in major crisis. The 2004 and 2007 enlargements did complicate matters for the European Union, in particular the prolonged debate over the constitution, but the extent to which monetary integration in particular should be held responsible is questionable. And although Europe's political and economic struggles have weakened the momentum for major initiatives, they have not led to the collapse of European integration, not do they look likely to do so.

Nevertheless the continued divergence in the economic performance of Eurozone members means that the European Union should be proactive in promoting cohesion. The need for improving the redistributive capabilities of the European Union was recognized during the planning for EMU in the study group report headed by Thomasso Padoa-Schioppa (1987). The report advocated the augmentation of structural funds in order to protect cohesion. Subsequently the Structural Funds and Cohesion Fund were used to compensate the countries that likely would be on EMU's periphery (Ireland, Portugal, Spain and Greece). Those same countries wound up growing more rapidly than the core countries like Germany when EMU was instituted. Contrary to expectations prior to EMU, Barry (2003) argues that 'while most dimensions of integration will be beneficial for convergence, not all of them will necessarily be so' (2003: 918). For example, countries such as Spain, Portugal and Ireland benefited from lower interest rates in the aftermath of EMU while Germany experienced slow growth. Thanks to corporate reforms and keeping wage rises low, Germany has become more competitive, leading to imbalances with other EMU members as its trade surplus rises. Prior to EMU, other states like Italy could have devalued their currency to restore competitiveness. The only options they have now are to reduce their own wage growth and economic demand, which will lead to higher unemployment or Germany will have to become more acceptant of inflation. Neither of these options is attractive and they will likely strain the Eurozone in the future. (I am indebted to William Paterson for raising this issue.)

Indeed, the process of monetary integration has changed the institutional and macroeconomic environment for EMU members, making it difficult to reform compensation policies that can not only take into account the changes associated with Eurozone countries but also the addition of the 2004 and 2007 enlargement countries (Barry and Begg 2003). Politically speaking, 'the real challenges are about EU regional policy in richer member states' (2003: 175), as these regions clearly need support. However it is debatable whether this should come from Brussels or from the national capitals. Taking away funds from the richer countries may be appropriate from the perspective of equitable distribution among all the Member States, particularly when so many of them are now substantially poorer than the EU15. However this would also remove an important symbol of the European Union's value to these Member States at a time when the popularity of the European Union is on the wane.

Even a traditionally pro-EU country such as Italy has felt a backlash in the wake of competitiveness problems since the euro's introduction. Italy had traditionally dealt with such problems through periodic devaluations, but the euro removed that option and the country's poor economic performance led Italian labour and social welfare minister Roberto Maroni to go so far as to suggest a referendum be held for withdrawing from EMU and going back to the lira (*La Repubblica*, 3 June 2005). The suggestion was denounced by the ECB, as its chief economist Ottmar

Issing termed it 'economic suicide' and President Jean-Claude Trichet dismissed it as 'totally absurd'. The Maastricht Treaty has no provisions for such a withdrawal, although it would not be the first time a sovereign nation reneged on an international agreement. The return to the lira would not be a panacea to Italy's economic problems, and the redenomination of Italian debt (public and private) in what surely would be a weak currency likely would negate the advantages of devaluation. The lira-ization of Italy's economy would be complicated and costly. Also, the likely prospect that Italy would become politically isolated in Europe makes withdrawal unlikely (Scott 1998). Nevertheless European Central Bank Governing Council member Christian Noyer acknowledged, 'It is possible for a country to leave the euro zone because member states are sovereign' (Bloomberg 4 July 2005).

Despite enduring state sovereignty, monetary union nevertheless has had political spillover effects and contributed to greater economic cooperation. In the wake of the Maastricht Treaty efforts were made to tackle the economic side of EMU, with issues such as employment, social policy, and fiscal policy coordination coming under discussion. These were dealt with in detail in previous chapters, but it is worth noting again that the subsequent issue areas took on a much looser structure than the delegation of fiscal policy to an independent central bank. Instead the Member States retain control of the content of policies, and even the application of agreements has been loose. Other recent attempts at further integration such as the Services Directive, slow progress in integrating labour markets and the difficulties surrounding the former Constitutional Treaty (later renamed Lisbon Treaty) point to a more considerable easing of integration momentum than existed at the time of Maastricht.

What about public sentiment? According to a spring 2007 Eurobarometer survey, support for EU membership was up four points since autumn 2006 at 57 per cent. Countries making particularly significant gains included Spain, Germany, Poland and the United Kingdom. The survey suggests that the economic recovery has changed Europe's mood, and that citizens are less worried about losing their jobs and more willing to contemplate widening the European Union's borders further to include poorer countries.

However, a 2007 FT Harris poll indicates that scepticism still prevails among the European electorate, with over two-thirds of the French, Italians and Spanish polled indicating that the euro had 'negative impact', with over half of the Germans agreeing. Only

5 per cent of the French gave the single currency positive marks in terms of its impact on the economy, although a majority of Germans, Italians and Spanish acknowledged its generally positive benefits (*Financial Times*, 28 January 2007).

Nevertheless this recent uptick is an anomaly given the overall declining support for the euro over recent years, largely attributed to hikes in the price of frequently used services. Officials still have reason to be concerned about the reputation of the euro among the general population. More than half of the citizens in the FT poll prefer their pre-euro currency, with almost two-thirds of Germans polled still longing for the mark. EU Commissioner for Monetary Affairs Joaquin Almunia warned governments not to use the euro as a scapegoat for domestic economic difficulties, as many are still not convinced of the advantages offered by the euro. This would only be exacerbated by the blame-shifting game played by numerous governments (*Financial Times*, 22 November 2006). The credit crisis that began in 2007 was also at least partially blamed on the mishandling of the ECB, with a 2008 FT Harris poll reporting that only 5 per cent of the Spanish and 8 per cent of the Germans polled thought it handled the crisis appropriately, with 56 and 48 per cent disagreeing (*Financial Times*, 25 August 2008).

Theoretical considerations

Ideas

Theory has not only helped shape the monetary integration process, the academic agenda has naturally been influenced by developments in the Eurozone. The lack of a unified theory of monetary union in the economics profession made broad quantitative assessments on the impact of EMU risky; thus economists looked at specific aspects of EMU to quantify its potential benefits. The Commission's 'One market, one money' study, for example, concluded that although optimal currency area theory gave 'useful insights ... [it] cannot be considered a comprehensive framework' (Commission 1990: 46).

Nevertheless it is instructive to consider how the Eurozone matches up to economic theories. Ardy et al. (2006) assess the suitability of EMU based on the Maastricht Treaty's convergence criteria and optimum currency area theory. The criteria predictably would pose difficulties for several countries, though only the debt figures remained problematic by the mid-1990s. In addition, ERM membership may not be necessary for exchange rate stability, as both Italy and Finland had not been members for two years but in spite of that were deemed to have stable exchange rates.

In terms of the labour market integration needed to offset economic shocks envisaged by optimum currency area theory, Ardy et al. (2006) note that the national labour markets still differed substantially in terms of flexibility and unemployment rates. In particular Greece, Germany, Italy, Belgium and Spain suffered from a significant amount of long-term unemployment. Spain and Italy also suffered from reduced levels of labour participation. Such circumstances make it politically difficult to open up labour markets across the EU/Eurozone, thus impeding the Eurozone from achieving an important characteristic (per optimum currency area theory). However a consensus does not exist in the economics literature on how monetary union impacts labour market flexibility. According to some studies monetary union may not result in increased labour market flexibility (Sibert and Sutherland 2000, Soskice and Iversen 2001) while others come to the opposite conclusion that monetary union promotes more flexibility (Bertola and Boeri 2002, Blanchard and Giavazzi 2003). The latter results go against the Frankel and Rose (1997) thesis that the Eurozone could become an optimal currency area post-EMU as trade and financial integration lead to a correlation of business cycles. Rather than moving closer towards becoming an optimum currency area, a 'rigidity' trap of tight monetary policy and involuntary fiscal consolidation has hindered rather than promoted Member States from undertaking structural adjustment (Silvia 2004).

Diverging business cycles (one of the criteria for the UK government deciding to join EMU) also persist. Crowley and Lee (2005) noted the divergence of business cycles in France from those in Germany and Italy since 1997, which supports the work done by Buti and van den Noord (2004) on the return of political business cycles since the start of EMU. One proposal to alleviate such pressures is the coordination of electoral cycles (Sadeh 2006), as elections have been found to have an important influence on exchange rate movements and policy (Chang 2004, Leblang 2003).

The convergence criteria found in the Maastricht Treaty differ from Britain's five economic tests, underscoring that various economic ideas can be used to rationalize/justify/assess monetary integration. Some of the debates include the relationship between inflation and growth (with Keynesian ideas competing with more monetarist ones), and the relationship between monetary policy and fiscal policy. For example, in the 1970s the Philips curve (positing a trade-off between inflation and growth) was discredited because of the Lucas critique. Earlier ideas (now associated with Mundell I) which were Keynesian in nature saw monetary policy as a way to stabilize the economy given wage and price rigidities. These ideas gave way to monetarism, which argued that an activist monetary policy would do more harm than good. On the one hand, the ECB espouses the logic that economic growth rests on the foundation of sound money and inflationary policies would not be beneficial. On the other hand, certain governments continue to publicly protest against the ECB's restrictive monetary policies, which they argue stifle economic growth. Their arguments therefore are based on conflicting economic assumptions, with the perspectives of some governments advocating greater activism on the part of the ECB. On the national level we can also see the belief in the manipulation of economic policy despite the discrediting of such intervention in the economics profession decades earlier. As Ardy et al. (2006) have argued, governments have a stronger reaction to some conditions than others. For example, fiscal policy exhibits a stronger counter-cyclical tendency during economic downturns than upturns. Similarly the threat of deflation evokes a stronger response than inflation.

Economic ideas have also adjusted to changing political and economic conditions. Rising capital mobility is one condition that has had far-reaching consequences. According to ideas that have been dubbed as Mundell II:

> In a world of free mobility of capital, the exchange rate ceases to be a stabilizing force. Instead ... the exchange rate becomes a target of destabilizing speculative movements and thus a source of large asymmetric shocks ... implying that the exchange rate could be used to stabilize the economy after an asymmetric shock should be abandoned ... joining a monetary union should not be seen as a cost arising from the loss of the exchange rate as an adjustment mechanism, but as a benefit of eliminating a source of asymmetric shocks.
>
> (de Grauwe 2006: 714)

While the economics profession has embraced different ideas regarding monetary integration, this academic work has not always been transposed into policy. Economic ideas alone can only give a partial explanation of the form that EMU has taken over the last decade.

Even the commitment to the sound money paradigm (Dyson 1994, 2000) was pragmatic more than dogmatic for many countries (McNamara 2006), indicating the need to examine interest-based explanations.

Interests

The desire for membership in the first round of monetary union created a powerful incentive to undertake numerous reforms that would bring economic conditions in line with the demands of the Maastricht Treaty's convergence criteria. However, after the start of EMU in 1999 reform fatigue kicked in and instead many Eurozone states became complacent. Rather than aggressively pursuing reform, governments have taken to criticizing EMU on various grounds, blaming it for the economy's economic woes. Monetary union did not act as an economic panacea for all participants but had different consequences and thus diverging needs and preferences.

For example, interest groups have different preferences regarding monetary integration and European integration. Prior to EMU some had theorized a strong role for commercial and financial interests in government preferences (Frieden 1998) and others saw interests as more ambiguous and tempered by ideas (McNamara 1999). Verdun (2008) argues that economic interest groups have played a more important role than previously assumed in both the governance and policymaking of the European Union, but it can be difficult to make generalizations. Bieler (2008) has argued that transnational labour has exhibited different preferences in different countries, with British transnational labour rejecting neoliberal ideas (and policies) and their counterparts in Sweden being more accepting of them.

Sadeh (2006) maintains that EMU is expensive from a social standpoint, given the economic and political idiosyncrasies still present in the Member States. However necessary they might be to the long-term success of EMU, policy reforms are politically difficult to make, and governments that have been in power for a long time are less likely to make necessary adjustments. Differences in economic traits such as business cycles, degree of openness and inflation have political repercussions on a government's longevity and hence the types of policies and reforms that are feasible.

Though much of the focus of analysis for EMU has been on economic effects and motivations, it was also viewed as a step towards greater political integration. Studies on the negotiations of the Maastricht Treaty suggest that monetary and political integration go together, as they are mutually self-reinforcing and encourage greater linkages (Baun 1996). Indeed both central bankers and academic economists openly questioned the economic case of monetary integration and how its creation and success would rest on political decisions. EMU occurred because of political dynamics rather than economic logic. As Thomasso Padoa-Schioppa (2004: 1981) wrote, 'Ultimately, the security on which a sound currency assesses its role cannot be provided exclusively by the central bank. It rests on a number of elements that only the state, or more broadly, a polity can provide.' Former Bundesbank president Karl Otto Pöhl spoke of the German government's desire for political union overriding the central bankers' contention that an ECB was 'manifest nonsense' (quoting and agreeing with former British Chancellor of the Exchequer Nigel Lawson). He termed the end result 'a compromise, and not a very good one'. Indeed, the euro would be 'a big step in the direction of a Federal Europe' (Keegan 2002). Former German Chancellor Helmut Kohl emphasized this point repeatedly:

> One cannot say this often enough. Political union is the indispensable counterpart to economic and monetary union. Recent history, and not just Germany's, teaches us that it is fallacious to think one can sustain economic and monetary union permanently without political union.
> (speech to the German Bundestag 1991, cited in Starbatty and Bofinger 2002)

Economist Paul de Grauwe (2006) has gone so far as to term EMU 'fragile' because it is insufficiently integrated to deal with the possibility of a disgruntled Eurozone state seceding. Its lack of a central budget renders it incapable of handling asymmetric shocks. A political union would enable the European Union to assume more traits of an optimum currency area, but such a move would occur in the distant future, if ever. Indeed, the 1987 Padoa-Schioppa report warned, 'there would have to be further adaptation of attitudes and behaviour among private agents (employers and trade unions), as well as of political attitudes, for monetary union to be a sufficiently low-risk proposition' (1987: 9). Such attitude changes require time and require more than the creation of new institutions, no matter how well designed.

Given the unlikelihood of political integration, is the prospect of a Eurozone break-up likely? According to Barry Eichengreen (2007), the technical costs and political ramifications should be enough to dissuade those who would consider doing so. The costs include those of a more practical nature, such as the need to alter computer codes and refit cash withdrawal machines. More serious would be the threat it would pose to the banking system and financial markets. Significant economic costs would ensue as well, such as an increase in debt servicing and the impact on interest rates, the seriousness of which would depend on the specific circumstances of the departure, in particular what institutions and mechanisms would be used to replace the ECB and the SGP and the extent to which they were deemed credible. According to Hallerberg and Wolff (2006) the impact of fiscal deficits on sovereign risk premia is lower for EMU countries because of the credibility conferred by the latter, implying the need for suitable institutional substitutes should a country leave the Eurozone. From a political perspective, Eichengreen notes that such an exit would be highly damaging to both EMU and the former Eurozone member, the latter likely becoming a second-tier country within the European Union.

Institutions

The somewhat disappointing economic conditions after over a decade of monetary union have been blamed on the governance system. What can the ECB do as opposed to the national governments? Confusion and ambiguity have resulted in various conflicts, some are readily resolved when a situation requiring a clarification arises (such as the responsibility for foreign exchange intervention), while others are more protracted and played out in the financial press (such as the argument between Trichet and Juncker over who is Mr Euro, discussed in Chapter 4). Both the ECB and certain Member States have tried to shift blame from one to the other.

Fitoussi (2006) has connected the relationship between the European Union's governance structure with its slow growth. On the one hand, the ECB does not have the mandate to respond to economic threats that do not impact price stability, making it less reactive than the Federal Reserve. On the other hand, the Member States' room for manoeuvre is constrained by the SGP. This means that the institutions that could impact growth (such as the ECB) cannot do so legitimately, whereas actors that enjoy the legitimacy to react to shocks (Member States) do not have the means to do so. Hence the Eurozone has not reacted to economic threats as aggressively as the United States. These policies are the result of path dependency (Pierson 2000), specifically the enduring impact of the Maastricht Treaty convergence criteria and the economic ideas behind them.

Conclusion

There is reason to be optimistic. By 2006 business and household confidence had improved, and the unemployment rate dipped below 8 per cent, the Eurozone's best result since 2001. The Eurozone also weathered the energy shock nicely (OECD 2007). External demand is solid, Member States have made some reforms in their respective labour markets and changes to welfare systems, and increased immigration too has enhanced the long-term prospects of the economy (IMF 2007).

What would improve the Eurozone's prospects? Completing the internal market could go a long way in fostering economic growth that would enable governments to undertake further structural reforms. At the top of most lists is reforming labour markets so that wages and hiring and firing practices can be more flexible (Baldwin 2006b). In addition, opening up the Eurozone's protected services sector could also allow Member States to take advantage of this important sector of economic growth. Although the 2006 Services Directive was a step in the right direction, it was considerably weaker than the initial proposal and excluded important sectors.

Finally, more can be done in terms of financial market integration. Specifically the implementation of the Financial Services Action Plan (in particular the MiFID) and integrating systems for clearing and settlement offer the European Union a major opportunity as well as a challenge for EU supervisory bodies (IMF 2007, OECD 2007). Ben Bernanke (2005) argues that 'the most significant effects of monetary unification have been felt, and will continue to be felt, in the development of European financial markets'. The euro has already done much to develop financial efficiency. Most notably, sovereign debt yields have converged substantially. For example, from 1990 to 1996 the spread on government bonds between Germany and Italy was 430 points. Similarly, Spanish government bond spreads averaged 350 basis points. Since the introduction of the euro, spreads have been minimal to nonexistent. In addition the development of euro-denominated government debt (as well as corporate debt) has made markets more liquid, although it has not attained the levels of the US Treasury (Bernanke 2005).

In terms of improving legitimacy and bolstering support for the Eurozone and its institutions, the ECB recently scored a public relations coup in the selection of Jean-Claude Trichet as the *Financial Times'* 2007 Person of the Year. The paper lauded the rapid injection of liquidity into financial markets in response to looming crises in August and December of that year. The beginnings of the US subprime crisis in the summer of 2007 prompted the ECB on 9 August to unilaterally inject almost €95 billion in overnight liquidity. Similarly in December markets were surprised by the injection of €350 billion into markets (*Financial Times*, 23 December 2007). The *Financial Times* wrote:

> As the drama unfolded, the ECB appeared to be setting the pace among central banks. In the ultimate compliment, the venerable US Federal Reserve and Bank of England copied the tactics of an institution not yet 10 years old. Mr Trichet is one of the few to emerge from the turmoil with his reputation enhanced, leading the *Financial Times* to name him today as Person of the Year.
>
> (*Financial Times*, 24 December 2007)

Conclusion

An efficient and legitimate EMU?

In 2008 celebrations occurred in both Brussels and Frankfurt in honour of the tenth anniversary of Economic and Monetary Union (EMU) and the European Central Bank (ECB). Although the major success of creating a new currency that has become the second most important in under a decade was justifiably emphasized, monetary union also had some disappointments and unexpected surprises. Weak economic growth in the Eurozone, economic divergence among Member States, and the slow pace of structural reforms have frustrated EMU's potential. Public scepticism in many states towards greater integration, including monetary integration, remains significant.

This reflects the problems of legitimacy that the European Union faces more generally, and needs to be addressed if the European Union is to tackle major challenges in the future, including developing the capacity to assume a leadership position in international monetary fora. EMU's legitimacy was based on the technocratic expertise of economists and central bankers, but the transference of power to supranational institutions was incomplete. A shared sovereignty emerged in which the independent European Central Bank and national governments together created European economic policy. While the contrasting incentives of these sets of actors (supranational and national) need not necessarily have caused problems, the poor delineation of accountability for policy contributed to the penchant for scapegoating and blame-shifting rather than collectively assuming responsibility.

This concluding chapter revisits some of the major themes of the book and reflects on the legitimacy of monetary integration more generally. Despite technocratic justifications for monetary integration, it clearly rests on political foundations. Then-Bundesbank president Karl Otto Pöhl (1990: 36–7) wrote 'references to alleged huge savings in transaction costs for the countries of a single currency are not in the least convincing ... [and] can be accounted for only in a broader political perspective, with the long-term objective of creating a political union'. For Germany in particular, the economic consequences of giving up the mark for a new currency were ambiguous, as it had less to gain from monetary union than other countries. Political reasons for monetary integration include greater political cooperation, in particular binding Germany to Europe after its sudden unification (Garrett 1993, Sandholtz 1993, Baun 1996). EMU's design under the Maastricht Treaty promised enough to appease the needs of the most important interests affected by integration (Verdun 1996), including: the German government's desire for greater political cooperation, non-German governments' wish for greater monetary sovereignty in the face of the mark-dominated European Monetary System of fixed exchange rates that preceded EMU (Dyson and Featherstone 1999), national central banks' concerns for price stability, and commercial interests' desire for stable exchange rates and increased trading opportunities (Moravcsik 1998).

This disparate set of interests ultimately sought three (potentially interrelated) objectives from monetary union: increased political cooperation, greater influence and stronger economic growth. With monetary union well into its first decade, much remains to be achieved on all three fronts, although EMU has unfairly shouldered much of the blame for this. First, the political cooperation that resulted from the Maastricht Treaty falls far short of the German government's desire for political union. The three-pillar structure introduced many new competences into the European Union yet left decision making an intergovernmental affair. Even after the much-vaunted 1992 programme, a truly single market has yet to emerge in Europe, as critical sectors like services remain under national control. The 2004 enlargement of the European Union did little to invigorate integration propensities. Indeed, the post-Maastricht Treaty grand project of the European Union was its draft constitution, which failed after negative referendum results in France and the Netherlands. Schild (2005) warns that the constitutional debate in France indicates a rise in the European Union acting as a scapegoat for economic and political ills.

The potential projection of power as a result of monetary union also included a larger role on the international stage (in addition to the European one for non-German countries). Europe has long used monetary cooperation as a hedge against the dominance of the US dollar and its fluctuations. The creation of an alternative international currency threatened to dethrone the dollar and give Europe more influence in international monetary and financial affairs. Although the euro is undoubtedly a major international currency, it will be some time before it replaces the dollar as the international reserve currency. The euro does not offer enough advantages in terms of reduced transaction costs and greater stability in order for market actors to switch out of the dollar. The countries within the Eurozone would need to harmonize further their policies (Portes and Rey 1998) and better coordinate their position in international fora like the International Monetary Fund and the G8 before the euro could assume the leading role in international monetary affairs that the United States has played during the postwar period.

Arguably the most important 'deliverable' of monetary union was economic growth. In addition to the oft-mentioned political rationale of political stability, one of the primary motivations for European integration in general is that membership offers opportunities to improve competitiveness and long-term growth prospects. The economic success of countries like Ireland, Spain and even the United Kingdom is partly attributable to membership of the European Union and the access to larger markets (goods and capital) and structural funds that membership offers. Monetary union based on the successful German model would presumably lead to greater competitiveness and economic growth. While some countries (like Ireland and Finland) have enjoyed an economic boom in the wake of monetary union, other countries remain mired in slow growth (notably France and Italy), with some having actually lost competitiveness. As the *Economist* (27 April 2006) remarked, 'A solid currency, maybe, but a shame about the economic performance.'

There are limits to how much interest rate policy (which is under the purview of the ECB) can affect economic growth. National policies remain critical to a country's economic competitiveness and growth prospects. Although the Eurozone's growth rate appears sluggish, some economies have thrived. Indeed, the most economically vibrant countries in the Eurozone have already implemented important reforms, particularly in labour markets. The larger Eurozone economies in particular have to make serious headway into politically painful economic reforms. Facing weak economic growth with no relief in sight, it is difficult for democratically elected governments to ask constituents to make further economic sacrifices, especially after numerous reforms had to be made in order to qualify for monetary union in the first place. The reward for monetary union was supposed to be economic growth. Instead, EMU policies may actually have a contractionary bias (Arestis and Sawyer 2003). Governments began falling under the confines of the strictures of the Stability and Growth Pact just as European economic policy became more politicized post-EMU.

Governments within the Eurozone continue to make major economic policy decisions without the input of their counterparts. For example, Germany's government under Angela Merkel decided to increase its VAT starting from 2007 without taking into account the reservations of countries like France and Belgium, which were concerned about the impact this would have on Eurozone growth (*Le Monde*, 6 June 2006). In addition, national budgets are prepared and submitted to national parliaments via different procedures at different times of the year.

The open-ended nature of macroeconomic coordination in the European Union can be blamed on the continued divergence of preferences among Member States (Ardy et al. 2006). This necessitates the use of the principle of subsidiarity and the need for flexible policy instruments and interpretations in order to hold together a still-disparate group of economies whose political loyalties lie primarily at the national rather than the European level. De Grauwe (*Financial Times*, 17 August 2005) argues that the problem lies in the fact that the institutions managing the Eurozone economy (the ECB and the Commission) do not bear political responsibility for the outcomes. The national governments, which can be voted out of office by unhappy constituents, use the fiscal policy instruments still at their disposal in order boost employment, the natural response given their accountability structure. Thus:

> The legitimization of the Eurozone governance structure by the new classical theory can only mask the weakness of this governance. Its weakness has everything to do with the fact that the power to manage the Eurozone economies has been given to European institutions that bear no political responsibility for their actions, while the national governments which have lost their macroeconomic instruments, are made accountable before their national electorates for the failures of macroeconomic management at the European level. Despite its intellectual backing, this poor governance will turn out to be unsustainable.
>
> (de Grauwe 2005)

While the ECB has a legal obligation to pursue price stability, the Member States are accountable to national electorates. Although they potentially can be fined if they fail to respect their obligations to the European Union, this fate is less threatening (and increasingly less likely) than being thrown out of office. Indeed, the ability of voters to elect a new government and thereby achieve a change in policy lies at the heart of a democracy, despite international obligations that a previous government may have made (Collignon 2004). Governments also recognize their obligation to (and interest in) introduce policies that voters want even if they are different from those employed by the previous government. The reluctance of governments to further delegate policymaking power to supranational institutions and lock in a specific preference has led to a preference for soft law, a situation that has become increasingly apparent over time. In particular, the Lisbon Strategy featured the soft-law-based open method of coordination for policy rather than the traditional community method so as to allow Member States to retain their ability to run independent policies (despite the possibility of being persuaded to run policies more in line with those of their EU partners).

The widespread perception that EMU has not contributed to an economically dynamic Eurozone means that EMU has been found wanting in both input legitimacy (popular support resting on shared values) and output legitimacy (superior economic outcomes than could be achieved without delegation of policy). The legitimacy of the European Union becomes increasingly salient as its policies become more far-reaching and impinge on the lives of its citizens. While some have argued that EU policy in general, and monetary policy in particular, need not live up to some idealized standard of popular support and democratic legitimacy (Jones 2002, Moravcsik 2002), arguments of the equivalency of delegation at the domestic level to delegation at the EU level remain problematic. Delegation occurs at the domestic level for reasons of efficiency and expertise, thus legitimizing the delegation of policy on the expectation of superior outcomes than could be had otherwise (Majone 1998), even in the absence of widespread popular support. The complexity of the European Union's political system makes outcome-oriented legitimacy necessary in order to resolve its democratic deficit problem (Scharpf 1999).

But the open-ended nature of EMU governance exacerbates the delicate balancing act of the Eurozone for achieving market credibility along with democratic legitimacy, as the ECB and the

Member States have been competing with one another in order to increase their own claims towards legitimacy. The ECB lacks input legitimacy and its output legitimacy is rather shaky: although it has delivered on its mandate of maintaining stable prices and interest rates are low throughout the Eurozone, growth and employment levels do not match expectations. It must therefore retain the legitimacy it derives as a technocratic body that cannot be influenced by short-term political demands in order to boost its credibility with its ultimate judge, financial markets. If financial markets were to question the stability of Eurozone macroeconomic policy and we saw a return to the currency speculation (this time against the euro) of previous decades, this would be a devastating blow to this fledgling institution. Therefore the ECB remains vigilant in regard to its policymaking territory, which it must defend against possible encroachments from the Member States. Given its lack of strong public support and its relatively short history, its legitimacy and therefore its independence is still under threat. This fight for its continued survival has caused the ECB to react sharply to Member State attempts at engaging in a dialogue.

Democratic governments cannot reasonably be expected to act counter to the expressed wishes of their constituencies, resulting in tension within Ecofin and the Eurogroup and at times bringing them into conflict with the ECB. The most logical disciplinary force for governments is not the Commission, the ECB or even one another but the actor that had precipitated much of the convergence prior to EMU: financial markets. Financial markets hold the most effective and credible punishment for non-adjustment. Indeed, monetary integration's design was specifically tailored to enhance the Eurozone's credibility with markets. When exchange rate cooperation once again came upon the European agenda, the primary objective was exchange rate stability in light of the dollar's volatility during the 1970s (Ludlow 1982). Another benefit from EMS membership emerged, that of increased credibility as governments' commitment to the pursuit of price stability became more credible (Giavazzi and Pagano 1988). EMS participation raised the costs of devaluation, which were decided jointly by member states. The steady decline in long-term interest rates between Germany and other member states confirm the market's lowered expectations of devaluation and inflationary policies in the run-up to monetary union.

However, post-EMU the market has seemingly failed to react to both the deteriorating fiscal conditions in the Eurozone's largest economies and the subsequent political battles that emerged over it, as long-term interest rates remained stable. On the other hand, the market's non-reaction to fiscal developments in the Eurozone could indicate that the markets, not viewing the SGP as a credible institution anyway, had already assessed the long-term conditions regarding savings and investment, which have not changed substantially over the last few years despite the SGP's difficulties. The battle between Ecofin and the Commission and the reform of the SGP therefore would not be considered major events. The chance of any of the Eurozone governments defaulting on their debt is negligible (Fitoussi 2005, Wyplosz 2005). However, there is still cause for concern, as Eurozone governments would essentially share the costs of fiscally profligate members through higher interest rates (Dehesa 2005).

While the market could effectively discipline Member States, its complacency towards the current situation has done nothing to enhance the legitimacy of EMU. One mechanism that has been attempted is the dialogue between the ECB and the European Parliament, which would supposedly make the former more accountable and transparent and ultimately more legitimate. However, the paucity of publicity in major media outlets as to the outcome of these hearings makes it difficult to argue that this in fact enhances EMU's legitimacy in more than a theoretical fashion. In addition, the EP's lack of sanctioning mechanism should it disagree with the ECB's actions further underlines the weakness of this mechanism (Chang 2002). Thus resolving the credibility and legitimacy of EMU through the ECB is unlikely in the short run.

Another suggestion has been to increase the power of the Commission. As a neutral actor, it would be in a stronger position to treat the Member States equally and mitigate charges regarding the political bias inherent in EMU (Wyplosz 2005). However, Member States are unlikely to relinquish their prerogative over the application of sanctions.

The most radical idea proposed has been political union, which would provide the European Union with both the coercive power and ability to redistribute resources needed to stabilize EMU (de Grauwe 2006). While the European Union has been steadily expanding its authority into new issue areas, the idea of political union is still highly speculative and theoretical. Nevertheless, it does highlight some of the major problems associated with monetary union. First, while the weaknesses of monetary union have been highlighted (often by EU actors themselves), its strengths rarely receive much attention. The lack of coercive power of the European Union to prevent exit means that on some level the option remains; EMU is not necessarily viewed as irrevocable. For this reason more needs to be done to publicize the benefits that have been achieved as a result of monetary union. Second, the redistributive consequences of monetary integration also need to be recognized. It was acknowledged early on that some countries (Greece, Portugal, Spain and Ireland) would have a difficult time achieving the Maastricht Treaty convergence criteria, thus contributing to the construction of cohesion funds. While the European Union could not undertake redistribution on the same scale as a national government could, it would be useful to introduce measures to monetary integration that could be seen as helping Member States rather than solely waiting to punish and reprimand them.

The design and implementation of monetary integration exhibit some of the worst elements of the democratic deficit that plagues the European Union more generally. First, its legitimacy rests on an ex-post legitimacy based on outcome, but the ideas behind the policies and institutions do not enjoy the necessary support at the national level. Second, the institutional configuration of EMU has created inconsistent monetary and fiscal policies with an unclear structure of accountability, contributing to suboptimal economic outcomes and public dissatisfaction with EMU.

The ECB and national governments must conduct monetary policy in a more efficacious manner that gives both parties incentives to cooperate with one another rather than exploit disagreements for political gain. In particular the nature of European integration makes it difficult to separate sectors like monetary integration from perceptions of European integration in general. Therefore dissatisfaction with monetary integration and government unwillingness to abide by restrictions it places on states corresponds to the generally pessimistic environment that Europe finds itself in. Political will must be found domestically (making balanced budgets a priority in conjunction with and not counter to the general direction of the government's policy programme), at the EU level (the reinvigoration of integration more generally, most likely via a new grand project), transnationally (market pressure on bond ratings spurring policy changes) or in some combination.

The issue of EMU's legitimacy raises the theoretical themes that have been used throughout this book: ideas, interests and institutions. The legitimacy of monetary union was founded on technocratic ideas regarding the type of institutions and policies that would lead to a better economic performance. Nevertheless these policies were not politically neutral and favoured some interests over others. Those interests can be seen at the international, European and domestic levels, as outlined in previous chapters. Some of the countries, if not worse off economically than they had been pre-EMU, at the very least find that this is the perception among their domestic population, which is dangerous for the legitimacy of EMU and European integration. Divergence within the Eurozone will pose a major challenge for the European Union in the future as it struggles to maintain cohesion among the Member States and provide tangible results that monetary union was in the general interest of the European Union. Finally the institutionalization and governance structure of monetary union has proven to be controversial given the uneven economic outcomes that have resulted.

The prospect of monetary union in Europe was initially greeted in some quarters with excitement and optimism and in others with scepticism and derision. Perhaps we should not be surprised that the reality of EMU is mixed, providing neither a panacea to all of the European Union's economic ills nor contributing to European and international conflict. The day-to-day business of running monetary union remains a challenge, one that is distinct from negotiating its initial agreements and constructing its institutional architecture. The euro is now a reality for hundreds of millions of European citizens, and that number is growing. Consolidating the gains of monetary union and capitalizing on its potential require political leadership. This can come from any number of actors and institutions, with the ECB and the Commission likely to lead the way in strengthening financial cooperation in Europe and trying to rationalize its governance system across a complex web of economic policies. Bringing about a currency that spurs serious debate over its potential as the international reserve currency is a remarkable achievement to have accomplished within a decade. Nevertheless it is important to remember that monetary integration is a work in progress rather than a completed project. Political will and leadership is still needed to ensure the continued stability and success of the euro.

Glossary

acquis communautaire All of the legislation governing the European Communities and European Union that new Member States are obliged to accept and implement.

Balance of payments Refers to the external commercial and financial transactions undertaken by a country.

Balassa–Samuelson effect Balassa (1964) and Samuelson (1964) noted that developing countries have higher inflation than advanced economies due to their higher productivity in tradable goods.

Basel–Nyborg Agreement 1987 agreement that raised available financing for European central banks, thereby making the EMS more symmetrical.

Black Wednesday 16 September 1992, the day that the British pound (as well as the Italian lira) withdrew from the Exchange Rate Mechanism of the EMS because of heavy speculation.

Broad economic policy guidelines (BEPG) Non-binding Council recommendations for Member State governments used to coordinate economic policy in which the Council, acting by a qualified majority on a recommendation from the Commission, formulates draft guidelines that are sent to the European Council. After considering the latter's input, the Council, again acting by qualified majority, adopts a recommendation setting out the BEPG of the Member States and the Community and informs the European Parliament (Article 99 of the EC Treaty).

Bretton Woods A town in New Hampshire at which a 1944 conference launched the IMF, World Bank and GATT. Also used in reference to the decision to establish the dollar exchange standard. Although the fixed exchange rate system collapsed in the 1970s, the institutions persist.

Bundesbank Germany's central bank that pursued a monetary policy prioritizing price stability that was imitated by other states under the EMS and was the inspiration for the ECB.

Capital controls Limits placed on the amount of foreign assets that a domestic citizen can legally acquire (or domestic assets that can be acquired by foreigners).

Cardiff Process Voluntary coordination of product, labour and capital markets based on the open method of coordination and used in the creation of the BEPG.

Cohesion The effort to reduce structural disparities between regions through regional policy (structural funds and cohesion funds).

Cohesion fund Part of EU regional policy, the objectives of which include convergence, regional competitiveness and employment, and European territorial cooperation.

Cologne Process The non-binding coordination of employment policy via a dialogue between Member State governments.

Committee of Permanent Representatives (COREPER) Body that assists the Council of the European Union in dealing with proposals put forward by the Commission and acts as a liaison with national capitals.

Community method Refers to the system of governance used in the first pillar of the European Union, the most salient features being the Commission's agenda-setting role, the use of qualified majority voting in the Council, the European Parliament as a co-legislator and the Court of Justice's ability to interpret Community law.

Contract model A model of domestic fiscal rules and budgetary procedures in which budgetary rules and targets are specified in advance, in contrast with a delegation model. This rules-based approach is more appropriate for coalition governments, according to Hallerberg (2004).

Convergence criteria The Maastricht Treaty's convergence criteria state that in order to pass to the third stage of EMU a country must meet targets for government debt and deficits, inflation, interest rates and exchange rate stability.

Corners view Also known as the bipolar view, argues that intermediate exchange rate regimes are unsustainable, making hard pegs and floating rates (the two corners) the only viable option.

Delors Committee A committee charged with the study and proposal of concrete stages leading to economic and monetary union, resulting in a three-stage plan towards EMU published in 1989.

Democratic deficit The charge that the European Union is insufficiently transparent and accountable, generally directed towards institutions like the independent European Central Bank and the unelected Commission. The European Union's general response has been the delegation of further power to the European Parliament.

Derogation Refers to a Member State that has not yet adopted the euro. Denmark and the United Kingdom, unlike other EU Member States with derogation, are exempt from participating in Stage three of EMU.

DG ECFIN European Commission's Directorate General for Economic and Financial Affairs undertakes economic and budgetary surveillance, offers assessment and advice, and assists in policy coordination. Its principal instruments are the Integrated Guidelines, the excessive deficit procedure, the Stability and Growth Pact, assessments of the Stability and Convergence Programmes and the national reform programmes for growth and employment submitted by Member State governments in the framework of the Lisbon Strategy.

Edinburgh Protocol Added to the Maastricht Treaty in order to ensure Danish participation, gave Denmark opt-outs on the issues of European citizenship, cooperation in internal (police) and external (defence) security and monetary union.

Economic and Financial Committee (EFC) A consultative body that provides support for Ecofin and is composed of no more than two representatives from the Member States, the European Commission and the ECB.

Economic and Monetary Union Consists of economic policy coordination and monetary integration. It was achieved in three stages, culminating in the 1999 introduction of the euro. The United Kingdom and Denmark have an opt-out clause and do not have to adopt the euro, whereas all of the other EU Member States are expected to do so upon fulfilling the convergence criteria.

Economic and Financial Council (Ecofin) One of the 'Councils of Ministers', consists of representatives of the governments of the Member States in charge of economic and financial matters. Ecofin is the legal representative of the Member States in matters relating to EMU.

Economists Those countries (such as Germany and the Netherlands) arguing monetary union required policy convergence prior to the introduction of a common or single currency. Their ideas contrasted with those of the monetarists.

Embedded liberalism Theory in political science that argued states pursued liberal international economic policies (such as the lowering of trade barriers) while maintaining domestic policies that would compensate those made worse off through liberalization.

Employment guidelines The guidelines proposed by the Commission and approved by the Council that outline the common priorities of the Member States, upon which Member States are encouraged to coordinate national employment policies. Since 2005, the employment guidelines have been integrated with the macroeconomic and microeconomic policies and are set for a three-year period.

Epistemic community A network or group of experts sharing a common set of causal beliefs that can influence policy by explaining cause and effect relationships, providing policy advice, and helping to identify and define the interests of governments and/or important groups.

Essen Strategy Refers to the decision of the European Council in Essen in December 1994 to pursue the following (non-binding) objectives: improve vocational training, promote productive investments through moderate wages policies, enhance labour market efficiency, support local initiatives that would lead to new jobs and increase access to employment for specific groups, for example, young people, long-term unemployed people and women. Developed further with the Treaty of Amsterdam.

EURIMF Provides European states with a venue in which to exchange viewpoints. It is composed of the European executive directors of the IMF and other Member State representatives for those countries without directorships, as well as a representative from the Commission delegation in Washington and one from the ECB.

Euro The name of the European single currency adopted by the Madrid European Council on 15 and 16 December 1995.

Euro area/Eurozone The area encompassing those EU Member States that participate in the third stage of EMU and use the single currency, the euro. As of 2009 there are 16 members.

Eurogroup An informal gathering of the Ecofin members participating in the Eurozone, during which they discuss matters of shared interest in regards to the single currency. The Eurogroup typically meets prior to Ecofin meetings, and the Commission and the ECB are invited to participate.

European Central Bank (ECB) Responsible for monetary policy in the Eurozone, its main task being the pursuit of price stability. It is one of the most independent central banks in the world. The current president is Jean-Claude Trichet.

European Council An EU institution comprised of the heads of state or government of the EU Member States and the president of the European Commission. They meet at biannual summits to discuss the general direction of the European Union's development, as well as convening intergovernmental conferences to make major treaty changes.

European Currency Unit (ECU) Prior to Stage Three of EMU, the ECU was a basket currency consisting of a weighted average of the national currencies of the EU Member States. The ECU was replaced by the euro on a one-for-one basis on 1 January 1999.

European Employment Strategy (EES) Also known as the 'Luxembourg Process', the EES coordinates Member State employment policies using the (non-binding) instruments of employment guidelines, national action plans, joint employment reports, and council recommendations. Since the 2005 revision of the Lisbon Strategy, the EES consists of Integrated Guidelines for Growth and Jobs (the Guidelines will now be presented jointly with the guidelines for the European Union's macroeconomic and microeconomic policies for a period of three years), the national reform programmes for each Member State, the Commission's annual report on growth and employment and recommendations adopted by the Council.

European Monetary Fund (EMF) Proposed institution that would manage the basket of currencies under the United Kingdom's hard ECU plan.

European Monetary Institute (EMI) A temporary institution created on 1 January 1994 to improve central bank cooperation and monetary policy coordination during Stage Two of EMU and to prepare for the creation of the euro. It was replaced by the ECB on 1 June 1998.

European Monetary System (EMS) A fixed-but-adjustable exchange rate regime established in 1979, with the main components being the ECU, the exchange rate mechanism (ERM) and various credit mechanisms. It was replaced by ERM II on 1 January 1999, and membership within the ERM II without realigning for two years is a convergence criterion for Eurozone membership.

European System of Central Banks (ESCB) The central banking system of the European Union made of the ECB and the national central banks of all EU Member States. Non-Eurozone Member States, however, retain control over their monetary policy, whereas Eurozone members have delegated authority to the European Central Bank.

Eurostat Statistical Office of the European Union, its databases are available for free online. Publishes official harmonized statistics of the European Union based on data from national statistical centres.

Eurosystem The central banking system of the euro area made up of the ECB and the national central banks of those EU Member States that have adopted the euro.

Excessive deficit procedure Part of the Stability and Growth Pact, governed by Article 104 of the Treaty establishing the European Community, obliging Member States to avoid excessive deficits in national budgets (defined as 3 per cent of GDP). The Commission reports on the situation, and if Ecofin decides an excessive deficit exists, it first makes recommendations to the relevant Member State. If the latter fails to rectify the situation, fines can be levied and its eligibility for funds from the European Investment Bank can be affected.

Exchange Rate Mechanism II Established in 1999, an exchange rate peg in which a central rate is set between the national currency and the euro, with a normal fluctuation band of ±15 per cent. Should the national currency reach the margins of the bands, foreign exchange intervention and financing are expected, with some very short-term financing available.

Executive Board of the ECB One of the decision-making bodies of the ECB composed of the president and the vice-president of the ECB and four other members, all of whom are appointed by Eurozone heads of state or government.

General Council of the ECB One of the decision-making bodies of the ECB composed of the president and vice-president of the ECB and the governors of the national central banks of all EU Member States.

German dominance theory The view that the German Bundesbank dominated the European Monetary System, obliging other Member States to follow its policy (in particular interest rate movements) in order to remain within the system.

Gouvernement économique/**economic government** The primarily French attempts to instil greater political accountability in monetary union through a political counterweight to the independent

ECB. The Eurogroup was originally envisaged to play such a role, though objections by other Member States led to it being an informal body without decision-making power. Nevertheless successive French governments continue to call for its creation.

Governing Council of the ECB The supreme decision-making body of the ECB consisting of the Executive Board and the governors of the national central banks of the Eurozone countries.

Hard ECU Idea promoted by the United Kingdom to create a parallel currency (the hard ECU) that would compete with the national currencies as an alternative to monetary union and a single currency.

Harmonized Index of Consumer Prices (HICP) The index of consumer prices calculated and published by Eurostat, used by the ECB to define and access Eurozone inflation levels.

Hegemonic stability theory An international relations theory that posits an international economic and financial system with a preponderant power (the hegemon) is more stable because the hegemon has the incentive and capacity to enforce order. Major proponents include Charles Kindleberger and Robert Keohane.

Inflation An increase in the general price level.

Integrated guidelines Part of the revised Lisbon Strategy that brings together the BEPG and employment guidelines.

Intergovernmentalism In contrast with the Community method that gives the Commission, Parliament and Court strong roles, intergovernmentalism refers to decision making dominated by the Member States in which the Commission shares the right of initiative, the Parliament is informed rather than acts as a co-legislator, and the Council votes require unanimity. Andrew Moravcsik has offered a theory of *liberal intergovernmentalism* in which major EC decisions were formed in a two-stage approach, with national preferences formed first, then the outcome of negotiations determined by the relative bargaining power of participating states.

International Monetary Fund (IMF) One of the Bretton Woods institutions that was established in 1946 to promote international monetary cooperation and exchange rate stability as well as assist its members in rectifying balance of payments imbalances.

j-curve effect An expression used to describe the initial weakening and subsequent improvement of the trade balance after a currency depreciates.

Keynesianism Economic idea that posits that government intervention can stabilize the economy, based on the assumptions that the government can improve on the market and that unemployment poses a bigger problem than inflation. Although this theory fell out of favour in the mid-1970s, it has since gained more adherents. Often contrasted with monetarist theories.

Kok Report Commission report published in 2004 (chaired by Wim Kok) which assessed the European Union's progress in achieving the targets set by the Lisbon Agenda. This critical report led to the revamping of the Lisbon Strategy in 2005, advising it to focus on the creation of jobs and growth.

Lisbon Agenda/Strategy During the meeting of the European Council in Lisbon (March 2000), the heads of state or government launched a 'Lisbon Strategy' aimed at making the European Union the most competitive economy in the world and achieving full employment by 2010 through non-binding coordination mechanisms dubbed the open method of coordination. Revised in 2005 to focus more on jobs and growth (at the expense of social policy and the environment) and to streamline the process.

Luxembourg Process After the Treaty of Amsterdam brought employment policy under the auspices of the European Union, the Luxembourg Jobs Summit in 1997 launched the European Employment Strategy (EES), also known as the Luxembourg Process.

Maastricht Treaty/Treaty on European Union Also known as the Treaty on the European Union, this treaty that was signed in 1992 contained plans for monetary union in three stages, in particular the convergence criteria that needed to be fulfilled prior to membership. It also contained numerous institutional innovations such the extension of co-decision and the creation of the pillar system, thus creating the European Union.

Monetarism Economic theory that posits the following: the need to limit the growth of money so as to avoid inflation; that if inflation is expected to be high, interest rates will rise and the exchange rate will weaken; and that changes in money growth first affect output and later inflation rates. Thus stable monetary policy should be pursued so as to provide greater certainty for markets, and excessive government intervention is often destabilizing for the economy. This theory is often contrasted with Keynesianism.

Monetarist Those countries (such as France and Italy) arguing that economic convergence would naturally occur after monetary union, thus there was no need for coordination and policy harmonization prior to it. Their ideas contrasted with those of the economists.

Monetary Committee An advisory committee assisting Member States in coordinating monetary policy, composed of representatives from the Treasury and central banks of the Member States (one from each), two officials from the Commission, a chair and a secretary. They functioned as independent experts rather than as Member State representatives. In 1999 it was transformed into the Economic and Financial Committee.

Monetary policy Primarily refers to the setting of interest rates and exchange rate policy, which for the Eurozone states' responsibility has been delegated to the ECB.

Mundell I Refers to a 1961 paper by Mundell on optimum currency areas that assumes an efficient market that determines exchange rate flexibility in adjusting to asymmetric shocks and concludes that a single monetary policy cannot be optimal across nation states given segmented labour markets and insufficient integration which leads to asymmetric macroeconomic shocks.

Mundell II Based on a 1973 paper by Mundell that argues that capital mobility makes the exchange rate a source of instability because of currency speculation and so cannot be used as a tool of adjustment after an economic shock. Monetary union is therefore desirable because it removes an important source of asymmetric shocks and guards against exchange risk premia.

Mundell-Fleming conditions/unholy trinity/trilemma The concept that of the following three ideas, only two are possible at one time: free movement of capital, fixed exchange rates, and monetary policy autonomy.

National reform programme Until 2005 referred to as national action plans, national reform programmes are part of the Lisbon Strategy. They outline how the employment guidelines are implemented at the national level, and evaluate the progress made by the Member State over the previous year and its plans for the upcoming year.

Neofunctionalism Theory of European integration that posits integration as a self-sustaining process due to functional spillover (as a result of the interconnected nature of economies, making integration in one area lead to the need to integrate in related areas) and political spillover in which national actors turn to supranational institutions to handle problems that can no longer be adequately handled at the level of the nation state. Influential authors include Ernst Haas, Leon Lindberg, Wayne Sandholtz and Alec Stone Sweet.

Open method of coordination (OMC) Previously used in employment policy and the Luxembourg Process, was defined as an instrument of the Lisbon Strategy (2000). The OMC provides an intergovernmental framework for cooperation in which Member States jointly identify common objectives to pursue and engage in a dialogue to identify best practices. This is an example of soft law, which does not provide sanctioning mechanisms and instead relies on peer pressure. The OMC has been criticized for being too weak and exacerbating the European Union's democratic deficit.

Optimum currency area theory OCA theory argues that monetary unification is desirable if it can handle asymmetric shocks, with the most important indicators being labour mobility and the presence of fiscal transfers.

Price stability The primary objective of the Eurosystem, which has been defined by the Governing Council as a year-on-year increase in consumer prices (as measured by the HICP) for the euro area that is below but close to 2 per cent over the medium term.

Regional policy Regional policy tries to reduce structural disparities between EU regions, based on the principle of solidarity. Financing of projects comes from Structural and Cohesion Funds, and although it is relatively new (incorporated into the EC Treaty in 1992), in 2007–13 was the European Union's second largest budget item.

SCIMF (EU Sub-Committee on IMF matters) Subset of the Economic and Financial Committee. It was created in 2001 and works on the IMF and other related subjects.

Seignorage When its currency is held by foreigners, a country accrues seignorage via the return on extra assets, real or financial, minus interest paid to foreigners and administrative costs.

Single European Act The 1986 Single European Act (SEA) added new momentum to European integration with the objective of completing the internal market by the end of 1992, making important institutional changes to ease decision making, and expanding Community powers.

Snake In March 1972, the Member States created the 'Snake in the Tunnel' in which fluctuations of European currencies (the Snake) were managed within narrow limits against the dollar (the Tunnel). Within a few years the Snake was disbanded and essentially constituted a German-mark zone of Germany, Denmark and the Benelux countries.

Social policy Incorporated into the Treaty of Amsterdam, the Agreement on Social Policy was signed by the Member States (save Britain) and allows the European Commission to act in: improving workers' health and safety, working conditions, the consultation of workers, the inclusion of workers not participating in the labour market, and gender equality. While some social policy is done by co-decision, unanimity is maintained in most areas.

Sound money paradigm/stability culture This paradigm privileges price stability as a special economic objective and was institutionalized in the European Union with the ECB's independence, its mandate to focus on price stability, and the Stability and Growth Pact.

Stability and Growth Pact (SGP) The SGP was designed to ensure that the Member States maintain budgetary discipline after the introduction of the single currency. The SGP contains a preventive arm and a corrective arm. States are committed to maintaining a balanced or nearly balanced budget (with a deficit limit of 3 per cent), with offending states potentially undergoing the excessive deficit procedure which can result in a penalty that ultimately becomes a fine. Controversy surrounding the non-application of the SGP led to its reform in 2005 that made it more flexible in an effort to improve Member State ownership.

Structural funds The structural funds and the cohesion fund are the financial instruments of regional policy, which is intended to narrow the development disparities among regions and Member States. There are two structural funds: the European Regional Development Fund (ERDF) which supports the creation of infrastructure and productive job-creating investment, mainly for businesses; and the European Social Fund (ESF), which promotes the inclusion of the unemployed and disadvantaged into the workforce through training measures.

Subsidiarity The principle that the European Union should not take action (except when it has exclusive competence) unless it can be more effective than action taken at the national, regional or local level. It is closely related to the principles of proportionality and necessity, requiring that EU actions should not exceed the Treaty's objectives.

TARGET (Trans-European Automated Real-time Gross settlement Express Transfer system) A payment system comprising a number of national real-time gross settlement (RTGS) systems and the ECB payment mechanism (EPM). The national RTGS systems and the EPM are interconnected by common procedures (interlinking) to provide a mechanism for the processing of euro payments throughout the Eurozone (and some non-Eurozone EU Member States).

Time inconsistency An economic idea referring to the conflicting incentives of policymakers. A government may want to announce policies in order to influence market expectations, but later on it may be tempted to renege. Markets therefore distrust policy announcements and can incorporate inflation expectations into their calculations, which would have a negative impact on the economy. Therefore rules-based systems are needed in order to make policy credible, meaning that policymakers may be better equipped to achieve their objectives by having their discretion removed and rules instituted instead.

Werner Report The 1970 Werner Report contained a detailed description of the establishment of economic and monetary union in three stages up to 1980. According to the plan, countries would increase economic policy coordination, reduce exchange rate fluctuations and finally irrevocably fix their exchange rates. In addition to monetary policy, fiscal policy would also be centralized. The collapse of the Bretton Woods system in the early 1970s contributed to the early demise of the plan.

Bibliography

Abbott, K. W. and Snidal, D. (2000). 'Hard and soft law in international governance.' *International Organization* **54**(3): 421–56.

Afonso, A., Nickel, C. and Rother, P. C. (2006). 'Fiscal consolidations in the Central and Eastern European countries.' *Review of World Economics* **142**(2): 402–21.

Aghion, P. (2006). 'A primer on innovation and growth.' *Bruegel Policy Brief* 2006/06.

Ahearne, A. and Eichengreen, B. (2007). 'External monetary and financial policy: a review and a proposal.' In A. Sapir (ed.), *Fragmented Power: Europe and the Global Economy*. Brussels, Bruegel.

Ahearne, A. and Pisani-Ferry, J. (2006). *The Euro: Only for the Agile*. Brussels, Bruegel.

Ahearne, A., Pisano-Ferry, J., Sapir, A. and Véron, N. (2006). *Global Governance: An Agenda for Europe*. Brussels, Bruegel.

Ahearne, A. and von Hagen, J. (2006). *European Perspectives on Global Imbalances*. Brussels, Bruegel.

Alesina, A. (1988). 'Macroeconomics and politics.' In S. Fischer (ed.), *NBER Macroeconomics Annual 1988*. Cambridge, Mass., MIT Press: 13–52.

Alesina, A., Barro, R. and Tenreyro, S. (2002). *Optimal Currency Areas*, NBER Working Paper 9072.

Alesina, A, Giavazzi, F., Uhlig, H., Gali, J. and Blanchard, O. (2001). *Defining a Macroeconomic Framework for the Euro Area: Monitoring the European Central Bank 3*. London, Centre for Economic Policy Research.

Alesina, A. and Summers, L. H. (1993). 'Central bank independence and macroeconomic performance: some comparative evidence.' *Journal of Money, Credit and Banking* **25**(2): 151–62.

Allemand, F. (2005). 'The impact of the EU enlargement on economic and monetary union: what lessons can be learnt from the differentiated integration mechanisms in an enlarged Europe?' *European Law Journal* **11**(5): 586–617.

Allsopp, C. and Artis, M. J. (2003). 'The assessment: EMU, four years on.' *Oxford Review of Economic Policy* **19**(1): 1–29.

Allsopp, C. and Vines, D. (1996). 'Fiscal policy and EMU.' *National Institute Economic Review* **158**(1): 91–107.

Altavilla, C. (2004). 'Do EMU members share the same business cycle?' *Journal of Common Market Studies* 42(5): 869–96.

Amato, G. (1988). The Italian Memorandum to ECOFIN, 23 February. Published as 'Un motore per lo SME', *Il Sole 24 Ore*, 25 February.

Andrews, D. M. (1993). *Scapegoating, Exit Costs, and Credibility: The Politics of Exchange Rate Regimes*. Annual Meeting of the American Political Science Association, Washington, DC.

Andrews, D. M. (2003). 'The committee of Central Bank governors as a source of rules.' *Journal of European Public Policy* 10(6).

Andrews, D. M. and Willett, T. D. (1997). 'Financial interdependence and the state: international monetary relations at century's end.' *International Organization* 51(3): 279–511.

Angeloni, I. (2008). *Testing Times for Global Financial Governance*. Brussels, Bruegel.

Angeloni, I., Flad, M. and Mongelli, F. P. (2007). 'Monetary integration of the new EU member states: what sets the pace of euro adoption?' *Journal of Common Market Studies* 45(2): 367–409.

Annett, A., Decressin, J. and Deppler, M. (2005). 'Reforming the stability and growth pact.' *IMF Policy Discussion Papers*.

Apel, E. (1998). *European Monetary Integration 1958–2002*. New York, Routledge.

Archibugi, D. and Coco, A. (2005). 'Is Europe becoming the world's most dynamic knowledge economy?' *Journal of Common Market Studies* 43(3): 433–60.

Ardy, B., Begg, I., Hodson, D., Maher, H. and Mayes, D. (2006). *Adjusting to EMU*. New York, Palgrave Macmillan.

Arestis, P. and Sawyer, M. (2003). 'European Union must end the stability and growth pact and reform the European Central Bank.' *Ekonomia* 6(1): 95–111.

Aristotelous, K. (2006). 'Are there differences across countries regarding the effect of currency unions on trade? Evidence from EMU.' *Journal of Common Market Studies* 44(1): 17–27.

Arrowsmith, J., Sisson, K. and Marginson, P. (2004). 'What can "benchmarking" offer the open method of co-ordination?' *Journal of European Public Policy* 11(2): 311–28.

Artis, M. (2006). 'The UK and the Eurozone.' *CESifo Economic Studies*. Doi:10/1093/cesifo/ifj002.

Artis, M. J. and Winkler, B. (1998). *The Stability Pact: Safeguarding the Credibility of the European Central Bank*. CEPR Discussion Paper No. 1688.

Artis, M. J. and Winkler, B. (1999). 'Stability Pact: Trading off flexibility for credibility?' In H. Hallett, M. M. Hutchison and S. E. H. Jensen (eds), *Fiscal Aspects of European Monetary Integration*. New York, Cambridge University Press: 157–88.

Artus, P., Bénassy-Quéré, A., Betbéze, J.-P. et al. (2004). *Reformer le Pacte de stabilité et de croissance*. Paris, Conseil d'analyse économique.

Askari, H. and Chatterjee, J. (2005). 'The Euro and financial market integration.' *Journal of Common Market Studies* **43**(1): 1–11.

Aylott, N. (2005). 'Lessons learned, lessons forgotten: the Swedish referendum on EMU of September 2003.' *Government and Opposition* **40**(4): 540–64.

Backé, P, Thimann, C,, Arritabel, O., Calvo-Gonzalez, O., Mehl, A. and Nerlich, C. (2004). *The Acceding Countries' Strategies Towards ERM II and the Adoption of the Euro: an Analytical Review.* ECB Occasional Paper 10.

Balboni, F., Buti, M. and Larch, M. (2007). *ECB vs Council vs Commission: Monetary and Fiscal Policy Interactions in the Emu when Cyclical Conditions are Uncertain.* European Economy Economic Papers 277.

Baldwin, R. (2006a). *In or Out: Does it Matter? An Evidence-Based Analysis of the Trade Effects of the Euro.* Centre for Economic Policy Research.

Baldwin, R. E. (2006b). *The Euro's Trade Effects.* ECB Working Paper No. 594.

Balladur, E. (1988). 'Europe's monetary construction.' Memorandum to ECOFIN Council, Ministry of Finance and Economics, Paris, 8 January.

Banaian, K., Burdekin, R. and Willett, T. (1983). 'Central Bank independence: an international comparison.' *Economic Review*, Dallas, Tex., Federal Reserve Bank of Dallas: 1–13.

Bank for International Settlements (2007). *Quarterly Review.* Basel, Bank for International Settlements.

Barro, R. J. and Gordon, D. B. (1983). 'Rules, discretion and reputation in a model of monetary policy.' *Journal of Monetary Economics* **12**: 101–21.

Barry, F. (2003). 'Economic integration and convergence processes in the EU cohesion countries', *Journal of Common Market Studies* **41**(5): 897–922.

Barry, F. and Begg, I. (2003). 'EMU and cohesion: introduction.' *Journal of Common Market Studies* **41**(5): 781–96.

Bauchard, P. (1986). *La Guerre des Deux Roses.* Paris, Grasset.

Baun, M. (1996). *An Imperfect Union: The Maastricht Treaty and the New Politics of European Integration.* Boulder, Colo., Westview Press.

Bean, C. R. (1998). 'Discussion.' *Economic Policy* **26**: 104–7.

Becker, W. (2007). 'Euro riding high as an international reserve currency.' *EU Monitor* **46**.

Beetsma, R. and Bovenberg, L. (1999). 'Does monetary unification lead to excessive debt accumulation?' *Journal of Public Economics* **74**.

Begg, D. (1991). *Monitoring European Integration: The Making of Monetary Union.* London, Centre for Economic Policy Research.

Begg, I. (2006a). *Lisbon Relaunched: What Has Changed? Is It Working Better?* Brussels, Centre for European Policy Studies.

Begg, I. (2006b). 'Real convergence and EMU enlargement: the time dimension of fit with the euro area.' In K. Dyson (ed.), *Enlarging the Euro Area*. New York, Oxford University Press: 71–89.

Begg, I. (2008). *Economic Governance in an Enlarged Euro Area*. European Economy Economic Papers 311.

Begg, I., Eichengreen, B., Halpern, L., von Hagen, J. and Wyplosz, C. (2002). *Sustainable Regimes of Capital Movements in Accession Countries*. London, CEPR Policy Paper No.10.

Begg, I. and Green, D. (1998). 'The political economy of the European Central Bank.' In P. Arestis and M. Sawyer (eds), *The Political Economy of Central Banking*. Cheltenham, Edward Elgar.

Begg, I. and Schelkle, W. (2004). 'Can fiscal policy co-ordination be made to work effectively?' *Journal of Common Market Studies* 42(5): 1047–59.

Beichelt, T. (2004). 'Euro-skepticism in the EU accession countries.' *Comparative European Politics* 2(1): 29–50.

Bénassy-Quéré, A. (2003). 'Pact de stabilité: deux objectifs, deux règles.' *La Lettre du CEPII* 224.

Bénassy-Quéré, A., Mojon, B. and Schor, A.-D. (1998). *The International Role of the Euro*. Working Paper 1998-03, CEPII Research Center.

Bergsten, C. F. (1997). 'The impact of the euro on exchange rates and international policy cooperation.' In P. Masson, T. H. Krueger and B. G. Turtelboom, *EMU and the International Monetary System*. Washington, DC, International Monetary Fund.

Bergsten, C.F. (1999). 'America and Europe: clash of the titans?' *Foreign Affairs* (March/April).

Bergsten, C. F. (2005). 'The euro and the dollar: toward a "finance G-2"'? In A. S. Posen (ed.), *The Euro at Five: Ready for a Global Role?* Washington, DC, Peterson Institute.

Berman, S. and McNamara, K. R. (1999). 'Bank on democracy: why central banks need public oversight.' *Foreign Affairs* 78(2): 2–8.

Bernanke, B. S. (2005). 'The euro at five: an assessment.' In A. S. Posen (ed.), *The Euro at Five: Ready for a Global Role?* Washington, DC, Peterson Institute.

Bernhard, W. T., Broz, L. and Clark, W. R. (2002). 'The political economy of monetary institutions.' *International Organization* 56(4): 693–723.

Bernhard, W. T. and Leblang, D. (2002a). 'Democratic processes and political risk: evidence from foreign exchange markets.' *American Journal of Political Science* 46(2): 316–33.

Bernhard, W. T. and Leblang, D. (2002b). 'Political parties and monetary commitments.' *International Organization* 56(4): 803–30.

Bertola, G. and Boeri, T. (2002). 'EMU labour markets two years on: microeconomics tensions and institutional evolution.' In M. Buti and A. Sapir (eds), *EMU and Economic Policy in Europe*. Edward Elgar.

Bibow, J. and Terzi, A. (eds) (2007). *Euroland and the World Economy: Global Player or Global Drag?* Basingstoke/New York, Palgrave Macmillan.

Bieler, A. (2008). 'Labour and the struggle over the future European model of capitalism: British and Swedish trade unions and their positions on EMU and European co-operation.' *British Journal of Politics and International Relations* **10**(1): 84–104.

Blanchard, O. (2004). 'Peut-on éliminer le chômage en Europe ?' *Revue française d'économie* **18**(4): 3–31.

Blanchard, O. (2006). 'European employment: the evolution of facts and ideas.' *Economic Policy* **45**(1): 7–59.

Blanchard, O. and Giavazzi, F. (2003). 'Macroeconomic effects of regulation and deregulation in goods and labor markets.' *Quarterly Journal of Economics* **118**(3): 879–907.

Blanchard, O. J. and Giavazzi, F. (2004). *Improving the SGP through a proper accounting of public investment.* CEPR Discussion Papers No. 4220.

Blanchard, O. J. and Muet, P. A. (1993). 'Competitiveness through disinflation: an assessment of the French macroeconomic strategy.' *Economic Policy* 16: 12–56.

Blinder, A. S. 'Keynesian Economics'. [Online] <http://www.econlib.org/library/Enc/KeynesianEconomics.html> (accessed 11 November 2008).

Boeri, T. (2005). 'Euro adoption and the labor market.' In S. Schadler (ed.), *Euro Adoption in Central and Eastern Europe: Opportunities and Challenges.* Washington, DC, IMF: 91–104.

Bonker, F. (2006). 'From pace-setter to laggard: the political economy of negotiating fit in the Czech Republic.' In K. Dyson (ed.), *Enlarging the Euro Area.* New York, Oxford University Press: 160–77.

Borowski, J. (2004). 'Costs and benefits of Poland's EMU accession: a tentative assessment.' *Comparative Economic Studies* **46**(1): 127–45.

Borras, S. and Jacobsson, K. (2004). 'The open method of co-ordination and new governance patterns in the EU.' *Journal of European Public Policy* **11**(2): 185–208.

Bottazzi, L. and Giavazzi, F. (2005). 'The euro and the European financial industry.' In S. Schadler (ed.), *Euro Adoption in Central and Eastern Europe: Opportunities and Challenges.* Washington, DC, IMF: 109–24.

Bovi, M. (2003). *A Non-Parametric Analysis of International Business Cycles.* ISAE Working Papers No. 37.

Bowles, P. and Whit, G. (1994). 'Central bank independence: a political economy approach.' *Journal of Development Studies* **31**(2): 235–64.

Brown, G. (1997). Speech by the Chancellor of the Exchequer, Gordon Brown MP on EMU. 27 October 1997 [online] <http://www.hm-treasury.gov.uk/453.htm> (accessed 25 December 2008).

Brusis, M. and Dimitrov, V. (2001). 'Executive configuration and fiscal performance in post-communist Central and Eastern Europe,' *Journal of European Public Policy* **8**(6): 888–910.

Buch, R. and Hansen, K. M. (2002). 'Danes and Europe: from EC 1972 to Euro 2000 – elections, referendums and attitudes.' *Scandinavian Political Studies* 25(1): 1–26.

Buiter, W. H. (1999). 'Alice in Euroland.' *Journal of Common Market Studies* 37(2): 181–209.

Buiter, W. H. (2004). *To Purgatory and Beyond: When and How Should the Accession Countries from Central and Eastern Europe Become Full Members of EMU?* London, CEPR Discussion Paper No. 4342.

Buiter, W. H. (2006). 'The "sense and nonsense of Maastricht" revisited: what have we learnt about stabilization in EMU?' *Journal of Common Market Studies* 44(4): 687–710.

Buiter, W. H., Corsetti, G. and Pesenti, P. (1998). *Financial Markets and European Monetary Cooperation: the Lessons of the 1992–93 European Exchange Rate Mechanism Crisis.* Cambridge, Cambridge University Press.

Buiter, W., Corsetti, G. and Roubini, N. (1993). 'Excessive deficits: sense and nonsense in the Treaty of Maastricht.' *Economic Policy* (16): 58–100.

Buiter, W. H. and Grafe, C. (2002). *Reforming EMU's Fiscal Policy Rules.* London, Centre for Economic Policy Research.

Buller, J. (2006). 'Contesting Europeanisation: agents, institutions and narratives in British monetary policy.' *West European Politics* 29(3): 289–409.

Bun, M. and Klaassen, F. J. G. M. (2007). 'The Euro effect on trade is not as large as commonly thought.' *Oxford Bulletin of Economics and Statistics* 69: 473–96

Burdekin, R. C. K. and Laney, L. O. (1988). 'Fiscal policymaking and the central bank institutional constraint.' *Kyklos* 41(4): 647–62.

Buti, M. (2006). *Will the New Stability and Growth Pact Succeed? An Economic and Political Perspective.* European Economy Economic Papers 241.

Buti, M., Eijffinger, S. and Franco, D. (2003). 'Revisiting the stability and growth pact: grand design or internal adjustment?' *Oxford Review of Economic Policy* 19(1).

Buti, M., Eijffinger, S.C W and Franco, D. (2005). 'The Stability Pact pains: a forward-looking assessment of the reform debate.' CEPR Discussion Papers 5216.

Buti, M., Roeger, W. and Veld, J. (2001). 'Stabilizing output and inflation: policy conflicts and co-operation under a stability pact.' *Journal of Common Market Studies* 39(5): 801–28.

Buti, M. and van den Noord, P. (2004). 'Fiscal discretion and elections in the early years of EMU.' *Journal of Common Market Studies* 42(4): 737–56.

Calmfors, L. (1994). 'Active labour market policy and unemployment – framework for the analysis of crucial design feature.' *OECD Labour Market and Social Policy.* Paris, OECD: occasional paper.

Calmfors, L. and Driffill, J. (1988). 'Bargaining structure, corporatism and macroeconomic performance.' *Economic Policy* 3(6): 14–61.

Calmfors Commission. (1997). *EMU: A Swedish Perspective*. Norwell, Kluwer.

Cappiello, L., Hördahl, P., Kadareja, A. and Manganelli, S. (2004). *The Impact of the Euro on Financial Markets*. ECB Working Paper No. 598.

Cecchetti, S. G. and O'Sullivan, R. (2003). 'The European Central Bank and the Federal Reserve.' *Oxford Review of Economic Policy* 19(1): 30–43.

Cerps, U. (2005). Comments on 'The euro and the European financial industry'. In S. Schadler (ed.), *Euro Adoption in Central and Eastern Europe: Opportunities and Challenges*. Washington, DC, IMF: 124–27.

Chang, M. (2002). 'The logic of collective responsibility in European monetary integration.' *Journal of Public Policy* 22(2): 239–55.

Chang, M. (2003). 'Franco–German interests in European monetary integration: the search for autonomy and acceptance.' In J. Kirschner (ed.), *Monetary Orders: Ambiguous Economics, Ubiquitous Politics*. Ithaca, N.Y., Cornell University Press: 218–39.

Chang, M. (2004). *Realigning Interests: Crisis and Credibility in European Monetary Integration*. New York, Palgrave Macmillan.

Chang, M. (2006). 'Reforming the stability and growth pact: size and influence in EMU policymaking.' *Journal of European Integration* 28(1): 107–20.

Chinn, M. and Frankel, J. (2007). 'Will the euro eventually surpass the dollar as leading international reserve currency?' In R. Clarida (ed.), *G7 Current Account Imbalances: Sustainability and Adjustment*. Chicago, University of Chicago Press: 285–322.

Clark, W. R. (2002). 'Partisan and electoral motivations and the choice of monetary institutions under fully mobile capital.' *International Organization* 56(4): 725–49.

Clift, B. (2006). 'The new political economy of dirigisme: French macroeconomic policy, unrepentant sinning and the stability and growth pact.' *British Journal of Politics and International Relations* 8: 388–409.

Cobham, D. (ed.) (1994). *European Monetary Upheavals*. Manchester, Manchester University Press.

Coeuré, B. and Pisani-Ferry, J. (2005). 'Fiscal policy in EMU: towards a sustainability and growth pact?' *Oxford Review of Economic Policy* 21(4): 598–617.

Coeuré, B. and Pisani-Ferry, J. (2007). The governance of the European Union's international economic relations: how many voices? In A. Sapir (ed.), *Fragmented Power: Europe and the Global Economy*. Brussels, Bruegel.

Cohen, B. (1998). *Geography of Money*. Ithaca, N.Y., Cornell University Press.

Cohen, B. J. (2002). 'Bretton Woods system.' In R. J. B. Jones (ed.), *Routledge Encyclopedia of International Political Economy*. New York, Routledge.

Cohen, B. J. (2003). 'Can the euro ever challenge the dollar?' *Journal of Common Market Studies* 41(4): 515–95.

Cohen, B. J. (2006). 'The euro and transatlantic relations.' In T. L. Ilgen (ed.), *Power, Soft Power and the Future of Transatlantic Relations*. London, Ashgate.

Cohen, J. and Sabel, C. (2003). 'Sovereignty and solidarity: EU and US.' In J. Zeitlin and D. M. Trubek (eds), *Governing Work and Welfare in a New Economy: European and American Experiments*. Oxford, Oxford University Press.

Collignon, S. (2004). 'Is Europe going far enough? Reflections on the EU's economic governance.' *Journal of European Public Policy* 11(5): 909–25.

Collins, S. M. and Giavazzi, F. (1992). *Attitudes towards Inflation and the Viability of Fixed Exchange Rates: Evidence from the EMS*. National Bureau for Economic Research Working Paper No. 4057.

Commission (1990). 'One market, one money. an evaluation of the potential benefits and costs of forming an economic and monetary union.' *European Economy* Vol. 44.

Commission (1997). *EMU: A Swedish Perspective*. Norwell, Kluwer.

Commission (2002a). *Taking Stock of Five Years of the European Employment Strategy*. Brussels.

Commission (2002b). *Qualitative Study on EU Citizens and the Euro in the Months Following its Introduction*. Brussels, May.

Commission (2003). *The Future of the European Employment Strategy (EES): A Strategy for Full Employment and Better Jobs for All*. Brussels.

Commission (2006a). *Working Together for Growth and Jobs: Further Steps in Implementing the Revised Lisbon Strategy*. Brussels, Commission Staff Working Paper SEC (2006) 619.

Commission (2006b). *Global Europe: Competing in the World*. Brussels, European Commission External Trade.

Commission (2006c). 'Public finances in EMU 2006 – the first year of the Revised Stability and Growth Pact.' Communication from the Commission to the Council and the European Parliament.

Commission (2006d). *2006 EU Economy Review*. European Commission.

Commission (2007a). *Quarterly Report on the Euro Area*, Vol. 6, No. 2. Brussels, European Communities.

Commission (2007b). 'Preventive arm of the Stability and Growth Pact needs to be made more effective.' Brussels, Communication from the Commission to the Council and the European Parliament. 13 June 2007.

Commission (2008). 'EMU@ten.' *European Economy* 2.

Crowley, P. and Lee, J. (2005). 'Decomposing the co-movement of the business cycle: a time-frequency analysis of growth cycles in the Eurozone.' *Bank of Finland Discussion Paper* 12-05.

Cruijsen, C. d. and Demertzis, M. (2007). 'The impact of central bank transparency on inflation expectations.' *European Journal of Political Economy* **23**(1): 51–66.

Cukierman, A., Webb, S. and Neyapti, B. (1994). *Measuring Central Bank Independence and its Effect on Policy Outcomes.* Institute for Contemporary Studies Occasional Paper No. 58.

Daly, M. (2006). 'EU Social Policy after Lisbon.' *Journal of Common Market Studies* **44**(3): 461–81.

Danish Ministry of Economic Affairs. (1989). *Danish Government's Official Report on EMU.* 27 November 1989. Copenhagen.

Darvas, Z. and Szapáry, G. (2008). *Euro Area Enlargement and Euro Adoption Strategies.* European Economy Economic Papers 304.

De Boisseu, C. (2004). *Les systèmes financiers: Mutations, crises et régulation,* Economica Paris.

De Boisseu, C. (2005). 'Le rôle international de l'euro: une mise en perspective.' *Centre d'Observation Economique* **115**(5): 613–32.

De Grauwe, P. (2002). 'Challenges for monetary policy in Euroland.' *Journal of Common Market Studies* **40**(4): 693–718.

De Grauwe, P. (2005). 'The Eurozone's conundrum of power without responsibility.' *Financial Times,* 17 August.

De Grauwe, P. (2006). 'What have we learnt about monetary integration since the Maastricht Treaty?' *Journal of Common Market Studies* **44**(4): 711–30.

De Grauwe, P. and Grimaldi, M. (2006). 'Exchange rate puzzles: a tale of switching attractors.' *European Economic Review* **50**(1): 1–33.

De Grauwe, P. and Schnabl, G. (2005). 'Nominal versus real convergence – EMU entry scenarios for the new member states.' *Kyklos* **58**(4): 537–55.

De Haan, J., Amtenbrink, F. and Waller, S. (2004a). 'The transparency and credibility of the European Central Bank.' *Journal of Common Market Studies* **42**(4): 775–94.

De Haan, J., Berger, H. and Jansen, D. (2004b). 'Why did the stability and growth pact fail?' *International Finance* **7**(2): 235–60.

De Haan, J. and Eijffinger, S. C. W. (2000). 'The democratic accountability of the European Central Bank: a comment on two fairy tales.' *Journal of Common Market Studies* **38**(3): 393–407.

De Haan, J. and Hag, G. J. V. T. (1995). 'Variation in central bank independence across countries: some provisional empirical evidence.' *Public Choice* **85**: 335–51.

De la Porte, C. (2002). 'Is the open method of coordination appropriate for organising activities at European level in sensitive policy areas?' *European Law Journal* **8**(1): 38–58.

De la Porte, C. and Nanz, P. (2004). 'The OMC – a deliberative-democratic mode of governance? The cases of employment and pensions.' *Journal of European Public Policy* **11**(2): 267–88.

De Long, J. B. and Summers, L. (1992). 'Macroeconomic policy and long-run growth.' *Economic Review, Federal Reserve Bank of Kansas City* QIV: 5–29.

De Vreese, C. H. and Semetko, H. A. (2004). 'News matters: influences on the vote in the Danish 2000 euro referendum campaign.' *European Journal of Political Research* **43**(5): 699–722.

Dehesa, D. L. (2005). *Unsound Fiscal Policies and Financial Markets Discipline*. Brussels, European Parliament Committee for Economic and Monetary Affairs.

Dellas, H. and Tavlas, G. (2005). 'Wage rigidity and monetary union.' *Economic Journal* **115**(506): 907–27.

Delors, J. (2004). *Mémoires*. Paris, Plon.

Deroose, S. and Baras, J. (2005). 'The Maastricht criteria on price and exchange rate stability and ERM II.' In S. Schadler (ed.), *Euro Adoption in Central and Eastern Europe: Opportunities and Challenges*. Washington, DC, IMF: 128–41.

Deutsche Bundesbank. (1990). 'Statements on creating economic and monetary union in Europe.' Europe Documents No. 1655, 5 October.

DG ECFIN. (2007). Mission Statement. [online] <http://ec.europa.eu/dgs/economy_finance/organisation/mission_en.pdf> (accessed 25 December 2008).

Dimitrov, V. (2006). 'From laggard to pace-setter: Bulgaria's road to EMU.' In K. Dyson (ed.), *Enlarging the Euro Area*. New York, Oxford University Press: 145–59.

Donnelly, S. (2005). 'Explaining EMU reform.' *Journal of Common Market Studies* **43**(5): 947–68.

Driffill, J. (2006). 'The centralization of wage bargaining revisited: what have we learnt?' *Journal of Common Market Studies* **44**(4): 731–56.

Du Bois, P. (1999). 'Euro qui comme Ulysses: L'unification monétaire de l'Europe de 1992 à 1999.' *Relations internationales* 100: 393–407.

Duckenfield, M. (1999). 'Bundesbank–government relations in Germany in the 1990s: From GEMU to EMU.' *West European Politics* **22**(3): 87–108.

Duval, R. and Elmeskov, J. (2006). *The Effects of EMU on Structural Reforms in Labour and Product Markets*. ECB Working Paper No. 596.

Dvorak, T. (2007). 'Are the new and old EU countries financially integrated?' *Journal of European Integration* **29**(2): 163–87.

Dyson, K. (1994). *Elusive Union: The Process of Economic and Monetary Union in Europe*. London, Longman.

Dyson, K. (2000). 'EMU as Europeanization: convergence, diversity and contingency.' *Journal of Common Market Studies* **38**(4): 645–66.

Dyson, K. (2006). 'Euro entry as defining and negotiating fit: conditionality, contagion and domestic politics.' In K. Dyson (ed.), *Enlarging the Euro Area*. New York, Oxford University Press.

Dyson, K. (2007). 'Euro area entry in East-Central Europe: paradoxical Europeanisation and clustered convergence ' *West European Politics* 30(3): 417–42.

Dyson, K. and Featherstone, K. (1999). *The Road to Maastricht*. New York, Oxford University Press.

Dyson, K. and Padgett, S. (eds) (2006). *The Politics of Economic Reform in Germany; Global, Rhineland or Hybrid Capitalism?* London, Routledge.

Eberlein, B. and Kerwer, D. (2004). 'New governance in the European Union: a theoretical perspective.' *Journal of Common Market Studies* 42(1): 121–42.

Ecofin [online] <www.consilium.europa.eu/ueDocs/cms_Data/docs/press-Data/en/ecofin/96375.pdf> (accessed 11 November 2008).

Ederveen, S. and Thissen, L. (2004). *Can Labour Market Institutions Explain Unemployment Rates in New EU Member States?* Economics Working Papers, European Network of Economic Policy Research Institutes. Working Paper No. 027.

Egebo, T. and Englander, A. S. (1992). 'Institutional commitments and policy credibility: a critical survey and empirical evidence from the ERM.' *OECD Economic Studies* No.18.

Egert, B., Drine, I., Lommertzsch, K. and Rault, C. (2003). 'The Balassa–Samuelson effect in Central and Eastern Europe: myth or reality?' *Journal of Comparative Economics* 31(3): 552–72.

Eichengreen, B. (1992a). *Golden Fetters*. Oxford, Oxford University Press.

Eichengreen, B. (1992b). 'Is Europe an optimum currency area?' In S. Borner and H. Grubel (eds), *The European Community after 1992: Perspectives from the Outside*. London, Macmillan: 138–61.

Eichengreen, B. (1995). 'The European payments union.' In B. Eichengreen (ed.), *Europe's Postwar Recovery*. New York, Cambridge University Press: 171–82.

Eichengreen, B. (2007). *The Breakup of the Euro Area*. NBER Working Paper No. 13393.

Eichengreen, B. and Leblang, D. (2003). 'Exchange rates and cohesion: historical perspectives and political–economy considerations.' *Journal of Common Market Studies* 41(5): 797–822.

Eichengreen, B. and Wyplosz, C. (1993). 'The unstable EMS.' *Brookings Papers on Economic Analysis* 1: 51–124.

Eichengreen, B. and Wyplosz, C. (1998). 'Stability pact: more than a minor nuisance?' *Economic Policy* 67: 113.

Eijffinger, S. C. W. and de Haan, J. (1996). *The Political Economy of Central-Bank Independence*. Princeton, N.J., Department of Economics, Princeton University.

Eijffinger, S. C. W. and de Haan, J. (2000). *European Monetary and Fiscal Policy*. New York, Oxford University Press.

Eijffinger, S. C. W., Hoeberichts, M. and Schaling, E. (1998). *A Theory of Central Bank Accountability*. Tilburg Center for Economic Research Discussion Paper 98103.

Elgie, R. (1998). 'Democratic accountability and Central Bank independence: historical and contemporary, national, and European perspectives.' *West European Politics* 21(3): 53–76.

Elgie, R. (2002). 'The politics of the European Central Bank: principal-agent theory and the democratic deficit.' *Journal of European Public Policy* 9(2): 186–200.

Enderlein, H. (2004). 'Break it, don't fix it!' *Journal of Common Market Studies* 42(5): 1039–46.

Enderlein, H. (2006). 'Adjusting to EMU: the impact of supranational monetary policy in domestic fiscal and wage-setting institutions.' *European Union Politics* 7(1).

Engel, C. and Rogers, J. H. (2004). 'European product market integration after the Euro.' *Economic Policy* 19(39): 347–84.

Englund, P. (1999). 'The Swedish banking crisis: roots and consequences.' *Oxford Review of Economic Policy* 15(3): 80–97.

Eurobarometer (2002). EU 15 Report. *Eurobarometer* 57, Spring.

Eurobarometer (2007). *Introduction of the Euro in the New Member States*. Brussels, Eurobarometer.

Eurodad (2006). *European Coordination at the World Bank and International Monetary Fund: A Question of Harmony?* Brussels.

Europa Scadplus (nd) [Online] <http://europa.eu/scadplus/glossary/index_en.htm> (accessed 11 November 2008).

European Central Bank (2003). 'The adjustment of voting modalities in the governing council.' *ECB Monthly Bulletin*. May.

European Central Bank (2004). *The Monetary Policy of the ECB*. Frankfurt, European Central Bank.

European Central Bank (2005). *Review of the International Role of the Euro*. Frankfurt, European Central Bank.

European Central Bank (2006). *The European Central Bank, the Eurosystem, the European System of Central Banks*. Frankfurt, European Central Bank.

European Central Bank (2007). *Review of the International Role of the Euro*. Frankfurt, European Central Bank.

European Convention (nd) *Keywords*. [Online] <http://european-convention.eu.int/glossary.asp?lang=EN&content=C> (accessed 11 November 2008).

European Council (1988). Presidency Conclusions (Hanover, 27–28.06.1988), SN 2683/4/88. Brussels, Council of the European Communities, June.

European Union (2003). *Official Journal of the European Union*, L 158/59.

[online] <http:europa.eu.int/eur-lex/en/archive/index_2003.html> (accessed 11 November 2008).

Everts, S. (1999). *The Impact of the Euro on Transatlantic Relations.* Centre for European Reform.

Fabrizio, S. and Mody, A. (2006). 'Can budget institutions counteract political indiscipline?' *Economic Policy* 21(48): 689–739.

Favero, C., Freixas, X., Persson, T. and Wyplosz, C. (2000). *One Money, Many Countries: Monitoring the European Central Bank 2.* London, Centre for Economic Policy Research.

Federal Trust. (2005). *Flexibility and the Future of the European Union.* London, Federal Trust.

Federal Trust. (2006). *The Governance of the Eurozone.* London, Federal Trust.

Feldmann, H. (2003). 'The implementation of the Stability and Growth Pact: taking stock of the first four years.' *Journal of European Integration* 25(4): 287–309.

Feldmann, M. (2006). 'The Baltic States: using pace-setting on EMU accession to consolidate domestic stability culture.' In K. Dyson (ed.), *Enlarging the Euro Area.* New York, Oxford University Press: 127–44.

Feldstein, M. (1997). 'EMU and international conflict.' *Foreign Affairs:* 60–73.

Feldstein, M. S. (2005). *The Euro and the Stability Pact.* NBER Working Paper No. 11249.

Ferrera, M., Hemerijck, A. and Rhodes, M. (2001). *The Future of Social Europe: Recasting Work and Welfare in the New Economy.* Oxford, Oxford University Press.

Fitoussi, J.-P. (2005). *Fiscal Indiscipline: Why No Reaction Yet by the Markets?* Brussels, European Parliament Committee for Economic and Monetary Affairs.

Fitoussi, J.-P. (2006). *Macroeconomic Policies and Institutions.* Working Paper 2006–06. Paris, Sciences Pos.

Fitoussi, J.-P. and Saraceno, F. (2002). *A Theory of Social Custom of Which Soft Growth May be One Consequence. Tales of the European Stability Pact.* Paris, Observatoire Français des Conjonctures Economiques Working Paper 2002-07.

Fleckenstein, T. (2006). 'Europeanisation of German labour market policy? The European employment strategy scrutinised.' *German Politics* 15(3): 284–301.

Fleming, M. J. (1962). 'Domestic financial policies under fixed and under floating exchange rates.' *IMF Staff Papers* 9: 369–79.

Frankel, J. A. (1995). 'Still the lingua franca: the exaggerated death of the dollar.' *Foreign Affairs* 14(4).

Frankel, J. A. and Rose, A. K. (1997). 'Is EMU more justifiable ex post than ex ante?' *European Economic Review* 41: 753–60.

Fratianni, M. and von Hagen, J. (1990). 'German dominance in the EMS: the empirical evidence.' *Open Economies Review* 1(1): 67–87.

Freeman, J. (2002). 'Competing commitments: technocracy and democracy in the design of monetary institutions.' *International Organization* **56**(4): 889–910.

Frenkel, M. and Nickel, C. (2005). 'How symmetric are the shocks and the shock adjustment dynamics between the euro area and central and eastern European countries?' *Journal of Common Market Studies* **43**(1): 53–74.

Frieden, J. A. (1991). 'Invested interests: the politics of national economic policies in a world of global finance.' *International Organization* **45**(4): 425–51.

Frieden, J. (1998). 'The euro: who wins? who loses?' *Foreign Policy* 112: 24–32.

Gabel, M. and Hix, S. (2005). 'Understanding public support for British membership of the single currency.' *Political Studies* **53**(1): 65–81.

Galati, G. and Woodridge, P. D. (2006). *The Euro as a Reserve Currency: A Challenge to the Pre-eminence of the US Dollar?* BIS Working Paper No. 218.

Gamble, A. and Kelly, G. (2002). 'Britain and EMU.' In K. Dyson (ed.), *European States and the Euro: Europeanization, Variation, and Convergence*. New York, Oxford University Press: 97–119.

Garrett, G. (1993). 'The politics of Maastricht.' *Economics and Politics* **5**(2): 105–23.

Genscher, H. (1988). *A European Currency Area and a European Central Bank*. Memorandum to the General Affairs Council, Ministry of Foreign Affairs, Bonn, 26 February.

George, S. (1990). *An Awkward Partner: Britain in the European Community*. New York, Oxford University Press.

George, S. (1994). *An Awkward Partner: Britain in the European Community*, 2nd edn. New York, Oxford University Press.

Geraats, P. (2008). 'ECB credibility and transparency.' *European Economy Economic Papers* 330: 1–34.

Gerlach, S. (2004). 'The two pillars of the European Central Bank.' *Economic Policy* **19**(40): 389–439.

Gerstenberg, O. and Sabel, S. F. (2000). 'Directly-deliberative polyarchy: an institutional ideal for Europe?' [online] <http://www2.law.columbia.edu/sabel/EUGOVpapers.htm> (accessed 25 December 2008).

Gerstenberg, O. and Sabel, C. F. (2002). 'Directly-deliberative polyarchy: an institutional ideal for Europe?' In R. Dehouse and C. Joerges (eds), *Good Governance and Administration in Europe's Integrated Market*. Oxford, Oxford University Press.

Giavazzi, F. and Giovanninni, A. (1989). *Limiting Exchange Rate Flexibility: The European Monetary System*. Cambridge, MIT Press.

Giavazzi, F. and Pagano, M. (1988). 'The advantages of tying one's hands: EMS discipline and Central Bank credibility.' *European Economic Review* 32: 1055–75.

Gillingham, J. (2003). *European Integration 1950–2003: Superstate or New Market Economy?* New York, Cambridge University Press.

Gleich, H. (2003). *Budget Institutions and Fiscal Performance in Central and Eastern European Countries.* ECB Working Paper No. 215.

González-Páramo, J. M. (2005). *The Reform of the Stability and Growth Pact: An Assessment.* New Perspectives on Fiscal Sustainability, Frankfurt, ECB.

González-Páramo, J. M. (2006). 'The Revised Stability and Growth Pact: is it working?' Speech at the Conference, The ECB and its Watchers, 5 May 2006, Frankfurt.

Goodman, J. (1992). *Monetary Sovereignty: The Politics of Central Banking in Western Europe.* Ithaca, N.Y., Cornell University Press.

Gowa, J. (1983). *Closing the Gold Window.* Ithaca, N.Y., Cornell University Press.

Greskovits, B. (2006). 'The first shall be the last? Hungary's road to EMU.' In K. Dyson (ed.), *Enlarging the Euro Area.* New York, Oxford University Press: 178–96.

Grieco, J. M. (1995). 'The Maastricht Treaty, economic and monetary union, and the neo-realist research programme.' *Review of International Studies* 21(1): 21–40.

Grilli, V., Masciandaro, D. and Tabellini, G. (1991). 'Political and monetary institutions and public financial policies in the industrial countries.' *Economic Policy* (13): 342–91.

Gros, D. (2001). *The ECB's Unsettling Opaqueness.* Report to the Economic and Monetary Affairs Committee of the European Parliament.

Gros, D. (2003). *Reforming the Composition of the ECB Governing Council in View of Enlargement: How Not to Do It!* Report to the Economic and Monetary Affairs Committee of the European Parliament.

Gros, D. (2004). 'Profiting from the euro? Seigniorage gains from euro area accession.' *Journal of Common Market Studies* 42(4): 795–813.

Gros, D. (2005) *The Stability Pact is Dead! Long Live the Treaty?* Centre for European Policy Studies [Online] <http://www.ceps.be/wp.php?article_id=135> (accessed 11 November 2008).

Gros, D., Mayer, T. and Ubide, A. (2005). *EMU at Risk.* Brussels, CEPS Macroeconomic Policy Group.

Gros, D., Mayer, T. and Ubide, A. (2006). *A World Out of Balance?* Special Report of the CEPS Macroeconomic Policy Group. Brussels, CEPS.

Gros, D. and Thygesen, N. (1998). *European Monetary Integration.* London, Longman.

Guiso, L., Jappelli, T., Padula, M. and Pagano, M. (2004).'Financial market integration and economic growth in the EU.' *Economic Policy* 19(40): 523–77.

Gyrffy, D. (2007). 'Deficit bias and moral hazard on the road to the EMU: the political dimension of fiscal policy in Hungary.' *Post-Communist Economies* 19(1): 1–16.

Haas, E. (1957). *The Uniting of Europe*. Stanford, Calif., Stanford University Press.

Haas, P. M. (1992). 'Introduction: epistemic communities and international policy coordination.' *International Organization, special issue, Knowledge, Power, and International Policy Coordination* 46(1): 1–36.

Habermas, J. (1996). *Between Facts and Norms: Contributions to a Discourse Theory of Law and Democracy*. Cambridge, MIT Press.

Habermas, J. (2002). 'Toward a European political community.' *Society* 39(5): 58–61.

Hafer, R. W. and Kutan, A. M. (1994). 'A long-run view of German dominance and the degree of policy convergence in the EMS.' *Economic Inquiry* 32: 684–95.

Hall, P. (1985). 'Socialism in one country: Mitterrand and the struggle to define a new economic policy for France.' In P. G. Cerny and M. A. Schain (eds), *Socialism, the State and Public Policy in France*. London, Frances Pinter: 81–106.

Hall, P. (1986). *Governing the Economy*. Oxford, Oxford University Press.

Hall, P. and Franzese, R. J. (1998). 'Mixed signals: central bank independence, coordinated wage-bargaining, and European Monetary Union.' *International Organization* 52(3): 505–35.

Hallerberg, M. (2002). 'Veto players and the choice of monetary institutions.' *International Organization* 56(4): 775–802.

Hallerberg, M. (2004). *Domestic Budgets in a United Europe: Fiscal Governance from the End of Bretton Woods to EMU*. Ithaca, N.Y., Cornell University Press.

Hallerberg, M. and v. Hagen, J. (1999). 'Electoral institutions, cabinet negotiations, and budget deficits within the European Union.' In J. Poterba and J. v. Hagen (eds), *Fiscal Institutions and Fiscal Performance*. Chicago, University of Chicago Press: 209–32.

Hallerberg, M. and Wolff, G. (2006). *Fiscal Institutions, Fiscal Policy and Sovereign Risk Premia*. Discussion Paper Series 1: Economic Studies. Frankfurt, Deutsche Bundesbank.

Hallett, A. H., Jensen, S. E. H. and Richter, C. (2005). 'Europe at the crossroads: structural reforms, fiscal constraints, and EMU enlargement – an empirical analysis.' *Ekonomia* 8(1): 21–50.

Harmon, M. D. and Heisenberg, D. (1993). 'Explaining the European currency crisis of September 1992.' *German Politics and Society* (29): 19–51.

Hartmann, P. and Issing, O. (2002). 'The international role of the euro.' *Journal of Policy Modeling* 24(4): 315–45.

Hartwig (2007). 'Towards a communitarisation? Spill-overs between structural funds and the European employment strategy.' In I. Linsenmann, C. O. Meyer and W. Wessels, *Economic Government of the EU: A Balance Sheet of New Modes of Policy Coordination*. Basingstoke, Palgrave Macmillan.

Hay, C., Smith, N. J. and Watson, M. (2006). 'Beyond prospective accountancy: reassessing the case for British membership of the single European currency comparatively.' *British Journal of Politics and International Relations* 8: 101–21.

Heipertz, M. and Verdun, A. (2004). 'The dog that would never bite? What we can learn from the origins of the Stability and Growth Pact.' *Journal of European Public Policy* 11(5).

Heipertz, M. and Verdun, A. (2005). 'The Stability and Growth Pact – theorising a case in European integration.' *Journal of Common Market Studies* 43(5): 985–1008.

Heisenberg, D. (1998). *The Mark of the Bundesbank*. Boulder, Colo., Lynne Rienner.

Heisenberg, D. (2005). 'Taking a second look at Germany's motivation to establish economic and monetary union: a critique of "economic interests" claims.' *German Politics* 14(1): 95–109.

Henning, C. R. (1997). 'American interests and Europe's Monetary Union.' Testimony before the Committee on Budget. United States Senate, Washington, DC. 21 October.

Henning, C. R. (1998). 'Systemic conflict and regional monetary integration: the case of Europe.' *International Organization* 52(3): 537–73.

Henning, C. R. (2007). 'Organizing foreign exchange intervention in the euro area.' *Journal of Common Market Studies* 45(2): 315–42.

Henning, C. R. and Meunier, S. (2005). 'United against the United States? The EU's role in global trade and finance.' In N. Jabko and C. Parsons (eds), *The State of the European Union, Vol. 7: With US or Against US? European Trends in American Perspective*. Oxford, Oxford University Press.

Henning, C. R. and Padoan, P. C. (2000). *Transatlantic Perspectives on the Euro*. Washington, Brookings Institution, with the European Community Studies Association.

Herrmann, A. (2005). 'Converging divergence: how competitive advantages condition institutional change under EMU.' *Journal of Common Market Studies* 43(2): 287–310.

Hibbs, D. (1977). 'Political parties and macroeconomic policy.' *American Political Science Review* 71(4): 1467–87.

High Level Group of Representatives of Governments of the EC Member States (1989). *Report on Economic and Monetary Union (the Guigou Report)*, Paris.

HM Treasury. (1989). *An Evolutionary Approach to Economic and Monetary Union*. London, HM Treasury.

Hodson, D. and Maher, I. (2001). 'The open method as a new mode of governance: the case of soft economic policy co-ordination.' *Journal of Common Market Studies* 39(4): 719–46.

Hodson, D. and Maher, I. (2004). 'Soft law and sanctions: economic policy co-ordination and reform of the Stability and Growth Pact.' *Journal of European Public Policy* 11(5): 798–813.

Horn, G. (2003). *Consequences of the Modification of the Governing Council Rules*. Report to the Economic and Monetary Committee of the European Parliament.

Horng, D.-C. (2004). 'The European Central Bank's external relations with third countries and the IMF.' *European Foreign Affairs Review* 9(3): 323–46.

Hosli, M. O. (2005). *The Euro: A Concise Introduction to European Monetary Integration*. Boulder, Colo., Lynne Rienner.

Howarth, D. J. (2007). 'Making and breaking the rules: French policy on EU "gouvernement économique".' *Journal of European Public Policy* 14(7): 1061–78

Howarth, D. J. and Loedel, P. (2003). *The European Central Bank: The New European Leviathan?* New York, Palgrave.

Howarth, D. and Loedel, P. (2004). 'The ECB and the stability pact: policeman and judge?' *Journal of European Public Policy* 11(5): 832–53.

Hughes-Hallett, A. and Lewis, J. (2007). 'Debt, deficits, and the accession of the new member states to the euro.' *European Journal of Political Economy* 23(2): 316–37.

Hughes-Hallett, A. J. and McAdam, P. (2003). 'Deficit targeting strategies: fiscal consolidation and the probability distribution of deficits under the stability pact.' *Journal of Common Market Studies* 41(3): 421–44.

IMF (1996). *World Economic Outlook*. Washington, DC, International Monetary Fund, October.

IMF (2007). *Concluding Statement of the IMF Mission on Euro-Area Policies*. Washington, DC, International Monetary Fund.

Issing, O. (1999). 'The eurosystem: transparent and accountable or "Willem in euroland".' *Journal of Common Market Studies* 37(3): 503–19.

Issing, O. (2002). 'On macroeconomic policy coordination in EMU.' *Journal of Common Market Studies* 40(2): 345–58.

Issing, O. (2006). 'Central Bank independence – economic and political dimensions.' *National Institute Economic Review* 196(1): 66–76.

Issing, O., Gaspar, V., Angeloni, I. and Tristani, O. (2001). *Monetary Policy in the Euro Area: Strategy and Decision Making at the European Central Bank*. New York, Cambridge University Press.

Iversen, T. (1998). 'Wage bargaining, central bank independence, and the real effects of money.' *International Organization* 52(3): 269–504.

Jabko, N. (1999). 'In the name of the market: how the European Commission paved the way for monetary union.' *Journal of European Public Policy* 6(3): 475–95.

Jabko, N. (2006). *Playing the Market: A Political Strategy for Uniting Europe, 1985–2005.* Ithaca, N.Y., Cornell University Press.

Jacobsson, K. (2005). 'Trying to reform the "best pupils in the class"? The open method of coordination in Sweden and Denmark.' In J. Zeitlin and P. Pochet (eds), *The Open Method of Coordination – The European Employment and Social Inclusion Strategies.* Brussels, PIE Peter Lang.

Jacobsson, K. and Schmid, H. (2002). 'Real integration or just formal adaptation? On the implementation of national action plans for employment.' In C. de la Porte and P. Pochet (eds), *Building Social Europe Through the Open Method of Coordination.* Brussels, PIE Peter Lang.

Jacobsson, K. and Vifell, A. (2007). 'Towards deliberative supranationalism? Analyzing the role of committees in soft coordination.' In I. Linsenmann, C. O. Meyer and W. Wessels (eds), *Economic Government of the EU.* New York, Palgrave Macmillan.

Jacquet, P. and Pisani-Ferry, J. (2000). *Economic Policy Co-Ordination in the Euro-Zone.* Centre for European Reform.

Johnson, D. (2005). 'The new outsiders of Central and Eastern Europe, with specific reference to Poland.' *Journal of European Integration* 278(1): 111–31.

Johnson, J. (2006). 'Two-track diffusion and Central Bank embeddedness: the politics of euro adoption in Hungary and the Czech Republic.' *Review of International Political Economy* 13(3): 956–73.

Jones, E. (2002). 'Macroeconomic preferences and Europe's democratic deficit.' In A. Verdun (ed.), *The Euro: European Integration Theory and Economic and Monetary Union.* Lanham, Md., Rowman & Littlefield: 145–64.

Jones, G. and Kutan, A. M. (2004). 'Exchange rate management strategies in the accession countries: the case of Hungary.' *Comparative Economic Studies* 46(1): 23–44.

Kaelberer, M. (2001). *Money and Power in Europe: The Political Economy of European Monetary Cooperation.* Albany, N.Y., SUNY Press.

Kaelberer, M. (2003). 'Knowledge, power and monetary bargaining: central bankers and the creation of monetary union in Europe.' *Journal of European Public Policy* 10(3): 365–79.

Kaltenthaler, K. (1998). *Germany and the Politics of Europe's Money.* Durham, N.C., Duke University Press.

Kaltenthaler, K. (2002). 'German interests in European monetary integration.' *Journal of Common Market Studies* 40(1): 69–87.

Keefer, P. and Stasavage, D. (2002). 'Checks and balances, private information, and the credibility of monetary commitments.' *International Organization* 56(4): 751–74.

Keegan, W. (2002). 'Euro's reluctant father faces facts.' *Observer,* 17 February.

Kenen, P. B. (1983). *The Role of the Dollar as an International Currency.* Group of Thirty Occasional Paper No. 13.

Kenen, P. (1995), *Economic and Monetary Union in Europe: Moving Beyond Maastricht*. Cambridge, Cambridge University Press.

Kenner, J. (2002). *EU Employment Law: From Rome to Amsterdam and Beyond*. Hart Publishing UK.

Keohane, R. (1980). 'The theory of hegemonic stability and changes in international economic regimes, 1967–1977.' In O. R. Holsti, R. M. Siverson and A. George (eds), *Change in the International System*. Boulder, Colo., Westview Press.

Kerstin, J. (2004). 'Soft regulation and the subtle transformation of states: the case of EU employment policy.' *Journal of European Social Policy* 14(4): 355–70.

Khan, M. S. and Choudhri, E. U. (2004). 'Real exchange rates in developing countries: are Balassa–Samuelson effects present?' *IMF Working Papers* 04/188.

Kirshner, J. (1995). *Currency and Coercion: The Political Economy of International Monetary Power*. Princeton, N.J., Princeton University Press.

Kirshner, J. (1999). 'Inflation: paper dragon or trojan horse?' *Review of International Political Economy* 6(4): 609–18.

Kirshner, J. (ed.) (2003). *Monetary Orders*. Ithaca, N.Y., Cornell University Press.

Klosse, S. (2005). 'The European employment strategy: which way forward?' *International Journal of Comparative Labour Law and Industrial Relations* 21(1): 5–36.

Kohler-Koch, B. (1999). 'Catching up with change: the transformation of governance in the European Union.' *Journal of European Public Policy* 3(3): 359–80.

Kohler-Koch, B. and Rittberger, B. (2006). 'Review article: the "governance turn" in EU Studies.' *Journal of Common Market Studies* 44(s1): 27–49.

Kok, W. C. (2003). *Jobs, Jobs, Jobs: Creating More Employment in Europe*. Brussels, Employment Taskforce.

Kok, W. C. (2004). *Facing the Challenge: The Lisbon Strategy for Growth and Employment*. Brussels, High Level Group chaired by Wim Kok.

Kokoszczyski, R. (2002). 'Poland before the euro.' *Journal of Public Policy* 22(2): 199–215.

Krugman, P. (1990). 'Policy problems in monetary union.' In P. d. Grauwe and L. Papademos (eds), *The European Monetary System in the 1990s*. London.

Krugman, P. (2007). 'Will there be a dollar crisis?' *Economic Policy* 22(51): 435–67.

Kutan, A. M. (1990). 'German dominance in the European monetary system: evidence from money supply growth rates.' *Open Economies Review* 2(3): 269–93.

Kydland, F. E. and Prescott, E. C. (1977). 'Rules rather than discretion: the inconsistency of optimal plans.' *Journal of Political Economy* 85(3): 473–92.

Lane, P. R. (2006). 'The real effects of EMU.' *Journal of Economic Perspectives* **20**(4): 47–66.

Lane, P. R. and Milesi-Ferretti, G. M. (2007). 'Europe and global imbalances.' *Economic Policy* **22**(51): 519–73.

Lawson, N. (1993). *The View from No. 11*. New York, Doubleday.

Leblang, D. (2003). 'To devalue or to defend? The political economy of exchange rate policy.' *International Studies Quarterly* **47**(4): 533–60.

Leblond, P. (2006). 'The political stability and growth pact is dead: long live the economic stability and growth pact.' *Journal of Common Market Studies* **44**(5): 969–90.

Leiner-Killinger, N., Lopez-Perez, V., Stiegert, R. and Vitale, G. (2007). *Structural Reforms in EMU and the Role of Monetary Policy – A Survey of the Literature*. ECB Occasional Paper No. 66.

Lindahl, R. and Naurin, D. (2005). 'Sweden: the twin faces of a euro-outsider.' *Journal of European Integration* **27**(1): 65–87.

Lindberg, L. and Scheingold, S. A. (1970). *Europe's Would-Be Polity*. Englewood Cliffs, N.J., Prentice-Hall.

Linsenmann, I. (2007). 'Towards a horizontal fusion of governing structures? Coordination of coordination processes through the broad economic policy guidelines.' In I. Linsenmann, C. O. Meyer and W. Wessels (eds), *Economic Government of the EU: A Balance Sheet of New Modes of Policy Coordination*. Basingstoke, Palgrave Macmillan.

Linsenmann, I., Meyer, C. O. and Wessels, W. T. (eds) (2007). *Economic Government of the EU: A Balance Sheet of New Modes of Policy Coordination*. Basingstoke, Palgrave Macmillan.

Linsenmann, I. and W. Wessels (2006). 'Optimal economic governance in an enlarged European Union: scenarios and options.' In K. Dyson (ed.), *Enlarging the Euro Area*. New York, Oxford University Press: 108–24.

Lodge, M. (2005). 'The importance of being modern: international benchmarking and national regulatory innovation.' *Journal of European Public Policy* **12**(4): 649–67.

Loedel, P. (1999). *Deutsche Mark Politics*. Boulder, Colo., Lynne Rienner.

Loedel, P. (2002). 'Multilevel governance and the independence of the European Central Bank.' In A. Verdun (ed.), *The Euro: European Integration Theory and Economic and Monetary Union*. Lanham, Md., Rowman & Littlefield: 125–44.

Ludlow, P. (1982). *The Making of the European Monetary System*. London, Butterworths Scientific.

Mahieu, G., Ooms, D. and Rottier, S. (2005). 'Forum section: EU representation and the governance of the International Monetary Fund.' *European Union Politics* **6**(4): 493–510.

Majone, G. (1998). 'Europe's democratic deficit.' *European Law Journal* **4**(1): 5–28.

Marchat, P. (2005). 'L'assouplissement du pacte de stabilité et de croissance.' *Revue du Marché commun et de l'Union européenne* **489**: 362–9.

Marcussen, M. (2002). 'EMU: A Danish delight and dilemma.' In K. Dyson (ed.), *European States and the Euro: Europeanization, Variation, and Convergence*. New York, Oxford University Press.

Marcussen, M. (2005). 'Denmark and European monetary integration: out but far from over.' *Journal of European Integration* 27(1): 43–63.

Marcussen, M. and Zolner, M. (2001). 'The Danish EMU referendum 2000: business as usual.' *Government and Opposition* 36: 379–401.

Marsh, D. (1992). *The Bundesbank: The Bank that Rules Europe*. London, Mandarin.

Masson, P. and Turtleboom, B. (1997), 'Characteristics of the euro, the demand for reserves, and policy coordination under EMU.' In P. R. Masson, T. S. Krueger and B. G. Turtleboom, (eds), *EMU and the International Monetary System*. International Monetary Fund.

Mayes, D. G. and Viren, M. (2001). *Policy Co-ordination and Economic Adjustment in EMU: Will It Work?* Seventh Biennial Conference of the European Community Studies Association, Madison, WI.

McCubbins, M. D. and Schwartz, T. (1984). 'Congressional oversight overlooked: police patrols versus fire alarms.' *American Journal of Political Science* 2(1): 165–79.

McKinnon, R. I. (2004). 'Optimum currency areas and key currencies: Mundell I versus Mundell II.' *Journal of Common Market Studies* 42(4): 689–715.

McNamara, K. R. (1998). *Currency of Ideas*. Ithaca, N.Y., Cornell University Press.

McNamara, K. R. (1999). 'Consensus and constraint: ideas and capital mobility in European monetary integration.' *Journal of Common Market Studies* 37(3): 455–76.

McNamara, K. R. (2002). 'Rational fictions: central bank independence and the social logic of delegation.' *West European Politics* 25(1).

McNamara, K. R. (2006). 'Economic governance, ideas and EMU: what currency does policy consensus have today?' *Journal of Common Market Studies* 44(4): 803–21.

McNamara, K. R. and Jones, E. (1996). 'The clash of institutions: Germany in European monetary affairs.' *German Politics and Society* 14(3): 5–30.

McNamara, K. R. and Meunier, S. (2002). 'Between national sovereignty and international power: what external voice for the euro?' *International Affairs* 78(4): 849–68.

Mélitz, J. (1988). 'Monetary discipline and cooperation in the European monetary system: a synthesis.' In F. Giavazzi, S. Micossi and M. Miller (eds), *The European Monetary System*. Cambridge, Cambridge University Press: 51–79.

Meltzer, Allan H. 'Monetarism.' [Online] <http://www.econlib.org/library/Enc/Monetarism.html> (accessed 11 November 2008).

Menasce, E. and Gianella, C. (2006). 'CEEC–Eurozone: a convergence in business cycles.' euractiv.com, 17 March.

Mersch, Y. (2003). *The Reform of the Governing Council of the ECB.* Speech given at the European Banking and Financial Forum in Prague, 25 March.

Meyer, C. O. (2004). 'The hard side of soft policy co-ordination in EMU: the impact of peer pressure on publicized opinion in the cases of Germany and Ireland.' *Journal of European Public Policy* 11(5): 814–31.

Meyer, C. O. and Kunstein, T. (2007). 'A "grand débat Européen" on economic governance? Publicised discourses as indicators for the performance of policy coordination modes.' In I. Linsenmann, C. O. Meyer and W. Wessels (eds), *Economic Government of the EU: A Balance Sheet of New Modes of Policy Coordination.* Basingstoke, Palgrave Macmillan.

Meyer, C. O., Linsenmann, I. and Wessels, W. (2007). 'An economic government for Europe in the making? The evolution of policy co-ordination in turbulent times.' In I. Linsenmann, C. O. Meyer and W. Wessels (eds), *Economic Government of the EU: A Balance Sheet of New Modes of Policy Coordination.* Basingstoke, Palgrave Macmillan: 1–10.

Micco, A., Stein, E, and Ordoez, G. (2003). 'The currency union effect on trade: early evidence from EMU.' *Economic Policy* 18(37): 315–56.

Miles, L. (2005). 'Introduction: euro-outsiders and the politics of asymmetry.' *Journal of European Integration* 27(1): 3–23.

Mongelli, F. P. (2008). *European Economic and Monetary Integration, and Optimum Currency Area Theory.* European Economy Economic Papers 302.

Mongelli, F. and Varga, J. L. (2006). *What Effects is EMU Having on the Euro Area and Its Member Countries?* ECB Working Paper No. 599.

Moravcsik, A. (1993). 'A liberal intergovernmentalist approach to the EC.' *Journal of Common Market Studies* 31(4): 473–524.

Moravcsik, A. (1998). *The Choice for Europe.* Ithaca, N.Y., Cornell University Press.

Moravcsik, A. (2002). 'In defense of the "democratic deficit": reassessing legitimacy in the European Union.' *Journal of Common Market Studies* 40(4): 603–24.

Mosher, J. (2000). 'Open method of coordination: functional and political origins.' *ECSA Review* 31(3).

Mundell, R. A. (1960). 'The monetary dynamics of international adjustment under fixed and flexible exchange rates.' *Quarterly Journal of Economics* 74: 227–57.

Mundell, R. (1961). 'A theory of optimum currency areas.' *American Economic Review* 51: 657–65.

Mundell, R. (1973). 'Uncommon arguments for common currencies.' In H. Johnson and A. Swoboda (eds), *The Economics of Common Currencies.* London, Allen & Unwin.

Muscatelli, V. A. (1998). 'Political consensus, uncertain preferences, and Central Bank independence.' *Oxford Economic Papers* 50: 412–30.

Neck, R., Haber, G. and McKibbin, W. J. (2004). 'European monetary and fiscal policies after the EU enlargement.' *Empirica* 31(2–3): 229–45.

Nordhaus, W. (1975). 'The political business cycle.' *Review of Economic Studies* 42: 169–90.

Noord, P. van den, Döhring, B., Langedijk, S., Nogueira, J. M., Pench, L., Temprano-Arroyo, H. and Thiel, M. (2008). *The Evolution of Economic Governance in EMU*. European Economy Economic Papers 328.

Notermans, T. (ed.) (2001). *Social Democracy and Monetary Union*. Berghahn Books.

Oatley, T. and Yackee, J. (2004). 'American interests and IMF lending.' *International Politics* 41(3): 415–29.

Obstfeld, M. (1986). 'Rational and self-fulfilling balance-of-payments crises.' *American Economic Review* 76(1): 72–81.

Obstfeld, M. (1999). *EMU: Ready, or Not?* NBER Working Paper No. 6682.

Obstfeld, M. and Peri, G. (1998). 'Regional non-adjustment and fiscal policy.' *Economic Policy*: 207–59.

OECD Glossary of Statistical Terms [Online] <http://stats.oecd.org/glossary/index.htm> (accessed 11 November 2008).

OECD (1997). *La mise en oeuvre de la stratégie de l'OECD pour l'emploi, l'expérience des pays membres*. Paris, OECD.

OECD (2007). *Economic survey of the Euro Area 2007*. Paris, OECD.

Padoa-Schioppa, T. (1987). *Efficiency, Stability and Equity: A Strategy for the Evolution of the Economic System of the European Community*. Brussels, Commission of the European Communities.

Padoa-Schioppa, T. (2004). *The Euro and Its Central Bank: Getting United after the Union*. MIT Press.

Pagano, M. (2004). 'The European bond markets under EMU.' *Oxford Review of Economic Policy* 20(4): 53–554.

Pain, N. and Van Welsum, D. (2003). 'Untying the Gordian knot: the multiple links between exchange rates and foreign direct investment.' *Journal of Common Market Studies* 41(5): 823–46.

Papademos, L. (2006). 'The global importance of the euro.' Speech made at the European Banking Congress 2006, Frankfurt.

Papadimitriou, D. (2006). 'Persistent laggard: Romania as Eastern Europe's Sisyphus.' In K. Dyson (ed.), *Enlarging the Euro Area*. New York, Oxford University Press: 215–33.

Pauly, L. (2008). 'Financial crisis management in Europe and beyond'. *Contributions to Political Economy* 27.

Pearce, D. (1992) *The MIT Dictionary of Modern Economics*, 4th edn. Cambridge, Mass.: MIT Press.

Pierson, P. (2000). 'Increasing returns, path dependence, and the study of politics.' *American Political Science Review* 94(2): 251–67.

Pisani-Ferry, J. (2006). 'Only one bed for two dreams: a critical retrospective on the debate over the economic governance of the euro area.' *Journal of Common Market Studies* 44(4): 823–44.

Pisani-Ferry, J., Aghion, P., Belka, M., von Hagen, J., Heikenstein, L., Sapir, A. and Ahearne, A. (2008). *Coming of Age: Report on the Euro Area*. Brussels, Bruegel.

Pochet, P. (1999). 'The new employment chapter of the Amsterdam Treaty.' *Journal of European Social Policy* 9(3): 271–8.

Pöhl, K. O. (1990). 'Towards monetary union in Europe.' *Europe's Constitutional Future*. London, Institute of Economic Affairs: 35–42.

Portes, R. and Rey, H. (1998). 'The emergence of the euro as an international currency.' *Economic Policy* 13(26): 305–43.

Posen, A. (1993). 'Why central bank independence does not cause low inflation: the politics behind the institutional fix.' In R. O'Brien (ed.), *Finance and the International Economy*. Oxford, Oxford University Press 7: 41–65.

Posen, A. (1998). 'Central Bank independence and disinflationary credibility: a missing link?' *Oxford Economic Papers* 50: 335–59.

Posen, A. S. and Gould, D. P. (2006). *Has EMU had Any Impact on the Degree of Wage Restraint?* Washington, DC, Institute for International Economics.

Pouvelle, C. (2006). 'Le role international de l'euro depuis 1999: facteurs et enjeux.' *Bulletin de la Banque de France* (147).

Prange, H. and Kaiser, R. (2005). 'The open method of coordination in the European research area: a new concept of deepening integration?' *Comparative European Politics* 3(3): 289–306.

Puetter, U. (2004). 'Governing informally: the role of the Eurogroup in EMU and the stability and growth pact.' *Journal of European Public Policy* 11(5): 854–70.

Puetter, U. (2006). *The Eurogroup: How a Secret Circle of Finance Ministers Shape European Economic Governance*. Manchester, Manchester University Press.

Puetter, U. (2007). 'Providing venues for contestation: the role of expert committees and informal dialogue among ministers in European economic policy coordination.' *Comparative European Politics* 5(1): 18–35.

Qvortrup, M. H. (2001). 'How to lose a referendum: the Danish plebiscite on the euro.' *Political Quarterly* 72: 190–6.

Radaelli, C. (2003). 'The open method of co-ordination – a new governance architecture for the European Union.' *Swedish Institute for European Policy Studies* 1.

Rhodes, M. (2005). 'Employment policy: between efficacy and experimentation.' In H. Wallace, W. Wallace and M. Pollack (eds), *Policy-Making in the European Union*. Oxford, Oxford University Press: 279–304.

Rhodes, M. and Keune, M. (2006). 'EMU and welfare state adjustment in Central and Eastern Europe.' In K. Dyson (ed.), *Enlarging the Euro Area*. New York, Oxford University Press: 279–300.

Rogers, J. H. (2007). 'Monetary union, price level convergence, and inflation: how close is Europe to the USA?' *Journal of Monetary Economics* **54**(3): 785–96.

Rogoff, K. (1985a). 'Can international monetary policy coordination be counterproductive?' *Journal of International Economics* **18**(3/4): 199–217.

Rogoff, K. (1985b). 'The optimal degree of commitment to an intermediate monetary target.' *Quarterly Journal of Economics* (403): 1169–89.

Rollo, J. (2002). 'In or out: the choice for Britain.' *Journal of Public Policy* **22**(2): 217–38.

Rollo, J. (2006). 'EMU and the new member states: strategic choices in the context of global norms.' In K. Dyson (ed.), *Enlarging the Euro Area*. New York, Oxford University Press: 47–70.

Rose, A. K. (2000). 'One money, one market: estimating the effect of common currencies on trade.' *Economic Policy* 30: 9–45.

Rose, A. K. (2001). 'Currency unions and trade: the effect is large.' *Economic Policy* **16**(33): 449–61.

Ross, G. (1996). 'The limits of political economy: Mitterrand and the crisis of the French left.' In A. Daley (ed.), *The Mitterrand Era: Policy Alternatives and Political Mobilization in France*. New York, New York University Press: 33–55.

Ross, M. and Lättemäe, R. (2004). 'EMU accession issues in Estonia.' *Comparative Economic Studies* **46**(1): 146–58.

Ruggie, J. G. (1982). 'International regimes, transactions and change: embedded liberalism in the postwar economic order.' *International Organization* **36**(2): 379–415.

Sadeh, T. (2006). 'Adjusting to the EMU: electoral, partisan and fiscal cycles.' *European Union Politics* **7**(3): 347–72.

Sandholtz, W. (1993). 'Choosing union: monetary politics and Maastricht.' *International Organization* **47**(1): 1–39.

Sandholtz, W. and Zysman, J. (1989). '1992: Recasting the European bargain.' *World Politics* **42**(1): 95–128.

Santos, J. A. C. and Tsatsaronis, K. (2003). *The Cost of Barriers to Entry: Evidence from the Market for Corporate Euro Bond Underwriting*. BIS Working Paper No. 134.

Sapir, A. (2006). 'Is the euro ready for a global role?' *Europe's World*, Spring: 56–61.

Sapir, A., Wallace, H., Vinals, J., Rosati, D., Pisani-Ferry, J., Hellwig, M., Bertoli, G. and Aghion, P. (2003). *An Agenda for a Growing Europe: Making the EU Economic System Deliver (Sapir Report)*. Brussels, European Commission.

Sargent, T. and Wallace, N. (1981). 'Some unpleasant monetarist arithmetics.' *Federal Reserve Bank of Minneapolis Quarterly Review* **5**(3): 1–17.

Sarkozy, N. (2008). Allocution de M. Nicolas Sarkozy au parlement européen. 21 October 2008, Strasbourg.

Savage, J. D. (2005). *Making the EMU: The Politics of Budgetary Surveillance and the Enforcement of Maastricht*. Oxford, Oxford University Press.

Schadler, S. (ed.) (2005). *Euro Adoption in Central and Eastern Europe: Opportunities and Challenges*. Washington, DC, IMF.

Schäfer, A. (2006). 'A new form of governance? Comparing the open method of co-ordination to multilateral surveillance by the IMF and the OECD.' *Journal of European Public Policy* 13(1): 70–88.

Scharpf, F. (1999). *Governing Europe: Effective and Democratic?* Oxford, Oxford University Press.

Scharpf, F. W. (2002). 'The European social model.' *Journal of Common Market Studies* 40(4): 645–70.

Schelkle, W. (2004). 'EMU's second chance: enlargement and the reform of fiscal policy co-ordination.' *Journal of European Public Policy* 11(5): 890–908.

Schelkle, W. (2006). 'The theory and practice of economic governance in EMU revisited: what have we learnt about commitment and credibility?' *Journal of Common Market Studies* 44(4): 669–85.

Schild, J. (2005). 'Ein Sieg der Angst – das gescheiterte französische Verfassungsreferendum.' *Integration* 3.

Scott, H. S. (1998). 'When the euro falls apart.' *International Finance* 1(2): 207–28.

Sibert, A. and Sutherland, A. (2000). 'Monetary union and labor market reform.' *Journal of International Economics* 51(2): 421–35.

Silvia, S. (2004). 'Is the euro working? The euro and European labour markets.' *Journal of Public Policy* 24: 147–68.

Simmons, B. A. (1994). *Who Adjusts? Domestic Sources of Foreign Economic Policy during the Interwar Years*. Princeton, N.J., Princeton University Press.

Smaghi, L. B. (2004). 'A single EU seat in the IMF?' *Journal of Common Market Studies* 42(2): 229–48.

Smaghi, L. B. (2006). 'Powerless Europe: why is the euro area still a political dwarf?' *International Finance* 9(2): 261–79.

Smaghi, L. B. (2007). *The Euro as an International Currency: Implications for Exchange Rate Policy*. Speech given at the Euro50 Group meeting, 50 Years after the Treaty of Rome: Strengthening the Economic Leg of EMU, 2–3 July 2007, Rome.

Soskice, D. and Iversen, T. (2001). 'Multiple wage bargaining systems in the single European currency area.' *Empirica* 28(4): 435–56.

Starbatty, J. and Bofinger, P. (2002). 'Does the euro need political union to survive?' *Finanzplatz e.V. Newsletter*.

Stoltenberg, G. (1988). 'The further development of monetary cooperation in Europe', memorandum to Ecofin Council. Ministry of Finance, Bonn.

Subacchi, P. (2005). 'Reforming economic governance in Europe: exploring the road to effective coordination.' *International Affairs* 81(4): 741–56.

Szyszczak, E. (2006). 'Experimental governance: the open method of coordination.' *European Law Journal* 12(4): 486–502.

Tabellini, G. (1987). 'Central bank reputation and the monetization of deficits: the 1981 monetary reform.' *Economic Inquiry* 25: 185–200.

Talani, L. (2000). 'Who wins and who loses in the City of London from the establishment of European monetary union.' In C. Crouch (ed.), *After the Euro: Shaping Institutions for Governance in the Wake of European Monetary Union*. New York, Oxford University Press.

Talani, L. (2005). 'The European Central Bank: between growth and stability.' *Comparative European Politics* 3(2): 204–31.

Tavlas, G. S. (1998). 'The international use of currencies: the U.S. dollar and the euro.' *Finance and Development* 35(2).

Thatcher, M. (1993). *The Downing Street Years*. New York, Harper Collins.

Thimann, C. (2005). 'Real convergence, economic dynamics, and the adoption of the euro in the new European union member states.' In S. Schadler (ed.), *Euro Adoption in Central and Eastern Europe: Opportunities and Challenges*. Washington, DC, IMF: 24–32.

Tiilikainen, T. (2005). 'Finland: any lessons for the euro-outsiders?' *Journal of European Integration* 27(1): 25–42.

Tilford, S. (2006). 'Will the Eurozone crack?' London, Centre for European Reform. [Online] <http://www.cer.org.uk/publications_new/688.html> (accessed 25 December 2008).

Triffin, R. (1960). *Gold and the Dollar Crisis: The Future of Convertibility*. New Haven, Yale University Press.

Trubek, D. M. and Mosher, J. S. (2003). 'New governance, employment policy, and the European social model.' In J. Zeitlin and D. M. Trubek (eds), *Governing Work and Welfare in a New Economy. European and American Experiments*. New York, Oxford University Press: 33–58.

Truman, E. M. (2005). 'The euro and prospects for policy coordination.' In A. S. Posen (ed.), *The Euro at Five: Ready for a Global Role?* Washington, DC, Peterson Institute.

Tsoukalis, L. (1977). *The Politics and Economics of European Monetary Integration*. London, Allen & Unwin.

Turrini, A. (2008). *Fiscal Policy and the Cycle in the Euro Area: the Role of Government Revenue and Expenditure*. European Economy Economic Papers 323.

Van den Noord, P., Döhring, B., Langedijk, S., Martins, J. N., Pench, L., Temprano-Arroyo, H. and Thiel, M. (2008). *The Evolution of Economic Governance in EMU*. European Economy Economic Papers 328.

Van Poeck, A., Vanneste, J. and Veiner, M. (2007). 'Exchange rate regimes and exchange market pressure in the new EU Member states.' *Journal of Common Market Studies* 45(2): 459–85.

Verdun, A. (1996). 'The road towards European economic and monetary union: why is it accepted? Perceptions of EMU in the UK, France and Germany.' *Acta politica* 31 3: 283–314.

Verdun, A. (1999). 'The role of the Delors Committee in the creation of EMU: an epistemic community?' *Journal of European Public Policy* 2: 308–28.

Verdun, A. (2000). 'Governing by committee: the case of monetary policy.' In T. Christiansen and E. Kirchner (eds), *Committee Governance in the EU*. Manchester, Manchester University Press.

Verdun, A. (2008). 'Policy-making and integration in the European Union: do economic interest groups matter?' *British Journal of Politics and International Relations* 10(1): 129–37.

Verdun, A. and Christiansen, T. (2000). 'Policies, institutions, and the euro: dilemmas of legitimacy.' In C. Crouch (ed.), *After the Euro: Shaping Institutions for Governance in the Wake of European Monetary Union*. New York, Oxford University Press.

Verdun, A. and Christiansen, T. (2001). 'The legitimacy of the euro: an inverted process?' *Current Politics and Economics of Europe* 10(3): 265–88.

Véron, N. (2007). *Is Europe Ready for a Major Banking Crisis?* Brussels, Bruegel.

Von Hagen, J. (2002). *More Growth for Stability – Reflections on Fiscal Policy in Euroland*. ZEI.

Von Hagen, J. (2005). 'Fiscal policy challenges for European Union acceding countries.' In S. Schadler (ed.), *Euro Adoption in Central and Eastern Europe: Opportunities and Challenges*. Washington, DC, International Monetary Fund.

Von Hagen, J. and Eichengreen, B. J. (1996). 'Federalism, fiscal restraints, and European monetary union.' *American Economic Review*: 134–8.

Von Hagen, J., Hallett, A.H. and Strauch, R.. (2001). *Budgetary Consolidation in EMU*. European Economy – Economic Papers 148, Commission of the EC, Directorate-General for Economic and Financial Affairs (DG ECFIN).

Von Hagen, J. and Traistaru, I. (2005). 'Macroeconomic adjustment in the new EU member states.' In C. Detken, V. Gaspar and G. Noblet (eds), *The New EU Member States – Convergence and Stability*. Frankfurt, European Central Bank.

Vreese, C. H. D. and Semetko, H. A. (2004). 'News matters: influences on the vote in the Danish 2000 euro referendum campaign.' *European Journal of Political Research* 43(5): 699–722.

Vujcic, B. (2004). 'Euro adoption: views from the third row.' *Comparative Economic Studies* 46(1): 159–76.

Wallace, H. (2000). 'The institutional setting: five variations on a theme.' In H. Wallace and W. Wallace (eds), *Policy-making in the European Union*. Oxford, Oxford University Press: 3–37.

Weber, A. (1991). 'Reputation and credibility in the European monetary system.' *Economic Policy* 12: 58–102.

Werner Plan. (1970). *Report to the Council and Commission on the Realization by Stages of Economic and Monetary Union in the Community*.

Winkler, B. (2000). *Which Kind of Transparency? On the Need for Clarity in Monetary Policy-Making.* ECB Working Paper No. 26. Frankfurt, Germany, European Central Bank.

Wypłosz, C. (1989). 'Asymmetry in the EMS: intentional or systemic?' *European Economic Review* 33: 310–20.

Wyplosz, C. (2005). *Fiscal Indiscipline: Why No Reaction Yet by Markets?* Report to the European Parliament Committee for Economic and Monetary Affairs. Brussels.

Wyplosz, C. (2006). 'European monetary union: the dark sides of a major success.' *Economic Policy* 21(46): 207–61.

Zängle, M. (2004). 'The European Union benchmarking experience: from euphoria to fatigue?' *European Integration online Papers* 8(3): 1–22.

Zeitlin, J.and Pochet, P. (eds) (2005). *The Open Method of Coordination in Action: The European Employment and Social Inclusion Strategies.* Brussels, Presses Interuniversitaires Européennes-Peter Lang.

Zohlnhöfer, R. and Ostheim, T. (2005). 'Paving the way for employment? The impact of the Luxembourg process on German labour market policies.' *Journal of European Integration* 27(2): 147–67.

Zubeck, R. (2006). 'Poland: unbalanced domestic leadership in negotiating fit.' In K. Dyson (ed.), *Enlarging the Euro Area.* New York, Oxford University Press: 197–214.

Index